The Kingdom Within

The Kingdom Within

A Guide to the Spiritual Work of the Findhorn Community

Edited and Compiled by Alex Walker

FINDHORN
Press

ISBN 0 905249 99 2

British Library Cataloguing-in-Publication Data. A catalogue
record for this book is available from the British Library.

Cover photograph © Alan Watson
Cover design by Posthouse Printing

Back cover photograph by Findhorn Foundation Visual Arts
Layout and setting in Garamond by Findhorn Press
Printed and bound by Guernsey Press Ltd,
Guernsey, Channel Isles

Published by Findhorn Press, The Park, Findhorn,
Forres IV36 0TZ, Moray, Scotland

Dedicated to
MARIE KERR URQUHART
9.1.27 - 9.9.94

CONTENTS

We would like to make it clear that 'the Findhorn Community' (capitalised) referred to throughout this book refers to the Findhorn Foundation and its associated Community, and not the nearby Scottish village of Findhorn which has its own history and traditions.

The views contained in this book are those of the authors and not necessarily those of the Trustees of the Findhorn Foundation.

Good News

Drop your guns, and hear the news.
The war is won, and we've called a truce.
The key is found, and the circle complete,
And the higher ground is beneath our feet.

Like the turn of a page, or a change of gear,
A brand new age is already here.
And even while men pursue their doom,
A magical child is kicking in the womb.

I'm preparing for birth. I'm not the only one.
I'm a part of the Earth, I'm a drop of the sun.
I'm in step with the stars, I'm in league with the land.
I'm a functioning part of the Master's Plan!

Mike Scott 1993
From 'Dream Harder' by The Waterboys
© *Sony Publishing. Reprinted by permission.*

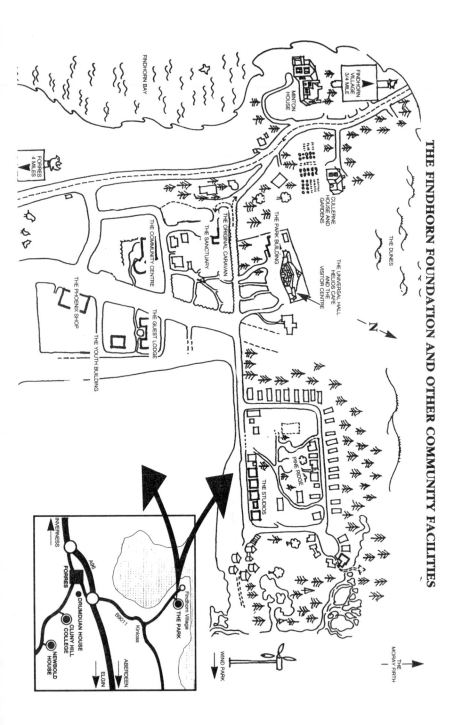

THE FINDHORN FOUNDATION AND OTHER COMMUNITY FACILITIES

One

Introduction

PURPOSE OF THIS BOOK

This anthology aims to provide those with an interest in learning more about the life and work of the Findhorn Community with a starting point for their studies. The material is essentially of three kinds:

1. A selection of key ideas about the philosophical background to and spiritual beliefs of the Community.
2. Some important factual information, particularly about the history of the Foundation, and the nature of the local environment in which it is located.
3. Guides to further reading.

Some of the contents are therefore universal in nature and some specific to life in the Findhorn Foundation and its associated Community.

Originally developed for the Foundation's own internal education programmes, this anthology is now available to a wider public in book form. However, although the collection is certainly intended as a means of creating a shared platform of knowledge for the Community and those interested in learning more about it, it is not intended to be either an ultimate authority or an exhaustive set of ideas.

As outlined below our work is to encourage individuals towards *experiences* of the divine rather than into discussions about divinity. We provide a training ground for spiritual seekers wishing to understand and express their own unique spirituality, rather than a college for learning either academic treatises or spiritual dogma. These papers are then an attempt to communicate what others are thinking and believing, not to dictate what you as a reader *should* believe.

Furthermore, the volume of publications about the Community is already so large that it is doubtful if any single individual has read it all. The wealth of material is truly daunting. It would therefore be futile to pretend that the ideas contained here can be anything other than an introduction to the Foundation and its work, and they are certainly not intended to be a summary of the 'New Age' as a whole. The reading lists presented are similarly only intended as introductions, not as a complete set or authorised bibliography.

It is also necessary to stress that this series is not intended to replace the original study papers first published in the 1970s and largely authored by David Spangler. They remain an invaluable part of our heritage, and contain a considerable amount of wisdom that is timeless in its appeal. However, twenty years have passed since their publication, and the context within which the Foundation is working — relative to the spiritual Community of which it is part, the wider community of West Moray, and the planetary situation as a whole — has changed to such a degree that this new series has been requested.

Some extracts from the original papers are incorporated in the body of the text presented here, but most of them have been excluded. Whilst our hope is that the material chosen is of primary relevance to this introduction to the life and work of the Community, this does not imply that the remainder is no longer relevant. Serious students of our life and work are encouraged to seek out this earlier collection, a full index to which is presented in the Appendix. Also in this Appendix is a description of terms such as 'Original' and 'Early' Study Papers, which those for whom such exactitude is important may choose to consult before proceeding further.

Finally, this is not a collection which has been created in such a way as to make it internally consistent with a high degree of rigour. There are certain common themes, and there are wide areas of agreement between all the contributors. There are nonetheless some differences of interpretation and an element of overlap in subject matter. Those who are kindly disposed to the ideas presented will perhaps enjoy such instances as a celebration of the diversity offered to those who delve into explorations of spirituality, and of humanity's relationship to the cosmos.

ROLE OF THE FOUNDATION & MEMBERSHIP

Alex Walker

Thus from the beginning, the intent of the Trust has not been to create a garden, nor to build a community, but to demonstrate a consciousness of attunement to the supreme link between all humanity, the Life of God.

David Spangler, *The Transformation of Findhorn*
(Early Foundation Study Paper)

The Findhorn Foundation

The Foundation is many things — a centre of spiritual activity, a community, a business, a charity, a focus for certain social activities, and so on. Each individual has a particular relationship to it which is likely to have certain unique elements. This diversity is part of its attraction, but complexity sometimes brings an element of confusion. The first part of this paper is an attempt to introduce some fixed reference points to which one can always return.

The easiest way to understand the Foundation is to look at it as a charitable trust with certain prescribed activities. This is an essentially legal definition, and in a later section we will look at a more complex set of ways to understand its purpose and role in the Community, but it is important to begin with this awareness.

The Trust Deed of the Foundation lists a number of purposes which encompass all the activities that may be undertaken. The most significant of these are:

- Spiritual education. The Foundation's work is based on:
  a) the belief that humanity is on the verge of a major evolutionary step which can be achieved through a change in consciousness, and
  b) that the essential truths of all the world's major religions and spiritual philosophies are similar in nature.

- Cooperation with nature. The Foundation's work in the gardens has been of consequence from its beginnings, and a sense of the need to take the natural world into account pervades every activity.

- The construction of a built environment which supports these activities. One of the principal aims of the Foundation is the replacement of all of the caravans on its original campus at the Park with permanent, ecologically sound buildings. Concomitantly there is an active commitment to the use of renewable energy systems, recycling, ecological waste treatment and environmental education.

Although not formally part of the Trust Deed it is clear that these activities have also resulted in:

- The creation of a community of consciousness which has both a residential component and a world-wide membership. This of course includes the many sister communities around the world which have been inspired by the work of the Foundation.

Going beyond these formal descriptions we can see that the Foundation is a centre of education and demonstration, but one which is at least as much an experiment as it is a role model. New ways of doing and being are constantly being tried out and inevitably not all of them are successful. There is a recognition that one can learn as much — perhaps more — from mistakes as from triumphs.

It is also a place which attempts to find unity in diversity. The main thrust of the educational work of the Foundation is the residential courses which show how a working community incorporating individuals from a wide variety of countries and religious backgrounds has been created. The Foundation maintains many international connections, and this work is carried out in a planetary context. It is not primarily a retreat centre or a 'mystery school' set apart from the rest of the world.

One other point is worth emphasising in this context. The founders of the Community often stressed that its activities needed to specialise in creating a positive future rather than in attempting to resolve society's existing tensions. The phrase "Don't heal the old, but build the new" is not often heard now, but it should be obvious that one small organisation cannot hope to solve all the world's problems. We salute those who struggle to feed those in need, heal the sick and house the poor, but our main role is to create practical workable solutions that will sustain healthy spiritual communities and societies, not to attempt to unravel dilemmas created by cultures rooted in materialism.

The Foundation thus has a unique role to play in both the Community that has grown around it and in the establishment of a better and more holistic human civilisation, but it is as important to avoid the potential glamour in this statement as it is to understand the nature of this role. A description of the Community and the relationship it has to the Foundation is to be found at the end of Section 2 below.

Vision Statements

Ideally an organisation would have one simple statement which sums up its main aims. This task of drawing up such a declaration, and achieving collective support for it is not so easy as it may seem, and there have been a number used by the Foundation in the past. The only one which is currently accepted, although in fact little used is:

The Findhorn Foundation honours the divinity within all life through active service to God, humanity and nature to achieve individual and planetary transformation.

This was conceived and accepted in 1992. More recently an attempt was made to change this to a longer and more comprehensive series of statements under the heading 'The Findhorn Foundation — Celebrating the Divinity Within All Life', but this did not find overall approval at a Community meeting called to discuss it in the autumn of 1993. The first statement still stands therefore.

An older statement, drawn up by Core Group in 1989 is still sometimes used:

We are a spiritual centre of transformation, education, healing, and demonstration, working with the qualities of love and wisdom to embody a vision of God, humanity and nature in co-creation and thereby offering hope, vision, inspiration and encouragement.

An even more simple statement is occasionally referred to:

We are here to create a positive vision for humanity and the planet.

It is important to add that all of these are *Foundation* vision statements. As a legally defined entity the Foundation can choose to outline (or limit) its activities in this way. The Community is, however, an abstract entity with, for the present at least, no coordinating centre or agreed determination of membership. The clarity of purpose available to the Foundation is not, then, applicable to the Community. On the other hand this allows the Community participants scope to extend their activities into any area into which spirit moves them.

It is then worth noting in this context that many of the original study papers are in some ways at least as applicable to the Community as they now are to the Foundation, particularly those dealing with the formative impulses of the centre.

Membership   *Alex Walker/David Spangler*

You come to give and not to get.
Dorothy Maclean

The concept of 'Foundation Membership', encompassing all forms of residential status, was the backbone of Foundation staffing from the 1970s for over twenty years. Such definitions are under constant review, and this category is no longer in formal use. There are now several legitimate ways to participate in Community life, and indeed to work within the Foundation. These categories include:

● Foundation Associate — essentially a volunteer.
● Foundation Student — a one- or two-year fee-paying apprenticeship, usually as a resident on Foundation property. This is often followed by a position in the next category.
● Foundation Staff, i.e. full-time employment in return for board and lodging and a small allowance.
● Foundation Employee — a waged position, invariably excluding accommodation. Such positions are small in number and often temporary.

● Community Member — a loose category with no formal definition, save that the individual claims some attachment to the spiritual work of the Community. The Foundation has utilised a number of Community members acting in a self-employed capacity in recent years.

The administrative challenges this situation creates are not addressed here. Even if it were appropriate, the rapidity with which these structures are changing would make any definitive statement out of date before the ink was dry. It is however germane to offer these words from David Spangler which address the inner nature of membership rather than its outer forms.

Fundamentally, the Community should be seen as a place of initiation, initiation being something which empowers a reorganisation in a person's life. This is a reorganisation of the psyche so that the person is never the same as before. In the Findhorn Community's case, this reorganisation should bring the person into a deeper communion with spirit and with the presence of the sacred. As such a place of initiation, this is a place where we can encounter in a mindful way the everyday qualities and presence of spirit.

Beyond any administrative meanings that may also be appropriate, the fundamental meaning of Community membership to me is this: a person is a member if he or she takes accountability to understand the inner qualities and blessings of this centre and to see that this essential spirit is embodied, empowered, and passed on clearly to others who have yet to come and receive benefit from this place.

The membership has then to be accountable for the vessel — to make sure that the well is dug and that the water is clear. Membership is more than simply being the drinker.

THE NEW AGE

Alex Walker

The idea that our world is currently in a process of transition from one 'Age' to another has many sources of inspiration. For some it is primarily an astrological event — the movement of our planet relative to the heavens so that we are increasingly coming under the influence of the sign Aquarius, rather than its precursor Pisces. For others it implies wider changes in the spiritual impulses that affect us, of which the signs of the zodiac are but a partial symbol.

Some see it as having a religious aspect involving the reinterpretation of the teachings of the great religions by a spiritual master or masters, perhaps also involving the return of the Christ or the appearance of the Lord Maitreya of the Buddhist tradition. Others begin with the perception of a need for a radical change within the human heart to overcome the obvious challenges of nuclear proliferation, environmental degradation, population explosion and rampant materialism, and simply have faith in divine intervention and their own creative potential to build the world anew. For many individuals the notion of a New Age includes all of these things.

However, it is not an organised movement with a specific membership or set of rules, and this has inevitably led to different interpretations of the nature as well as the origin of the concept. Indeed the term 'New Age' has come to mean many different things, some of them more the product of advertising agencies than spiritual reflection[1]. We use it in this Community to describe an idea which inspires those who believe that humanity is at a point in history when significant cultural and spiritual changes are occurring. Whatever their origin, these

---

[1] The description by journalists of some groups of British travelling people as 'new age' adds to the confusion. As far as we know these groups do not espouse any spiritual cause at all. Similarly, descriptions of the fundamentalist Christian sect who came to such a tragic end in Waco, Texas in 1993 as 'new age' seem simply mischievous.

changes are mostly concerned with a transition from one set of beliefs which insist on racial, national and religious separations towards another set which emphasise our common identity and the divinity within all life. In short, the idea is concerned with a transformation of consciousness and a resultant more positive future for us all.

Even more succinctly, if there is a single word which can be used to illuminate the concept of the New Age it is perhaps wholeness. The past epoch of recorded history has been one where differences have been emphasised; not only distinctions between groups within the human family but also separation between, for instance, humanity and nature, body and soul, masculine and feminine aspects of the personality and so on.

We believe that the future will be largely concerned with rediscovering and rebuilding our connectedness to each other, to nature and to the unseen spiritual realms, so that we may become whole as individuals, as a species, even as a planet. In fact, this search for wholeness or connectedness has already had a powerful impact on many areas of our culture.

It is now more common for physicists to compare their findings about the nature of matter with the experiences of Eastern mystics. Biologists have become increasingly concerned with ecological systems in addition to the behaviour of individual animals or species. Mathematicians have discovered chaos theory with all its implications about the delicate balance between our own activities and the cycles of the natural world such as weather patterns.

There is a growing interest in complementary medical techniques such as homoeopathy, acupuncture and clairvoyant healing, all of which rely on premises which are not exclusively scientific, and which tend to emphasise intuitive diagnoses and treatment of the whole person rather than a specific symptom or condition.

Change has been less dramatic in politics, economics and religion to date, but even here it is obvious that the future will not be a mere extrapolation of the past. In the North, the great political power bloc divisions of the mid-20th century have vanished and been replaced by a system of mutual acceptance and cooperation, albeit often still offered grudgingly. Indeed we have grown so used to hearing of Russian requests for Western assistance that we are in danger of forgetting just how extraordinary the idea would have appeared to a citizen of the 1980s.

Tragic events in the former communist countries notwithstanding, the rule of international law and order is slowly making it less and less likely that nations will use military force against one another in a way that has been commonplace throughout history. Hope is on the horizon in both the Middle East and South Africa.

Vision- and value-driven, as opposed to profit-driven, businesses are becoming more common in the West. The tragedies of poverty and deprivation in the South or Third World may seem as intractable as ever, but the globalisation of the world economy is slowly bringing a measure of wealth and dignity to parts of South East Asia. Recent advances in information technology are likely to reverse the flow of capital from the South to the North[2], so gradually creating a more level 'playing field'. Who knows what further developments are in store?

The Green movement may have failed to gain any significant political power, but few politicians can ignore the environmental agenda, even if it is still often on a level of expressed sympathy and concern rather than action. Recycling of resources is now a widely accepted and approved activity.

Within religious life the inter-faith movement is gaining ground, and it is no longer surprising to hear senior figures from one religion suggesting cooperation with adherents of other faiths. Although it is by no means universally welcomed, the ordination of women in the Anglican church is a symbol of the upheavals being experienced by religious organisations everywhere.

Yet for all this drama the concept of a New Age is something of a misnomer. It may prove to be a period of dramatic change, but the underlying motive forces are essentially spiritual ones, and the eternal verities of spiritual life are not new

---

[2] Payments on Third World debt currently result in the poorest countries of the world being net contributors of wealth to the richest countries.

at all! All that is different is our growing ability to understand those truths and to put them into action in novel ways.

Of course, the New Age is not without its critics, not least from some of its most prominent enthusiasts who frequently query the excesses perpetrated under this banner. Its very eclecticism makes it an unpalatable philosophy for those with fundamentalist religious views of any persuasion. It is also seen as a threat by many ordinary Christians — a theme which is explored further in Section 7. However we do not see our movement as a religion. Rather, it is a context within which all aspects of life, including religious observance, are taking place.

From a Western religious point of view perhaps the two most consequential hallmarks of this change will be:

An open view of spiritual seeking which tolerates the use of ideas and practices from more than one tradition, rather than a closed system in which individuals are tied to a single all-purpose philosophy.

An emphasis on experience as well as faith. Our view is that we are entering a time when spiritual insight is not just given to a few theologians, adepts, priests or shamans, but is available to all[3].

---

[3] These two features of openness and experience are more commonly part of Eastern religious practices (for example, most of the world's 30 million practitioners of Shinto are also Buddhists), hence the widespread view that the New Age movement is mainly concerned with the integration of Eastern ideas into Western theology. However, the unfolding energy patterns that are bringing these changes to the West are also having a profound impact on the East too, although in very different ways.

THE FINDHORN COMMUNITY
AS A NEW AGE CENTRE

David Spangler

Why is the Findhorn Community a New Age centre?

There are many surface reasons. One obvious one is that it identifies itself with the vision of a new emerging culture. This new culture may take a number of different forms, but at its core it is conceived as being more soul-infused, more attuned to the sacred, more holistic, compassionate and co-creative than anything we have experienced before. It is also a planetary culture, one which respects and honours local and individual diversity but which provides a space to experience and express the interdependence, interconnection and oneness — in short the identity — of humanity and of the planet as a whole.

One way the Community expresses this vision is through being a planetary centre. Though located in Scotland, it is home to people from many nationalities and religious backgrounds, all living and working together harmoniously and co-creatively.

The Community also interprets the meaning of a 'planetary centre' in another way, by seeking to foster a planetary awareness at an ecological and spiritual level. The development of its famous gardens through cooperation with the angelic and elemental forces of nature is an example of this. Liberating society from an overly materialistic perspective and restoring a sense of the inner worlds of spirit and the ways in which we may cooperate with them is usually considered part of the New Age package, an element of the emerging culture.

Another example is the current effort to create a model eco-village at the centre where the new paradigm of sustainability and ecological balance can be demonstrated and tested. In fact, the work of the Findhorn Foundation and Community to build an ecovillage and to experiment with new forms of technology such as solar and wind power and John Todd's 'Living Machines' is a new way of expressing the original commitment of the centre to demonstrate the elements of a new culture. It certainly is a modern manifestation of the original cooperative work with the nature spirits. As John Talbott, the coordinator of the ecovillage project, has said, the eco-houses which the Community has been building are the 'forty-pound cabbages of the 90s'.

By experience, the Community as a centre for interspecies, interdimensional and international cooperation inducts in us a living awareness of the planet as a whole being and of ourselves as partners with that wholeness. We can begin to grasp the meaning of the vision of an emerging planetary culture as a manifestation of a New Age.

However, in my mind, what makes the Foundation a New Age centre is not its community, its work with new paradigms, its ecological demonstrations, or even its cooperation with the angelic kingdoms. It is the fact that esoterically it has a connection with an overlighting spirit — which itself might be thought of as an angel — that embodies the inner qualities of a New Age. These are inner qualities of soul and outer qualities of creativity that are destined to unfold in humanity as it moves through its next stages of spiritual and cultural evolution.

This spirit, to my understanding, is not the same as the being sometimes called by the Community the 'Angel of Findhorn'. It is a planetary — indeed, in some respects, a cosmic — being of great love, light and wisdom who overlights all humanity and all the earth as a custodian of the next pattern of emergence.

What inner and outer capabilities this spirit is working to stimulate and nourish within humanity and the planet as a whole, I do not know. It will probably be centuries before the fullness of its work becomes apparent. However, initially it is energising two related qualities of energy, both of which are deeply anchored and active in the Foundation and Community.

One of these is the energy of transformation. Transformation is an openness to change in substantive ways that truly make a difference in our lives and in our world. The energy of transformation confronts us with those things in us that are blocks to our unfoldment, things that we must release or surrender, things that must be radically changed and not just rearranged; however, it also presents us with opportunities for growth, with new vision, and with the empowerment that comes from opening to new life and new possibilities. The energy of transformation can shatter habits to liberate new vision and creativity. It can accelerate change and growth. The presence of this energy has been evident in the Community since its inception, and encountering it has often been seen as one of the challenges people may meet when they come to the Community.

The second is a quality I call 'the spirit of newness'. Newness is a spiritual energy that acts within a structure or condition to open it out, to create spaciousness, and to energise or enliven it so that energy and life flow more freely and gracefully. This flow may then reinvigorate and reinstitute the structures and conditions that exist, or it may lead to new possibilities and the emergence of something new and unexpected. It is the factor that keeps an open system open. Newness is not the same as novelty, which is a phenomenon of form. Something that is spiritually new may look and act exactly like something that is old, but it has been renewed and revitalised and is open to the threshold of emergence. Newness is the energy within a structure that maintains what already is, if that is appropriate, but expands a space for emergence and discovery as well.

Transformation can lead to new forms, but newness leads to an enlivening and creative openness, even within old forms. Newness is not an event but a condition of being that is vital and creative. It can utilise well-worn, ancient processes, but prevents them from becoming habits. When I seek to attune to this quality, I often contemplate the meaning and power behind the statement in the New Testament: "Behold! I create all things new."

Both transformation and newness heighten an individual's inner life, like taking a large drink of spiritual caffeine. They enhance energy and make it dance in new ways. They are energies of opening and liberation, making possible new vision.

Both these energies provide a matrix and an openness for deeper qualities of soul to awaken and emerge, according to individual need and capacity, as well as the capacity of the group. They are precursors to the next steps of inner evolution.

While these two qualities are planetary and may be experienced anywhere, it is their focused presence plus the esoteric connection they provide to the inner life and activity of the spirit of the new emerging culture that to me makes this place a New Age centre. The Community and this centre for various inner and outer reasons is an inner lens that heightens the activity of these energies and the spirit that is behind them. This is both the Findhorn Foundation's privilege and its gift to the world, and its responsibility and challenge. Being a New Age centre esoterically is not an easy thing; it demands selflessness and a commitment to service, but it is a joyous thing as well. It is this joy and the creative vision it inspires that remains one of the Findhorn centre's greatest offerings to the needs of our world at this time.

NEW AGE RELIGION

Peter Russell

We are entering the most turbulent, most exciting, most challenging and most critical times in human history. We have reached a paradoxical stage in our evolution. Our development is now threatening our ..ontinued survival. And behind this global crisis is an inner, psychological crisis. For all that we have created has come from human thinking — and it is to human thinking therefore that we should look if we are to find the heart of the problem.

We have become caught in the belief that the material world — the world that we observe through the senses — is the most important part of our reality. And caught in the belief that if we are to find the happiness we seek, it is to this world that we should look. If we are not happy, we must get our surroundings to change. Have people take more notice of us. Create a more secure future for ourselves. Be in control of things. Gather the things that we believe will bring us peace of mind.

This material mind-set lies at the root of our love of money — and remember it is our *love* of money that Timothy (1, 6:10) declares to be the root of all evil, not money itself — for money gives us the means to exchange what we have for the promise of greater happiness. It is this material mind-set that leads us to treat each other as enemies, poison the air we breathe, carelessly eliminate other species that share our planet and plunder the resources of the living Earth. We exploit the world searching for fulfilment that is at best an illusion.

We seem to have forgotten that whether or not we are happy inside is as much a function of how we see the world as it is of the way the world is. It is a question of how we interpret what we see and how we judge it. For if we judge what we see to be a threat to our well-being, we will make ourselves upset. It is by learning to let go of our attachments to such judgements that we are able to be at peace, no matter how the world may be.

Strange as it might seem, belief is the antithesis of spiritual development. Through our beliefs we fix onto a particular per-spective of reality. It is not yet *seeing is believing'* so much as that we see what we believe. We tend to filter out those facets of reality that disagree with our own view of how things are. And in doing so we miss the whole. Yet has not spiritual growth always been an awareness of the whole — an expansion of our awareness?

To free our mind of its constraints is, and always has been, the essence of spiritual development. It tries to help us to let go of our attachments — all the things that we cling to, and all the ideas that we cling to. Yet paradoxically — as well as sadly — this need for security leads us to turn the very means of lib-eration into yet another belief. We turn our spiritual discover-ies into doctrines and dogmas. We create a church.

To paraphrase the Buddha, "Do not believe because I have told you it is so. Only when what I say accords with your own experience should you believe." For inner awakening is a mat-ter of stepping back from beliefs and assumptions. It is about seeing reality as it is, not through the lens of preconception.

This is why spiritual teachings have time and again sought to help us break free from our prejudices and assumptions — break free from our belief that it is through material salvation that we will find the inner peace we seek — break free from the boundaries of our ego.

Belief is a function of the ego, not of our true self. The true self has no need of belief; it knows itself as it is. Awakening is about letting go of any attachments we might have to our beliefs — however spiritual such beliefs might be — and experienc-ing ourselves as we are.

This is the 'new age' that we all truly aspire to. Not a new age founded upon some new set of beliefs — a new set of reli-gious doctrines and dogmas — but an age in which our minds are free from prejudices and our hearts are free from judge-ment. Such an age would indeed be new.

Our thanks to Resurgence magazine for permission to re-print this article.

THE PERENNIAL PHILOSOPHY

Alex Walker

According to a Findhorn Foundation Press release in 1992:

We see ourselves as a meeting place for individuals with different spiritual beliefs, not as some form of new religion or cult. Because much of what we do is primarily experiential and to do with inner or subjective experience it is sometimes difficult to describe. We rely heavily on the notion that all spiritual beliefs tend to incorporate a practice of silent meditation or prayer. We believe that it is faith in God, respect for nature and goodwill towards our fellow humans that are important, not the particular form of words used to describe these ideas.

The Foundation's Trust Deed also avers that:

The objects of the trust are the advancement of religion and religious studies and practices in any part of the world by teaching, example and demonstration of the validity of the essential truths of all religions and spiritual teachings and by such means to encourage and help those who sincerely seek by the increase of their Knowledge and the development of their Being to achieve a greater understanding of the purpose and meaning of life and its relationship to God's universal plan.

The above statements are not in any way unique. Indeed they are common to many spiritual groups. For example:

There is one religion and there are many covers. Each of these covers has a name: Christianity, Buddhism, Judaism, Islam etc, and when you take off these covers you will find that there is one religion. (Hazrat Inayat Khan, founder of the Sufi tradition in the West)

Western Europe rejected the perennial philosophy at the Renaissance and has been led step by step to the materialistic philosophy which rejects fundamental human values and exposes humankind to the contrary forces at work in the universe. The only way of recovery is to rediscover the perennial philosophy, the traditional wisdom, which is found in all ancient religions and especially in the great religions of the world. But those religions have in turn become fossilised and have each to be renewed, not only in themselves, but also in relation to one another, so that a cosmic, universal religion can emerge, in which the essential values of Christian religion will be preserved in living relationship with the other religious traditions of the world. This is a task for the coming centuries as the present world order breaks down and a new world order emerges from the ashes of the old. (Dom Bede Griffiths, Benedictine monk and founder of Shantivanam ashram)

The Foundation thus finds itself in good company and part of a genuine tradition. Nonetheless there are real difficulties with this approach, as Rev Dr Frank Whaling has pointed out:

The thesis of the transcendental unity of all religions also tends to elevate one aspect of religion to supremacy over the others. In the case of the perennial philosophy and the neo-Vedanta the emphasis is placed upon the mystical or metaphysical spirituality. According to them, this is what true religion is really all about. All other aspects, such as community, ritual, ethics, social involvement, sacred text, beliefs, aesthetic awareness, and more outward spiritualities are secondary. Ultimately they may even be non-essential.

Although there is not usually condescension or elitism in the approach based upon mystical spirituality, it is difficult for the imputation of elitism to be completely avoided. Insofar as their hierarchy of interests finds its summit in spirit, it is clear that interior spirituality must be at the height of their concern and that other elements of religious life will be graded lower. Insofar as most religious people are not greatly involved in interior spirituality (for example the Sufi and Hasidic groups in Islam and Judaism are fairly small) the implication must be that they live at a lower level of religious life.

The transcendent unity of all religions therefore is really the transcendent unity of a minority within each religious tradition. And this is achieved by hierarchical weighting of authentic religion in the direction of spirituality.

There are therefore genuine dangers in what one might call 'New Age fundamentalism'. It is common in the Community to hear individuals talking of the metaphorical mountain path to God, and somehow there is often an unspoken assumption that because the perennial philosophy is a pure stream uncluttered with religious iconography, it is therefore to be found close to the summit of the climb[4].

This may be a mistake. The stream may be pure, but your present position on this metaphorical mountain cannot be inferred from this alone. There are surely many individuals bravely battling towards the headwaters of formal traditions who are far above you. Do not underestimate the wisdom they have to offer. To do so can be a glamour — an ego-distortion which will become a distraction rather than a badge of achievement.

The perennial philosophy as the mystical centre of religious thought is the theory which you will work with while you live in this Community. Knowing this is not enough. Embodiment of its teachings is the practice which will take you along and up the path.

---

[4] For example: "Irrevocable commitment to any religion is not only intellectual suicide; it is positive un-faith because it closes the mind to any new vision of the world." Alan Watts; *The Book*; Vintage; 1972; page 10.

READING LIST

William Bloom (ed.); *The New Age*, Rider; 1991. An overview of some of the most important contributors to New Age thought.

William Bloom & John Button; *The Seeker's Guide: A New Age Resource Book*, Aquarian Press; 1992

Fritjof Capra; *The Tao of Physics*, Fontana; 1989. *The Turning Point: Science, Society and the Rising Culture*, Simon and Schuster; 1982

Marilyn Ferguson; *The Aquarian Conspiracy*, Paladin; 1982

Dom Bede Griffiths; *A New Vision of Reality*, Collins; 1989. The quotation is from page 296.

Willis Harman; *Global Mind Change*, Knowledge Systems; 1988

Hazrat Inayat Khan; *The Unity of Religious Ideals*, Sufi Order Publications; 1979. The quotation is from page 29.

Peter Russell; *The Awakening Earth*, Routledge; 1982

David Spangler; *Revelation — The Birth of a New Age*, Findhorn Press; 1972. Originally a series of lectures, this book is now out of print. Its message marked the turning point when the Community moved from imagining itself as preparing for a future New Age, to believing in itself as an embodiment of a transformation that had already arrived. Other Findhorn Press titles by the same author are listed in Section 2. *Conversations with John*, Lorian Press; 1981. *Further Conversations with John*, Lorian Press; 1982. *The New Age*, Morningtown Press; 1988. Musings on whether or not it is an appropriate appellation given the 'commercialism or the craziness that marks the two extremes of the New Age spectrum of activities'. He decides in favour.

David Spangler & William Irwin Thompson; *Re-Imagination of the World*, Bear and Co; 1991. William Irwin 'Bill' Thompson has had a long association with the Findhorn Community. Academic, poet, and founder of the Lindisfarne Association, he is the author of many other books including:

William Irwin Thompson; *From Nation to Emanation*, Findhorn Press; 1982. (Now out of print.)

Rev Dr Frank Whaling; *Interfaith Dialogue and Comparative Religion;* in *Compassion Through Understanding*, Edited by F. Whaling and K. Holmes; Kagyu Samye Ling Inter-Faith Symposium 1988; Dzalendara. The quotation is from page 157.

Gary Zukav; *The Dancing Wu Li Masters: An Overview of the New Physics*, Rider; 1992

Two

A Short History of the Findborn Foundation & Community

THE PREPARATION OF THE FOUNDERS

Alex Walker

The history of this period in the Community's development is extensively documented and rather than repeat a well known story at length, this section contains some key facts and dates about the founders and founding years as a source of reference.

Eileen Caddy was born in Alexandria, Egypt in 1917 and was educated at a boarding school in Ireland. In 1939 she married Andrew Combe, an RAF officer and they had five children together. He became involved in the Moral Re-Armament movement, and Eileen participated in some of their activities, although without enthusiasm. The couple first met Peter Caddy when they were stationed at Habbanya in Iraq. In 1953 whilst back in England, Peter and Eileen fell in love. Eileen's request for a divorce resulted in her becoming completely separated from her children. Her life had 'suddenly become a nightmare'. Shortly thereafter, whilst visiting a sanctuary in a private house in Ashwell Lane, Glastonbury, Eileen first heard the inner voice that was to direct the rest of her life. The words she heard were "Be still and know that I am God."

Peter Caddy was born in 1917 at Ruislip, about 30 miles from London. Unlike Eileen his early life was steeped in esoterics, including the work of Helena Blavatsky and the Rosicrucian Order. His first spiritual teacher was a Dr Sullivan, also known as Aureolis. He married Nora Meidling at 22 and soon after was commissioned into the RAF as a Catering Officer "having been turned down as a pilot because I was colour blind". He was a champion middle distance runner and when posted to India he completed several Himalayan expeditions, including a trek to Tibet.

Shortly after the war he met **Sheena Govan,** and not long thereafter she became his second wife. Sheena was a strong-willed woman and a spiritual teacher with a Quaker background who trained Peter for the next five years — a training which continued after Peter and Eileen married.

Dorothy Maclean hails from Ontario, Canada, and had a Presbyterian upbringing. She attended a degree course in business at the University of Western Ontario. During the Second World War she worked for British Intelligence in New York, meeting Sheena Govan en route. Later, whilst in Panama, she met and married her husband John, who introduced her to the teachings of a number of religious works including the Bhagavad Gita and those of the Sufi Order. Having moved to London they explored a variety of spiritual groups together. After they divorced Dorothy maintained contacts with one of these groups which was organised by Sheena.

It was at such a group meeting that Peter, Eileen and Dorothy first met. Under Sheena's tutelage Eileen and Dorothy began to develop their skills in receiving and recording guidance, whilst Peter continued his own very different training in intuition and obedience. During this period Peter took on a catering job at an Air University at Hamble in England for a while. Whilst there he purchased a second-hand Bournemouth caravan for £650. Peter and Eileen's first and second children, Christopher and Jonathon, were born during this time, but Eileen's relationship with Sheena became increasingly strained. Indeed matters became so bad that Eileen even attempted suicide when Peter was away in Ireland. She was rescued by her brother and for a brief period was in contact with Andrew again.

Peter continued his peripatetic lifestyle, finding employment in a variety of occupations, including that of a brush salesman in Glasgow. Dorothy was also in and out of work, often as a secretary. After a variety of happenings, including Eileen's traumatic stay in Sheena's cottage on Mull, and the unwelcome attentions of the press who scoured the Hebrides for stories about the 'Nameless Ones'[5], Peter finally applied for and obtained the position of manager of **Cluny Hill Hotel**. The three adults and two children moved there in March 1957.

Cluny Hill had been something of a white elephant, but during their stay they transformed the finances of the hotel, bringing it up to 'four star' standards in large measure by following Eileen's guidance. Peter and Eileen's third son, David, was born there. In their second season they were joined by **Lena Lamont** whom they had met in Glasgow, and who had also been part of Sheena's group. Now separated from Sheena they nonetheless continued their spiritual development, and established telepathic links with centres around the world who were aligning to spirit — the Network of Light. One of their contacts was with **Naomi Stephens** whom Peter had met in the Philippines years before.

It is clear that they felt they were involved in important undertakings — Eileen's guidance stressed this on several occasions. However, the management of the hotel chain were keen to see the successes at Cluny repeated elsewhere. It was therefore to the group's great surprise that they were asked to move to another hotel at **The Trossachs** in Perthshire. Despite their protests Peter, Eileen, Dorothy and Lena were all transferred there early in 1962. The premises were known as the 'graveyard of managers' and it is clear they felt that some malign force was at work against them. Their achievements at Cluny Hill were not so easily accomplished there, and at the end of their first season they were sacked, without any given reason, and with four hours' notice to leave. Peter, Eileen, Dorothy and the three children left for the Caddy caravan, which by then was located at Findhorn Sands Caravan Park.

On 13th October Eileen received the following guidance:

My child, on no account are you to feel you have failed completely at the Trossachs. Many invaluable lessons were learnt. Always keep positive about your return to Cluny Hill, but not under this company.

---

[5] A title invented by a journalist frustrated by the lack of sensational copy to be had. The original story broke after one of Sheena's followers left his wife in England. When asked the name of the group he was to join, the reply was of course that 'it didn't have one', hence this unfortunate sobriquet.

On 24th October she received:

This whole caravan is becoming charged with the most tremendous power and when it reaches a certain strength, nothing will be able to stop the vibrations from going forth and linking and holding together the Network of Light as a whole.

This site at Findhorn Sands was not available for residential occupation during the winter, and after a month's searching they found a space in a hollow at **Findhorn Bay Caravan Park**. None of them were impressed by the quality of the environment, which was by all accounts a site next to a garbage dump and a broken-down garage surrounded by weeds and brambles. Nonetheless it was a case of any port in a storm, and they moved the caravan there on 17th November 1962. Light snow fell as they arrived.

The Early Days

Dorothy Maclean

(From To Hear the Angels Sing, *pages 44-52)*

When we arrived, we discovered that across the bay, the last remaining portions of Britain's only desert were finally being conquered and planted by a system involving the cross-hatching of branches to protect seedling trees. That desert itself had been wealthy agricultural land until some few hundred years ago. Legend has it that, overnight, due to gales brought about as a punishment to a laird who had sold his soul to the devil, hundreds of acres of rich farm land and many dwellings were silted over[6]. Today the Culbin Desert has become the Culbin Forest.

The reality of our own situation was more like a desert. The five Caddys filled the two tiny rooms of the trailer and I, thanks to the kindness of a hotel owner in the village, was allowed to sleep a mile or so away in the hotel staff quarters, which were closed for the winter. Each day I hiked across the dunes to spend the day with the Caddys. An extremely severe winter, well below freezing for six consecutive weeks — which incidentally froze every trailer water pipe in the park — made it necessary for me to go back to my room in the late afternoon just to turn on my electric underblanket. Otherwise it would have taken me hours to warm up and sleep in the unheated room. Despite the nuisance of an extra trip before spending the evenings with the Caddys, those hikes, following the countless animal and human trails winding among the hillocks and dunes, were for me the highlight of that period.

It was a strange situation for all us three mature and active people more or less hanging around together for no known reason. We had no jobs, having tried to get them without success. This in itself was strange, since Peter and I were both

---

[6] See Sinclair Ross in Section 9 reading list for a more accurate description of these events.

qualified and had never before had any difficulty finding employment. Despite the fact that we had gone through hells and bits of heaven together, we certainly did not stay together there for any personal reasons. At first we felt sure that we would be spending just the winter there and would return to the hotel when it re-opened at Easter. It was only the reassurance of our inner guidance that kept us in the situation.

The first few months we spent repairing the caravan. Following Sheena's training to do everything with love, to the glory of God, and as perfectly as possible, we sanded every unevenness from the surfaces of the trailer inside and out, and achieved impeccable results. After all, there was no lack of time to pressure us into botched jobs. A mobile library supplied us with books. I read autobiographies and murder stories. Peter, who had always had a wish to start his own garden but had very little opportunity for practical gardening, mainly read gardening books. We were isolated from everyone and everything, our only contacts with the outside world being a trip to nearby Forres when Peter and I collected our weekly unemployment benefits. Although we kept in touch with what was happening in the world through television and newscasts, our vital interest was in changing human consciousness, which the news rarely mentioned. In any case, changing consciousness was an individual task; we were getting on with it as best we could

Our continuing inner work had different focuses at different times. In the early Findhorn days, and with another like-minded friend, Lena, who joined us in the spring[7], we spent a great deal of time telepathically contacting the Network of Light. Briefly, this network was like a communication grid on subtle levels, covering the world in triangular patterns. The 'stations', usually manned by a group of spiritually dedicated people, existed in most countries throughout the world. This network

---

[7] In fact there are several early references in the archives to Lena arriving with her three children before the end of November 1962. In any case, it is a mistake to think of this period as involving 'Peter, Eileen and Dorothy and the three children'. There were in fact four adults and six children for virtually the entire time.

had been charted by an American friend of ours [Naomi Stephens] through telepathy, and we ourselves linked with it telepathically, sometimes receiving from these groups, sometimes broadcasting to them, and always linking the whole together in love. We also had telepathic communication with beings known in certain esoteric circles as the Masters of the Seven Rays. Basically, these Masters are highly developed humans who have accepted responsibility to aid humanity. Focusing on these beings as I knew them, I would get on their wavelengths, there being a distinctly different energy feel about each one. I was developing the faculty to attune to and distinguish subtle vibrations.

Easter came and Peter had received no offer to resume the management of the hotel. Since it seemed that we were stuck there for another year, I ordered an annexe from local builders for my accommodation. To supplement our food supply and to fulfil his wish to have a garden next to the trailer, Peter began to cultivate a small patch of ground, six by eleven feet, on which he grew a quick crop of radishes and lettuce. More time passed without jobs materialising, while he continued the cultivation of more ground around the trailer. This was no easy task on sand dunes in which only gorse and coarse grass grew. Underneath there were fine crops of pebbles very suitable for soakaways, but not for gardens. Peter cut off the top layer, then Eileen and I, occasionally helped by the boys, picked out the pebbles for about a foot down. Then Peter laid the top turf in the hole, upside down, and we shovelled the sand back, mixing in any bits of available compost. Then Peter planted vegetables, or sowed seeds. The many gardening books he read were a mixed blessing, with one book suggesting one method and the next advocating a different procedure — and none of them written for garden vegetables in sand dunes in northern Scotland. Our days began to centre around the garden, and we pursued our gardening with the same kind of care and perfection that we had learned to put into everything. It was hard physical work, often dreary, but being outdoors made it enjoyable to me.

In one of my meditations early in May I received an interesting new directive from within:

To those who have an insight into life, everything has meaning. For example, there is a spiritual meaning behind the constant blowing of the wind, in spite of any unpleasant results it may bring.

The forces of Nature are something to be felt into, to be reached out to . . . One of the jobs for you as my free child is to sense the Nature forces such as the wind, to perceive its essence and purpose for me, and to be positive and harmonise with that essence. It will not be as difficult as you immediately imagine because the beings of the forces . . . will be glad to feel a friendly power. All forces are to be felt into, even the sun, the moon, the sea, the trees, the very grass. All are part of my life. All is one life.

I thoroughly approved of this suggestion, thinking it would be a good excuse for time spent on walks or lying in the sun. I have always felt best alone in Nature. To me, lying in the sun with as much skin exposed as possible is not only a sensual delight but almost a spiritual experience. I feel blissfully spaced out, as if absorbing some sort of wholeness, and not even exposure to the tropical sun in Panama cured me of the feeling. But when I showed this guidance to Peter, he took it to mean that I was to feel into the forces of Nature to give him information about the garden. Next morning I received:

Yes, you can cooperate in the garden. Begin by thinking about the nature spirits, the higher overlighting nature spirits, and tune into them. That will be so unusual as to draw their interest here. They will be overjoyed to find some members of the human race eager for their help. This is the first step.

By the higher nature spirits I mean the spirits of differing physical forms such as clouds, rain, vegetables. The smaller individual nature spirits are under their jurisdiction. In the new world to come these realms will be open to humans — or I should say, humans will be open to them. Just be open and seek into the glorious realms of Nature with sympathy and understanding, knowing that these beings are of the Light, willing to help but suspicious of humans and on the lookout for the false. Keep with me and they will not find it, and you will all build towards the new.

I was left with a sinking feeling in my stomach. I felt totally incapable; how could I attune to beings about which I knew nothing? These seemed to be neither the fairies of children's literature nor the creatures of myth. Anyway, I was afraid that I might be under some illusion. I stalled, yet I knew from experience that I couldn't forever disregard an inner directive. While I was filled with all these disbeliefs and questions, Peter had none at all. His background in positive thinking trained him to admit no doubts. He had his faith affirmed by following Eileen's guidance for years, and he immediately accepted all guidance from us in complete faith. Peter, all action himself, expected the same of us. When I told him I couldn't do what my guidance had suggested, he simply replied, in his usual supportive, though forceful manner: "Nonsense, of course you can." This too probably put me off, since I have always responded better to requests than to commands.

With a sincere desire to increase our own firmness in action, Peter had, in fact, shared with Eileen, Lena and me a series of lectures that had been part of his training. Included in these was the exercise of repeating the phrase "I am Power." I had considerable trouble with this exercise at first, because I don't like the thought of power with its implications of force. I would not repeat the phrase, although I had no compunction about repeating, "I am Love." Then, on analysing myself, I concluded that the word 'power' was not the culprit, but the word 'I'. I had been thinking of the limited human personality called Dorothy as the 'I', as the power, instead of the unlimited God-essence of Dorothy. When I changed my identification, I could happily repeat that phrase. I was going through this series again, and on repeating "I am Power" one day, some weeks after the earlier guidance to contact the forces of Nature, I slipped into a stream of power. I became so identified with power that I felt I could do anything, even attune to the essence of the spirits behind Nature, as had been requested of me, for I as God-essence could be one with the essence of any part of creation. Vegetables had been mentioned in my guidance, and as Peter was interested in receiving guidance related to the garden, I decided to choose the garden pea, since it was growing in our garden and I had known it since childhood. I had a clear sense of what the plant was in terms of its colour, shape, flower and taste, and moreover I loved eating peas. Drawing on my familiarity with and fondness for peas, I imagined and focused on their essence, or inner spirit. The response was surprisingly immediate:

> *I can speak to you, human. I am entirely directed by my work, which is set out and moulded and which I merely bring to fruition, yet you have come straight to my awareness. My work is clear before me: to bring the force fields into manifestation regardless of obstacles, of which there are many on this man-infested world . . . While the vegetable kingdom holds no grudge against those it feeds, man takes what he can as a matter of course, giving no thanks, which makes us strangely hostile.*
>
> *What I would tell you is that as we forge ahead, never deviating from our course for one moment's thought, feeling or action, so could you. Humans generally don't seem to know where they are going, or why. If they did, what powerhouses they would be! If they were on a straight course, how we could cooperate with them! I have put my meaning across and bid you farewell.*

Although unclear as to what it would mean, cooperation with the spirits of Nature was an acceptable idea, since to me cooperation was and is the way to relate. When I showed the typed message to Peter, he composed a list of questions for me to ask the spirits of the various vegetables, since he had been facing a number of challenges.

Thus began a day-by-day unfoldment in communication with the forces behind Nature. Peter, of course, would try to find a reason for a plant's malfunction himself, but when he found none or did not know what to do, he would give me questions. Then I would attune to the spirit of the particular vegetable for the answer. Having done it once, I couldn't use the excuse that it was an impossible feat. In fact I now realise that my own or anyone else's belief in our limitation is the greatest block to achievement. So circumstances, using Peter as their able instrument, kept forcing me to turn to the Nature forces. For instance, we had two sowings of dwarf beans; the first lot didn't come up, while the second lot seemed promising. The spirit essence of dwarf beans told me that the first lot had been sown too deeply and before the soil had sufficient nutrition, but that the other was fine and was being worked on by them. The spinach sprouted so well that Peter asked if it was too thick. I received:

> *If you want strong natural growth of the leaf, the plants will have to be wider apart than they are at the moment By leaving them as they are, you will get overall as much bulk in the leaves, perhaps a little tenderer but with not as strong a life force. I, of course, like to see plants given full scope, but the choice is up to you.*

Even at this early stage, no laws were laid down and human freedom of choice was integral to the cooperation. Whatever we asked, I received an answer of some sort, sometimes merely 'yes' or 'no', and sometimes an explanation. For example, we were told, on request, when to water each plant, where to put in new ones, which needed liquid manure, etc. For the first couple of years, until we became familiar with this unfamiliar view of garden growth, Peter had frequent questions. However, he acted at once on suggestions given. Otherwise, I believe, the cooperation would not have continued.

As to who these Nature beings were, I quickly realised that each was not the spirit of the individual plant but was the 'overlighting' being of the species. I discovered that the being behind the garden pea held in its consciousness the archetypal design of all pea plants throughout the world, and looked after their welfare. Obviously such beings must function in more than our three dimensions, but my previous telepathic contact had made this concept familiar. A slight acquaintance with Theosophical literature, together with my inner promptings and the tremendous purity, joy and praise which these beings emanated, led me to conclude that they were some type of angel. As the word angel had a very restricted and stereotyped image in my mind, contrary to the impression of lightness, freedom and formlessness given by these beings, I decided, generally, to call them 'devas', a Sanskrit word meaning 'shining one'. The word was no doubt often used in India, but it was not hackneyed or conventional to my mind.

The Pea Deva was the first to come into my awareness. The second which my inner guidance suggested I should contact was a being overlighting that particular geographical area. I called it the Landscape Angel. I was told it would answer general questions concerning the soil at first, and later it would act as envoy for the whole angelic world. The Landscape Angel was very keen on compost, indicating that man had to play his part in this cooperation and that we couldn't expect them to do all the work, especially to grow vegetables in unnourishing sand. This Angel gave fairly detailed instructions on compost making, when to turn the compost, whether it should be mixed with the soil or laid on top as a mulch. Imperceptibly, the Landscape Angel gave us a more holistic approach to the garden, helping us to see it as part of the larger environment. We began to see the soil as part of a living organism and the plants as links with their environment, a focus of energy integrated and interacting with its surroundings. As my inner guidance said:

> As you read and try to understand that book (Agriculture, by Rudolf Steiner), you come across what are called cosmic influences on the Earth emanating from the various planets. Think of that planet as a living Being, and also as the forces being relayed by Beings and being received by Beings. There is no such thing as dead matter. Everything is living and everything has a place in my one life; and that life force is more than what you call magnetism. It is an influence consciously wielded on the higher levels. You are simply surrounded by life; you are a life force moving among other life forces. As you recognise this and open up to them, you draw near to them and become one with them, and work with them in my purposes.

The Landscape Angel said that since Peter, through me, had voiced the need for the ingredients necessary to make the soil live, he would be shown these ingredients as we did not have the money to buy them. Indeed he was: grass cuttings from the trailer park; soot from an ancient dump used by local chimney-sweeps; seaweed from the shore; and horse manure that we collected with buckets and spades from a field, to the puzzlement of both horses and passers-by. Once we obtained a bio-dynamic preparation for compost. All of us, including the children, went through the ritual of mixing it in a big vat, going round and round giving it the prescribed number of turns. It was fun and hard work; in fact this whole period was healthy, hard work for us all.

BUILDING THE COMMUNITY

Alex Walker

Not long after they moved the 'original caravan' to its new — and, unbeknown to them, permanent — location, Eileen received guidance that she should meditate in the caravan park public toilets[8] to overcome the difficulties of trying to find quietude in the cramped confines of their new home. Another test of her character, but one which proved its value, and for the next seven years she spent several hours per night there writing down her messages from God.

Eileen was not the only one tested. Dorothy and Peter had frequent clashes, and the group's tiny income was a continual source of stress, yet somehow the garden and the Community in miniature prospered.

The first person to join the founders was **Naomi**, who placed a caravan[9] on the site of what is now the sanctuary in the spring of 1964. Although in her seventies she worked hard to develop the links between the fledgling Community and the Network of Light, and under her tutelage they were able to reach and identify the centres more clearly. Naomi continued to live in the Community until 1966.

Guidance for the garden suggested:

> *You are to have as many varieties of fruits and vegetables as possible. Contact with the devas is essential, and this can only be done when each plant is actually grown.*

In the second season 65 kinds of vegetable, 21 fruits and 42 herbs were cultivated. This was also the first year of giant brassicas. One cabbage weighed in at 38lbs, and another at 42lbs (19kg). Flowers were not grown in the garden for another two years.

---

[8] Later converted to an apothecary.

[9] This caravan — latterly called 'Dorothy's' as she also used it as an office for a number of years — was re-sited just north of Doris's bungalow. It was finally scrapped in 1991.

This was also a time of many 'manifestation' stories. For example, in the spring of 1963 Peter had planned a concrete patio for the area next to the caravan. No money was available to buy materials but a few days later a neighbour arrived and told them that a truck had left a whole load of slightly damp cement in bags in a dump across the road. According to Peter: "Though it may seem an astounding coincidence, events like this had become normal in our lives."[10]

Although passers-by had noticed the extravagant growth even in its first year, by the summer of 1965 the developments in the garden were coming to the attention of a wider group of people.

In the August of 1965 Peter set off on a journey which took him to **Glastonbury**, where he met Tudor Pole, the founder of the Chalice Well Trust, and **Liebe Pugh** who had formed a group known as the Universal Link at Lytham St Annes in north-west England. He returned with the first genuine guests to the Community — Dr and Mrs Daniel Fry from Glastonbury.

On another trip Peter went to a conference at Attingham Park hosted by **Sir George Trevelyan**[11]. It must be remembered that at that time esoteric spiritual endeavours in the Western world were still confined to a tiny minority of fringe groups who often had little or no knowledge of one another. Books on these subjects were few and far between. In the rarefied upper-crust atmosphere of this gathering Peter's approach to life was considered outrageous by many of the participants, although Sir George himself was clearly impressed.

Despite his best attempts Peter had been unable to find a job of any kind, although Dorothy managed to find work as a secretary in the local area. Peter and Eileen presumed they were going back to Cluny Hill and were perhaps disappointed

---

[10] *Findhorn Garden*, page 5.

[11] The grandfather of the new age movement in Britain, Sir George was for a time a teacher at Gordonstoun school before entering into his public works. Founder of the Wrekin Trust, and a trustee of the Findhorn Foundation during the 70s and early 80s, he has published several books including *Summons To A High Crusade*; Findhorn Press; 1986.

when Eileen's guidance announced:

*There is no hurry for you to go back to Cluny Hill; that will
be brought about when this place is completed, and there is
still much more to be done here.*

Later in the year Peter and Eileen visited the sacred island
of **Iona** off the west coast of Scotland, staying at the St Columba
hotel. It was the only time Eileen had left Findhorn in nearly
three years[12]. Whilst on the island she received guidance to the
effect that the linking of the three centres of Glastonbury, Iona
and Findhorn was 'very important'. Meditations to further these
links continue to this day.

In the autumn of 1965 the County Horticulture Adviser visited the garden, and he was so impressed he asked Peter to
take part in a radio broadcast.

Early in 1966, R. Ogilvie Crombie (**Roc**), an elderly poly-
math from Edinburgh, visited the Community for the first time.
He had met Peter casually at a gathering in Edinburgh, and his
interest in the happenings at Findhorn had been aroused. It
seems that his visit awakened a long dormant[13] ability in Roc;
shortly after this visit he had his famous encounter with Kurmos the faun (see Section 3). Roc's connections with Pan and
the nature spirits have been well documented.

Yet Roc was not merely there to provide an additional perspective on gardening and nature. He also played an important part in the occult development of the Community. It is
clear that he acted as an advisor to Peter in many things, and
was occasionally instrumental in having Peter ask individuals
to leave that he felt were working against the appropriate development of the Community, consciously or otherwise. Although
Roc was a great support to Peter and Dorothy, Eileen had considerable resistance to this role as her training was very much
to remain positive and invoke the energies of the Christ. Her

---

[12] There are indications that Peter was seriously considering going to live
there, e.g. letter to Kathleen Fleming of 22.10.65 in Foundation Archives.

[13] Roc's connection with nature does of course go back much further than
this time. He had visited the Faerie Glen on the Black Isle as early as
1903.

guidance told her:

This is an example of where there needs to be unity in diversity.

Much later, during channelling sessions with David Spangler, the reply to a question would sometimes be, "Ask your Protector," meaning Roc. Although Roc never lived in the Community he continued to play this guardian role until his death in 1975.

In the Spring of 1966 five guests came for Easter, including Anthony Brooke[14] and Monica Parrish of the Universal Foundation. At Whitsun there were 17 guests. Also in that year the connection with Liebe Pugh was strengthened, Eileen and Peter both visiting her at Lytham St Annes. This visit had a profound effect on Eileen in two ways. First of all she felt a tremendous inner connection with Liebe and continued corresponding with her until her death just a few months later. Secondly this was the occasion when Eileen met **Joanie Hartnell Beavis** who had been working with Liebe for some time[15]. Joanie was to become Eileen's closest friend and support after she moved to Findhorn in 1967.

On Christmas Eve of 1967 Eileen, Peter and Joanie went to the power point on Cluny Hill. There Eileen had a series of dramatic visions. Shortly afterwards she received:

The day many have been waiting for is over. The cosmic power released at that appointed moment, felt by you and many others, has begun to reverberate around the universe. Nothing will stop it. It will gather momentum and power and it will be sensed by many as time goes on. Some may be disappointed because there was no outer manifestation. Nothing has gone wrong. It is simply that man has misinterpreted what has been prophesied. It has often happened that way.

This is the beginning of the universal happenings all over the world. This place will become world renowned, for nothing

---

[14] Anthony Brooke is also known as 'the last white Raj of Sarawak'.

[15] Joanie's first meeting with Liebe Pugh had been suggested by Robert and Aileen Ross Stewart. Ross, as he was universally known, became the first chairman of the Foundation's trustees.

will stop the expansion of work going on here. This release of cosmic power into the whole of the universe is far greater than you can ever imagine. Your feeling of uplifted consciousness is the start of great changes that will be felt by each individual everywhere. Forge ahead from strength to strength with My hallmark deeply imprinted, and be at perfect peace.[16]

In 1968 *God Spoke to Me* was published, six cedarwood bungalows were erected to house the growing Community, and Peter planted 600 beech trees as a hedge — a physical and psychic barrier around the gardens. During this year a perplexed government investigator decided to remove Peter's unemployment benefit, but by then the 'Findhorn Trust' had been conceived as a legal umbrella under which the growing activities of the Community could be organised. At about the same time a resident of the Samye Ling centre at Eskdalemuir visited the Community for the first time — **Craig Gibsone,** later destined to be a focaliser of the Foundation.[17]

This was also the year when Sir George Trevelyan first visited. Shortly thereafter he wrote to Lady Eve Balfour, founder of the Soil Association and author of *The Living Soil,* giving an enthusiastic account of his visit. On Lady Eve's recommendation **Professor Lindsay Robb**, a consultant to the Soil Association, arrived in early 1969. After his tour of the garden with Peter and Roc he wrote:

The vigour, health and bloom of the plants in this garden at midwinter on land which is almost barren, powdery sand cannot be explained by the moderate dressings of compost, nor indeed by the application of any known cultural methods of organic husbandry. There are other factors at work, and they are vital ones.

---

[16] Corroboration for the importance of this time was received in a transmission of 'Limitless Love and Truth' by David Spangler. See William Irwin Thompson; *Passages About Earth*: page 160ff, and also the study paper on Sri Aurobindo and the Mother in Section 9 below.

[17] His recollection is that the gardens, although beautiful and clearly a factor of major significance, were not as eye-catchingly extravagant as earlier reports indicate.

The Park sanctuary was constructed in 1969, and Eileen received guidance to build the original part of the Community Centre[18]. On 19th March a BBC programme about the Community was broadcast and over 600 visitors came during the year, nearly 200 of them as residential guests.

One prestigious visitor to the Community at this time was **Richard St Barbe Baker,** the indefatigable 'Man of the Trees'. He was one of the very few individuals to receive a personal Deva message through Dorothy.

---

[18] The original building comprised the kitchen, entrance hall and the serving area adjacent to the kitchen. The main dining area was added in the 70s, and the circular two-storey extension in 1987.

THE COLLEGE

Alex Walker

In the 60s the Community was a magical place, but one where the expectations were no less than a full day's work, seven days a week, and a serious-minded commitment to both work and spiritual practice. 1970 saw the arrival of **David Spangler** and **Myrtle Glines**, and this event ushered in a whole new era in which education rather than the gardens became the focus of activity, and a younger generation of new members began to take themselves more lightly.

David was born in Columbus, Ohio in 1945, but he spent six formative years in Morocco from 1951 to 1957. During this period he began having intense mystical experiences, and contacts with spiritual beings. He began a course in biochemistry at Arizona State University, but his inner experiences prompted him to leave and begin a career as a lecturer and philosopher. His intellectual influence on the Community's development in the 70s was enormous. To him we owe the idea of the Community as a college, and the wealth of written and lecture material he contributed over the three years of his residence here, and occasions subsequent to that, is prodigious.

His lectures and study papers, fully listed in the Appendix, cover a wide range of topics including education, esoterics, art, nature, sexuality, government, etc. According to an early Foundation pamphlet his book *Revelation: the Birth of a New Age,* which contains transmissions from a source known as '**Limitless Love and Truth**' "contains, more than any other, the philosophical basis for what is evolving in the Foundation. With all this expansion into the realm of the intellect, David also reminded us constantly that, above all, life is the school, and work and relationships are as good a teacher as any classroom. David helped to expand our consciousness, and bring into it an awareness of the Community's planetary and universal role in the new age."

The impact of all this work was evident from the growth in Community size. In 1970 there were about 20 members, by

1972 there were 120, and by 1974 over 150, with 25 guests per week arriving in the summer months. These changes did not suit everyone. Lena, an intensely shy woman, moved first to Pineridge, and then left the Community altogether sometime in 1971.

Also in 1971 Eileen was told in meditation that she should cease giving out guidance for the Community, a state of affairs that has, with rare exceptions, remained to this day.

In 1972, acting on legal advice that the deed of the original trust was not really adequate to encompass the work of the Community, the **Findhorn Foundation** was created on 9th May (which date is therefore the Foundation's birthday as opposed to the Community's anniversary which is celebrated on 17th November). The first trustees were Captain Robert Ross Stewart, Sir George Trevelyan, Pauline Tawse (who was later to donate the Park Building[19] to the Foundation), John Hilton and Joanie Hartnell Beavis. In the same year a house on Iona — **Traigh Bhan**, meaning white beach — was gifted to the Foundation by Jessica Ferrara who had lived there for some years.[20]

---

[19] Then the residence of Alex and May Gibson, the owners of Findhorn Bay Caravan Park. After they sold the Park Building, they moved to Cullerne House.

[20] Katherine Collis was intimately involved in this process, and the Foundation continues to honour the connection between Traigh Bhan and the Lorians.

THE FOUNDATION IN THE 70S AND 80S

Carol Riddell

(Extracts from The Findhorn Community, *pp 80-89)*

Directly or indirectly, David drew to us many young people, who brought with them guitars, long hair and a lifestyle with a definite Californian flavour of casual manners and sun shorts. They drank in the wine of early Findhorn Community esoterics and began to build. The majority did not stay very long. In the early 70s the average length of membership seems to have been only about six months. But others took their place, and many were practically minded. The flavour of the Community began to change — cramped living conditions, sing-songs, artistic groups, collective projects and a gentle resistance to authority are characteristic of this 'middle-period' Findhorn Community.

In this period an area called Pineridge in the north-east of the Caravan Park was 'colonised' and transformed, the Community centre was extended to accommodate the many new members and guests, the craft studios went up[21] and the present publications building was completed. The Community started to produce audio tapes, and there was a strong emphasis on the performing arts. The mood was one of dynamism and expansion. By 1974 the physical layout of the Park was much as it is today. There were 180 members, and an education programme was in place.

Over a seven-year period, Peter and Eileen released their control over the Community. In 1972[22] Eileen was directed to cease sharing her guidance with everyone else:

Let go, stand back and allow all those in the Community to live a life guided and directed by Me. Let them learn from experience to live positively, demonstrating the laws of manifestation in their own lives. If this means that the work is held up for the time being, let it be held up. Until life is lived,

[21] In 1971.

[22] Other sources, e.g. *Flight Into Freedom,* state this occurred in 1971.

lessons are not learned, and these lessons are far more important than expanding without learning, living on what others have learned.

In Eileen's view, Peter had become rather dependent on her guidance; its withdrawal was a challenge for him. But without sharing her guidance, Eileen herself became unsure of her role in the Community. An examination of copies of *Findhorn News,* circulated to supporters of the Community in this period, shows how important the guidance was. Up to 1971 practically every item of information is backed by a piece of guidance. By August 1971 David Spangler's work begins to fill the magazine, which Peter edited at this period. The withdrawal of guidance increased the strain in Peter's relationship with Eileen, for her guidance-receiving ability was, for him, one of the ties between them. He began to turn to others for support, and also formed a 'core' group of seven, the nucleus of a management group, which soon grew to 12 members[23]. But often the delegation of responsibility did not provide results that met his standards.

> *To prepare for my leaving the Community for short periods of time, we have decided to form a Core Group of seven members who would be responsible for the Community while I was away . . . During the past few months I have been sharing all that has been happening with the Core Group, and am now gradually withdrawing to enable them to take on the running of the Community.*
>
> (From 'View from the Centre', by Peter Caddy, *Findhorn News,* April, 1974.)

Peter also set up a 'focalisers' group of those responsible for departments in the diversifying Community (March, 1974)[24].

---

[23] Histories can perhaps only ever be a metaphor for truth rather than a description of some absolute. It may already be obvious that the various personal recollections of our past on offer are not always in complete accord. It has been suggested that this sentence does not take into account the fact that Eileen continued to share her guidance with Peter for some time after she ceased to do so for the Community. Such guidance supported the formation of Core Group.

[24] or Spring 1973, in response to the departure of the Lorians.

Key decisions were discussed in Community meetings. In addition, in 1973, not only David Spangler but also Dorothy Maclean[25] left the Community — soon to organise the Lorian Association in the United States.

Peter's heart opened to a young Swedish woman to whom he had given responsibility in the Community. Although there was no sexual relationship, Eileen reacted sharply. The Community was thrown into a period of uncertainty but there was no challenge to Peter's overall authority. An editorial in the February 1975 *Open Letter* — which replaced *Findhorn News* — reports:

> *We at [the] Findhorn [Community] are embarking on the first lap of a new cycle in our development; the phase of building the foundation of the Community is reaching completion and now we are involving ourselves in a deeper and more conscious commitment to the New Age through training and education. Individual wholeness comes first, and the changes that Peter and Eileen Caddy are experiencing within their own relationship are reflected in the changes in the whole Community.*

Early in this transition period, in 1973, the decision to build our 'Universal Hall' (originally the 'University Hall') was made. Eileen's guidance for the Hall was clear. A functional hall was to be put up fast, with the emphasis then turning to proper housing for members, who had to live in very cramped conditions in caravans. But although this guidance was shared, the Core Group were now receiving advice and ideas from many sources. The divine inspiration of the Findhorn Community required the development of inner attunement by the membership, so that each could individually harmonise with higher truth. But the Community had in the past relied on others for its decision-making process, and was not experienced at this level of inner work. It was much more exciting to embark on

---

[25] And several other prominent Community members including Roger and Katherine Collis, Kathi and Milenko Matanovic. Some students of Community history perceive in this exodus of talent the beginnings of the financial and management problems of the later 70s.

the building of a major monument, a project which kindled the collective enthusiasm of the young members, rather than on the construction of a utilitarian hall. The more superficially attractive view prevailed.

Ten years later we had the monument, a superb building in stone, beautifully furnished and decorated, with magnificent mural paintings. It also contributed greatly, however, to a very large debt, and the collective energy of the Community for construction was exhausted.

In the period up to 1979, when he left, Peter delegated more authority to the Core Group. This group still used meditation and attunement as a basis for its decision-making, but without Eileen's guidance a current of more ordinary, administrative decision-making became stronger. The Core Group was self-selective; as someone dropped out, so someone else would be attuned to by the group.

In an article in the *Open Letter* of December 1975 Nick Rose commented:

> *Like the rest of [the] Findhorn [Community] the Core Group is divinely ordinary. It is prey to the lures of glamour and illusion like any other group. It is striving to improve its communication with the Community. It is trying not to impose a vision in such a wilful and purposeful manner that it inhibits the growth of personal vision.*

In the Findhorn Community, Divine will unfolds itself unhurriedly, without the stress and impatience which our cultures regard as the norm. We have to relearn patience and right timing. The Core Group provided stability during a time when membership turnover was high and individuals had a shorter period in the Community for spiritual development. Only in the later part of the 1980s did a new trend in management emerge.

Expansion and Glamour

Throughout the 70s thousands of guests visited the Findhorn Foundation, were inspired and returned to spread their inspiration in changed lives. This is the true and simple history of the Findhorn Foundation, and it continues today. The more detailed events and dramas are the stage settings within which this process of transformation and development of love occurs.

Peter and Eileen were not exempt from change. Peter's relationship with Eileen became steadily more distanced. His priorities were changing, and he left the Community in 1979 to develop himself by means of a new series of relationships. He remarried in 1982, and his new wife demanded from him a large share in the physical upbringing of their child. Peter was, in his seventies, required to learn the more mundane aspects of fatherhood. Through a further marriage he has been experiencing the more devotional aspects of religion so familiar to Eileen in her moments of inner surrender.

Eileen, on the other hand, has gradually conquered her shyness to become a lecturer and spiritual guide, unafraid before mass audiences of thousands. In this respect Peter and Eileen's example, which has demanded great readjustment relatively late in life when others are thinking of 'taking it easy', has been inspirational to us.

While they were still together, Eileen and Peter were given the gift of returning to Cluny Hill, as promised in Eileen's guidance many years earlier. In the intervening period the hotel had become very run down, and the Community purchased it for the ridiculously small sum of £60,000[26]. At the time, though, it was a huge step to take. It was a relatively collective Community decision[27], although the then Community treasurer[28] resigned over it. So Cluny Hill Hotel became **Cluny Hill College**.

---

[26] On 17th November 1975.

[27] Meaning that Peter brought Community members to Cluny Hill for tours of the premises, and that the Community at large was informed of the process rather than being involved in the decision as such. In fact there was a serious division of opinion on this issue. From this point on Peter was often on tour. On his return, Core Group resolutions would sometimes be overturned. It would be some time before the Community as a whole would actively participate in major decisions.

[28] John Hilton, an ex-bank manager who had been at loggerheads with Peter for some time over the deficits the Foundation had been running up. His resignation was not immediate but came some months later.

The purchase of Cluny set loose an impulse for property acquisition which turned out to be a double-edged sword for the Community. Eileen's guidance spoke of the development of a 'Village', eventually growing into a 'City of Light'. Members began to feel that God was guiding the process, so all we had to do was acquire, and He would make sure of the funds[29]. The key year was 1978. We were given **Drumduan House**, and its gardens were lovingly renovated at great expense. It was finally occupied by the Moray Steiner School in 1987. **Station House** was bought as members' accommodation and refurbished. In a more controversial decision Core Group decided to buy **Cullerne House** and grounds.

A group of members borrowed money to purchase another old house, **Newbold**. We accepted the custodianship of an island called **Erraid**, on the west coast of Scotland, off the island of Mull. Erraid is owned by two Dutch families, but we were offered its use for a small community for ten months of the year.

We were getting big and over-extended and the debts were mounting up. At the end of the 1970s we were far out-spending our income, and owed more than £300,000 to private individuals and to the bank.

With hindsight it is clear that a superficial interpretation of divine protection led to irresponsibility and carelessness, a kind of collective materialism similar to that evident in the former Soviet Union, where no one felt responsible for property that belonged to the abstract 'State'. Even in 1985 after a new, strict financial policy had long been in place, I arrived in Drumduan garden, which had not been properly worked for two years, to find four lawn mowers in the garden shed, none of them functional. With a little attention we managed to get three in working order!

* * *

---

[29] Several individuals have pointed out that this was by no means a unanimous feeling. The influence of David Spangler's work on the 'New Laws of Manifestation' was of crucial importance at this time, and of course in the absence of the author a variety of interpretations were extant.

The attraction and glamour of esoterica also reached their peak in the late 1970s. David Spangler had warned the Community about glamour in an open letter written from America in 1975:

Glamour is the greatest challenge facing us today. It causes us to step off the balanced track and wander in culs de sac. It is a form of entrancement, bewitchment, hypnotism. It generates illusion (and is a product of it, as well) and it hinders communication. In fact, that is its greatest danger and characteristic. Glamour distorts communication and communion by altering the perspective of a single quality so that other qualities can no longer relate to it. It is like loud music playing when you are trying to quietly think or to converse with others; it is like over-inflating a tyre on your automobile so that the vehicle tilts and cannot run on a level. It fosters the creation of private worlds in which our attention is trapped and others cannot truly communicate with us.

. . . The Christ is found in life's processes, high and low, and not just in special events or people who may satisfy certain needs for stimulation and glamour. Building for the New Age is not tripping from charismatic happening to charismatic happening, like a junkie looking for his daily 'fix'. The Christ, the New Age, planetary transformation are not meant to be addictions; our work is not really expressed in terms of visions, lights, sounds, seizures of energy, and hallelujahs . . . Being the Christ is an everyday commitment to life as it is and as it is unfolding to become in revelation of its Divine Essence, a life seen beyond frills or glamour, lived in recognition of the uniqueness of each day and of the Divinity that is the fabric from which that uniqueness is woven.

(*Reflections on the Christ,* pp 102, 113)

In spite of David's warnings, the Community had to learn its lesson about glamour. The problem came to a head with the 'crystal incident' in 1978. A small group of people began visiting the Community, and some became members, who felt that only with certain kinds of decoration and design, and particularly through the use of crystals, could the appropriate energy be properly channelled here. Indeed, it was not so much divine energy, but the energy of the fabled past civilisation of Atlantis which was to be incorporated into our almost completed Universal Hall through a special configuration of crystals and wires. The whole conception was not properly communicated to the membership, and Peter's authority was still such that there was considerable acceptance of the new idea.

A specially cut quartz crystal, about the size of a grapefruit, was prepared and suspended on gold wires[30] in the centre of the Hall. The gold wires led to the supporting pillars, from which silver wires led down into the foundations. In the basement, a smaller crystal was embedded in the floor, and a piece of meteoritic iron sat above it. A third crystal was fixed to a light in the centre of the ceiling. The Hall was closed for some time before this occult arrangement was finished and then, around Christmas 1978, a special ceremony of invocation was held to inaugurate the energy transfer. Craig Gibsone remembers walking out of the ceremony and leaving the Community[31], so great was his disgust. He returned only in 1983.

A year and a half later, during a presentation by a visitor from the Edgar Cayce Foundation, the wires snapped and the crystal fell, smashing a two-inch-thick glass panel in the floor and narrowly missing the speaker, who had 'providentially' not chosen to stand in the centre of the Hall. The crystal shattered into many pieces, to almost everyone's great relief. Eileen was not present at the talk, but her comment when informed of the event was: "Thank God[32]." She collected the crystal fragments and, following her guidance, they were returned to the earth from which they came. This curious incident ended a period which taught the Community some hard lessons.

'Psychic glamour' is widespread in the 'new age' movement nowadays. It caters for people who are dissatisfied with the

---

[30] Or wire.

[31] These events did not happen simultaneously. Several months passed before Craig's departure.

[32] Although she had supported the original idea. Eileen was on Core Group for much of the 1970s.

cruder aspects of materialism, but who still retain a desire to purchase personal transformation quickly for a fee. Such demands are fulfilled by a large coterie of 'psychic entrepreneurs' who advertise their wares in the host of 'new age' magazines. Many people still visit us expounding their 'visions' or new techniques, trying to set us to rights. We enjoy them and thank them, and they pass on elsewhere. We are becoming more and more conscious of the simplicity and directness of the divine message — that our purpose is to find the divine within, the criterion for which is the practice and experience of unconditional love. Our work is too important to be side-tracked.

The Early 1980s: Caution and Retrenchment

As a result of the controversies surrounding the acquisition of property and the distortion of glamour, a number of members left the Community. We entered a phase of caution and uncertainty, like a child who has been disciplined. Strict accounting became the watchword, and the attempt to take responsibility for our debts and reduce them a primary goal. Instead of a warm welcome for anyone who claimed paranormal abilities, the Community became very cautious about psychics.

When I arrived at the Findhorn Foundation in 1983, my practice of what I then called 'psychic healing' and clairvoyance was regarded with considerable caution, and I was advised to give it up for a few years while I adjusted to the Community. In 1984 when I started an intensive organic vegetable garden at Cullerne, I noticed a beautiful rose quartz crystal in an out-of-the-way corner of the Park, and thought it would be a lovely decoration for the centre of the garden. Not knowing about the 'crystal incident', I was taken aback by the hornets' nest this proposal stirred up, and had to release the idea. We were still in reaction against crystals, which are in themselves harmless enough things. But when the rose quartz crystal was finally put in one of the Cullerne gardens a couple of years later, guests started doing rituals around it and it had to be removed once more.

When Peter left, he handed on the focalisation of the Community to François Duquesne. It was a critical time. François's cautious and rational approach to finance and organisation was essential for this period of retrenchment. The Community needed to reconnect with a coherent vision. François deeply felt the need for the 'village' of Eileen's guidance to be made into a reality. He strongly supported expansion beyond the Educational Foundation of the Trust Deed into a spiritually based Community, embracing business activity.

The great opportunity in this direction was the purchase of the Caravan Park, which François negotiated. The Park, where the Community was founded, came up for sale in 1983. It was obvious that we should become custodians of this land. Furthermore, the maintenance of the commercial side of the business for some years could give us a source of income, which we sorely needed in our indebted state. The owner, knowing that we were the only likely customer, drove a hard bargain. A sustained campaign was launched, in which each member took responsibility for manifesting funds for the cost of a particular area of the Park. This gave individuals a direct stake in fund-raising. Appeals were sent to previous Community members and visitors; auctions and fund-raising events followed each other in quick succession. We were able to raise what we considered an appropriate price for the land but the owner held out for another £80,000. We had to go further into debt, with the affirmation that we would pay this new debt off within a year, which we did. The Park was purchased in November 1983, the high point of François's time as focaliser[33].

Current Trends

The purchase of the Caravan Park marked a positive turning point. A programme for steady debt reduction was in place, the membership was smaller and its average age began to go up. Members stayed longer. Some independent businesses started to form. People began to come here to live their lives with and around us without being members of the Foundation. For the first time a real distinction between the Community and Foundation emerged. There has been a move towards the decentralisation of responsibility, which means that individual members become less dependent on a centralised leadership.

In 1988, Foundation members were involved in a long period of collective and individual attunement to create a new spiritual Core Group. This process represents the most determined attempt yet to move towards a spiritual democracy, based not merely on simple voting, but on contact with inner vision.

Although our financial crisis is by no means over, within very limited means the Foundation is beginning to build permanent accommodation for members.

Finally, a Community of people is growing who want their lives to have a spiritual centre and who find support in the Findhorn Foundation ambience.

Note that the process of creating a new Core Group is one that changes quite frequently. This subject is covered in more detail in Section 10.

---

[33] 1983 was a genuine *annus mirabilis* in comparison to the previous years of struggle and difficulty. That year saw an all-out community effort to secure four key objectives. These were:

- the purchase of the caravan park
- the completion of the Universal Hall, which had lain semi-finished since the mid-70s. The construction and decoration of the foyer and café were completed hours before the commencement of the 3rd World Wilderness Congress in October.
- a re-invigoration of life at the Park, which had become very moribund due to the general decline in membership and the particularly harsh winter in 1981/2 which had sent many single people scampering for the relative warmth of Cluny. In early 1983 the Wednesday evening KP crew consisted of a single individual who enterprisingly usually left a note in the hatch asking the five or so souls who were likely to eat there to wash their own plates.
- the successful implementation of a balanced budget.

In no subsequent year have such clear objectives been identified and fulfilled.

Foundation and Community

Alex Walker

Future trends for the Foundation are hard to predict, but it seems likely that the redevelopment of the caravan park with permanent buildings will take up a considerable amount of time and energy for the foreseeable future. The success of the educational programmes has been proven over more than fifteen years, and although it will require constant effort to ensure their continued excellence, the Foundation's special place in the minds of those seeking spiritual alternatives seems assured. There are several initiatives to develop links between the Foundation and academia at present and they may well prove to be a major area of importance in the future.

The role and nature of spiritual practice in the Foundation also goes through changes from time to time. The current separation of Core Group, with its spiritual focus, from Management Committee, with its administrative focus, will presumably remain for the time being and may prove to be the point of inspiration for a greater element of overt spiritual practice and celebration, and a renewed interest in retreats.

Quite apart from these conscious elements of policy there appears to be a less predictable element of learning that goes on in the collective. The effects of this process may be compared to the pendulum of a clock which swings from one side to another. For example the financial excess of the mid-70s gave way to the austerities of the following period. This may seem to be an obvious example of cause and effect but other examples are more enigmatic. For instance in the days of the 'Cullerne Garden School' during the early 80s, the work ethic was absolutely predominant and phenomenal energy was put into the physical structures. Unfortunately this left little time for dealing with the human side of affairs and when the Garden School collapsed it was quickly replaced by a group which, for a while, had more of an interest in 'process' and a laissez faire attitude to productivity which was the antithesis of the earlier activities.

There are many other examples — too many members, too few members; too little accommodation, too much accommodation (this seems to be a bi-annual cycle); authoritarian structures versus relative anarchy; broken-down buses, new Mercedes Benzes; intense activity in the studios, empty studios; and so on.

Perhaps these are simply very ordinary events, and it is too tempting to read esoteric symbols into them, but there does appear to be a kind of collective learning process by which one emphasis has to be replaced at a later date by its opposite, a situation which it is not always easy to apprehend in the short term.

However, from 1988 to 1993 the most significant area of expansion in the Community took place outside of the Foundation itself, and it is to this that we now turn.

NFD Ltd
New Findhorn Directions Ltd, the Foundation's wholly owned trading company, was created in 1979. From 1979 to 1983 its principal activity was Weatherwise Solar, now a semi-independent company called AES Ltd. From 1983 to 1987 its main activity was running the commercial part of Findhorn Bay Caravan Park. Since then it has taken on a number of activities once run as Foundation departments, such as Findhorn Press and the Phoenix shop, and added a number of new ones such as the Wind Park. Of course the activities of the company remain in every way very close to the Foundation as can be seen from its mission statement below. Nonetheless it is significant that NFD's trading turnover now exceeds the value of total Foundation income from education, donations etc.

A recent trend has been to encourage wider investment in some of these activities and at the time of publication Findhorn Press has become an independent organisation.

NFD's Mission Statement
'Celebrating Business As Sacred.'
In order to achieve this:
1. We commit ourselves to integrating an awareness of the presence of God into all our levels of activity including

inter-personal relationships and our decision-making processes.

2. We commit ourselves to the creation of an environment that supports the physical, emotional and spiritual well-being of our customers, employees, managers, suppliers and shareholders.

3. We commit ourselves to the fostering of businesses that promote excellence in their products and services, always maintaining an attitude of respect for the Earth.

4. We commit ourselves to implementing all of the above in such a way as to generate sufficient profit for the further development of the company and the support of other areas of the Findhorn Foundation, like-minded organisations and our local community, and to be a source of inspiration world-wide.

The Board of Directors
May 6th 1992

Our Mission Statement reflects the hopes and intentions of many people. We do not believe it always accurately portrays the way things are at NFD so much as the way we would like things to be. It is our dissatisfaction with current reality, when compared with what is possible, that spurs us toward excellence and toward creating a better person, company and world. When NFD fails to measure up to its stated Mission Purpose, as it inevitably will at times, we should not despair. Rather let us take up the challenge together to bring our reality closer toward our vision.

The Wider Community

Even more growth has occurred in the wider Community. Some of this has involved the creation of educational organisations such as Newbold Trust and Moray Steiner School, and the programmes at Minton House. A great deal of it involves individuals operating small companies or as sole traders in a wide number of activities.

Integrating this growth has not been easy. Numerous titles have been given to different groups such as independent members, associates etc and there has sometimes been significant confusion about the role of such individuals relative to one another and to the Foundation. On more than one occasion we have been warned that we are in danger of creating several different and to a greater or lesser degree antagonistic communities, rather than one united by a common vision. Moves are now afoot to create a Community organisation of some kind, but at the time of writing it is not yet clear what its role will be.

Much of the confusion stems from the fact that the Foundation is the owner of virtually all the available collective facilities in the Community, but finds itself unable to provide for everyone's needs. Conflicting views about appropriate uses of for example the Community Centre and the Hall have therefore arisen.

The Basis of the Spiritual Community

Any group of individuals has a complex web of interactions which no simple description can ever provide anything more than a general guide to understanding. Nonetheless, comprehension of the Community as a whole can be aided by reference to the diagram opposite.

Its main features are:

- There is a spiritual impulse here around which all connected with the Community are aligning themselves.
- The 'Hub' of this Community is Core Group. The facilities directly associated with this are the sanctuaries, the Quiet Garden, Traigh Bhan etc.
- Gathered around this Hub are a variety of organisations and individuals who choose to consciously support this centre — the Foundation's education and building programmes, NFD, Moray Steiner School, and all Foundation associates and members of the 'Selectorate'[34] are part of this inner ring. Note however that the alignment is to the spiritual core, not necessarily to the Foundation itself.

---

[34] The Selectorate is the name given to a group made up of Foundation members/employees and long-term Community residents. See Section 10 for further details.

SCHEMATIC DIAGRAM
OF THE
SPIRITUAL COMMUNITY

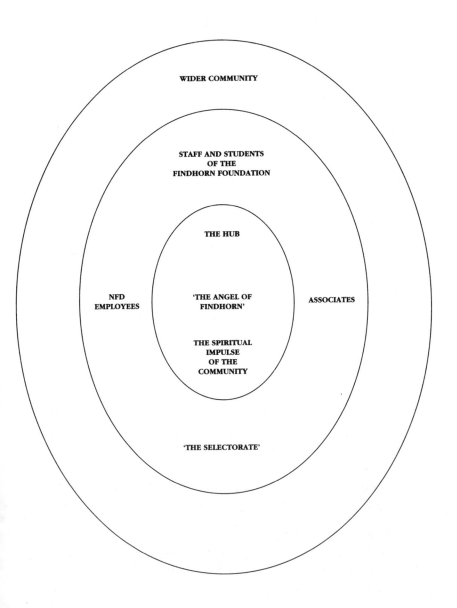

- There is an 'outer ring' of groups, individuals and organisations who are here in part at least because of the spiritual impulse at the centre, but who do not necessarily wish to formally associate themselves with our work for whatever reason.
- Beyond this metaphorical outer ring there is of course the wider community of West Moray who have no association with our work.

There is no suggestion that those in the outer ring (or beyond) are any less spiritual than those nearer the centre. It is simply that they are choosing to express their spirituality in a way which is different from ours.

The above section is an amended extract from 'A Five Year Strategic Plan for the Findhorn Foundation: Part B'; unpublished Foundation report; 1992.

Other Items of Useful Information
This section contains a brief selection of items of information not included in the main text, but which readers may find of interest.

Past Focalisers of the Foundation

> Peter Caddy 1962-79
> François Duquesne 1979-83
> Jay Jerman 1983-87
> Craig Gibsone 1987-91
> Judy Buhler-MacAllister 1992 -

As explained in Section 10, Roger Benson and Joan Jerman were considered as co-directors of the Foundation for some time during Craig's tenure.

Judith Bone became acting focaliser of the Foundation for several months during the 1991-2 interregnum.

The Founders Today
Eileen Caddy spends some of her time on speaking tours, and in visiting her extensive family, but her home base is very much at the Findhorn Foundation.

Dorothy Maclean is similarly still active, visiting the Community from time to time. She has her home in Washington State.

After Peter Caddy left the Community he spent some time in the United States where he married Paula McLaughlin. Together they had a son, Daniel. They subsequently divorced and Peter eventually married Renata Zurn. Sadly, Peter died in a car accident in February 1994, shortly before his 77th birthday. His ashes are interred in the grounds of the home where he and Renata lived together in southern Germany.

Lena Lamont is described as one of the 'four founders' in some early literature. Unfortunately our contacts with her and her family have ceased since she left and her present whereabouts are not known.

Community Facilities

Minton House. Purchased by Judith Meynell and others in 1983, Minton has run a variety of workshops and other events over the past ten years. In 1994 plans are afoot to set up a charity — the Minton Trust — to embrace many of these activities, particularly retreats, workshops, inter-faith dialogue and 'faith in business' oriented events. The house will also continue to offer both bed and breakfast and longer-term accommodation.

Moray Steiner School. Founded as a department of the Foundation in 1985 it was originally located at the 'Family House' on Pineridge and moved to Drumduan in 1987. The school is now an independent company limited by guarantee with charitable status. The creation of the school was one of the most important achievements of Jay Jerman's term as focaliser

Newbold House. After a brief period as part of the Foundation, Newbold became an independent trust in the 1970s. The many activities at Newbold are similar to those of the Foundation and are described in detail in the Foundation's guest brochure.

AES LTD. Aka Weatherwise Solar. 'Weatherwise' was one of the first divisions of NFD under the direction of Lyle and Liza Schnadt. In 1983 it became independent, returning as a partly owned subsidiary of NFD in the 90s.

One Earth Magazine publishes a wide range of information

about Community life. It was at one time a Foundation department, but it became independent in 1990.

Findhorn Bay Holistic Health Centre, which offers a
range of health care services for the Community, was formed
as an independent charity in 1993.

Trees for Life, whose work is discussed in Section 3, also
became an independent charity in 1993.

Information on these organisations, and a range of other
Community facilities is outlined in 'Welcome to the Findhorn
Foundation', an information pack first published by the Foun-
dation in 1994 as a guide to new members of the Community.

Reading List

Eileen Caddy;
God Spoke to Me; 1971; *Footprints on the Path*; 1976; *The Living Word*;
1977; *The Dawn of Change*,1979; *Opening Doors Within*; 1987. All
published by Findhorn Press. *Flight Into Freedom*; Element Books,
1988 (Eileen's autobiography). *Foundations of a Spiritual Community*; Findhorn Press, 1991 (originally published as *Foundations of
Findhorn*; 1976). A selection of extracts from Eileen's guidance edited
by Roy MacVicar. For some it contains the essence of spiritual life in
a New Age community and perhaps would be an adequate substi-
tute for this entire collection of study papers. *Opening Doors Within*
(video); Ironwood Productions; 1991. *The Spirit of Findhorn*; new edition 1994 (originally published by Fowler UK & Harper & Row USA
in 1975).
Peter Caddy; *The Findhorn Story*; unpublished draft; 16.11.1971.
Peter Caddy & Jeremy Slocombe; *In Perfect Timing*; unpublished
1993 draft of Peter's autobiography — we eagerly await its publication.
Findhorn Community; *Faces of Findhorn*; Findhorn Press; 1980.
(Now out of print.) *The Findhorn Garden*; second UK edition by Findhorn Press; 1988. Other publishing details appear in the reading list
for Section 3.
Paul Hawken; *The Magic of Findhorn;* Fontana; 1975. This is now a
very dated view of the Community, and although factually accurate,
its style is hardly that of understatement. It is important to note that
in Dorothy Maclean's view Sheena Govan is largely seen through
Eileen's eyes and comes across as a much less wise and loving person than she actually was, and that 'the village simpleton' a.k.a.
Munion who helped out Eileen on Mull was more than somewhat
maligned too.
Dorothy Maclean; *To Hear the Angels Sing*; first published by Lorian
Press; 1980. Now published by Morningtown Press, USA. Dorothy's
autobiography.
NFD Team Member Welcome Pack; New Findhorn Directions Ltd.;
unpublished internal document; 1993.
Psychic Magazine; *The Findhorn Experience* by Antoinette May;
July/August 1975. A four-page summary of the early days.
Carol Riddell; *The Findhorn Community: Creating a Human Iden-
tity for the 21st Century*; Findhorn Press; 1990.
David Spangler; *Links with Space*; 1971; *Revelation — The Birth of
a New Age*; 1972; *The Little Church*; 1972; *New Age Rhythms*; 1972;

Festivals in the New Age, 1976; *Laws of Manifestation*, 1976; *Towards a Planetary Vision*, 1977; *Vision of Findhorn Anthology*, 1977; *Relationship and Identity*, 1978; *Reflections on the Christ*, 1978; *Explorations*, 1980. All published by Findhorn Press and now out of print.
William Irwin Thompson; *Passages About Earth: An Exploration of the New Planetary Culture*; Harper and Row; 1973.

Three
Nature and Ecology

Man has never been far from Eden.
It has been as close as a heartbeat,
As a new breath, as a shift of thought.

When man ate the apple
Of the tree of good and evil,
He did not leave the garden
He simply sank into slumber.

If man would know of good and evil,
He must dream and be filled
With the wisdom of dreaming;

Man still dreams beneath that tree,
In Eden.
Let him now awake.

David Spangler, *New Age Rhythms*, p 57

From its earliest days the Findhorn Community has always involved experiments in cooperation with nature.

In this section, the first paper by Roc concerns his initial meetings with Pan and other nature spirits. It was originally published in *The Findhorn Garden*.

The second paper by David Spangler further explores the relationship between humanity and nature. It forms part of the Original Series of Foundation Study Papers.

The third paper by William Bloom examines our contemporary relationship with the unseen worlds, and was written especially for this book.

The next section is a brief overview of some of the developments in the field of ecology which have influenced us over the years.

The final piece itemises some of the current Community practices in the realm of cooperation with nature.

CONVERSATIONS WITH PAN

R. Ogilvie Crombie

(Originally entitled 'The Nature Spirits', the following is an extract from The Findhorn Garden; *Findhorn Press; 1988; pp 100-125.)*

Some people, possibly more than we realise, talk to the plants in their gardens and houses. Since nobody likes to be made to feel foolish, care is taken not to be caught in the act, and silent rather than voiced speech is used. Is it foolish to talk to plants? They do not move about like animals, and they are inarticulate; but they are alive and, in fact, have a kind of consciousness. People who are sensitive know this and are careful and considerate in the way they handle them.

It is essential to understand the true nature of the plants one cultivates in order to look after and handle them properly. (The word 'plant' is used here to include all members of the vegetable kingdom; trees, bushes, flowers, fruits, vegetables and so on.) That plants are sensitive is now becoming a well-known fact. For some years a considerable amount of scientific research has been devoted to demonstrating the reality of this sensitivity. Probably one of the first to study the subject was the remarkable Indian physicist Sir Jagadis Chandra Bose, who did his work in the early part of this century. For example, he believed that plants suffer severe shock in being transplanted, which delays their establishment in a new place and sets back growth. So before transplanting, he anaesthetised a plant by covering it with a glass bell jar into which he introduced chloroform vapour. Plants treated in this way took at once to their new environment, thus proving his point. The recent book of Cleve Backster and Marcel Vogel in the USA has demonstrated that plants are sensitive even to human thoughts.

Since the actual facts of these and other investigations now taking place throughout the world are well covered in other publications, there is no need to describe the specifics here. It is what these experiments imply that is vital to us. This does not mean that people with gardens ought, for example, to give trees a shot of anaesthetic before a branch is cut off or that flowers should be offered a whiff of nitrous oxide before being picked. It does mean that plants should be treated with care and consideration and, indeed, with appreciation for the service they give to man.

However, the true nature of plants cannot be described by scientific data only. My experience with the elemental kingdom has demonstrated that to me. But it was only after the research on plant sensitivity was published, opening up a deeper understanding of nature, that I became willing to speak publicly about the experiences I have had with the nature spirits, the elementals.

Their realm is intangible and non-material, and cannot be appreciated by the five physical senses, except in a condition of heightened awareness. The existence of the elemental kingdom cannot be proved to the satisfaction of the scientist, nor can the reactions of its inhabitants be demonstrated in the laboratory. Yet to one perceiving with the higher senses, it is as real as any of the more material kingdoms.

When we see the leaves change colour in Autumn, we might wonder how this is brought about. The botanist has one explanation, based on observation and analysis. The elemental kingdom has another, attributing the work to energy forms known as fairies and elves. Both are right. It all depends on the way you look at it.

What is meant by the elemental kingdom? Ancient and mediaeval philosophers believed that all matter was made of differing combinations of what they call the four 'elements' — earth, air, fire and water. They also believed that these elements were inhabited by beings or entities known as 'elementals'. While earth, air, fire and water are not elements in the present day meaning of the word, they remain useful concepts in esoteric and occult teachings, because they have a higher significance than the purely physical one. It is important to understand my interpretation of the word 'elemental', since certain schools of thought use the word to mean negative or evil entities from the lower astral plane. There are such entities which should preferably be termed 'pseudo-elementals', since the true elementals come from a higher plane and are part of the angelic hierarchy.

My own contact with such entities, in particular with earth spirits, first took place in the Royal Botanic Gardens of Edinburgh in March, 1966. These gardens, which cover a large area and contain many varieties of bushes, shrubs, flowers and trees, have for many years been one of my favourite places. In spite of being mainly a town dweller for all but ten years of my life, I have a great love for nature and, in particular, a deep sense of affinity for trees.

One beautiful afternoon I was wandering about the rock garden and other favourite spots. Eventually I began walking along a path skirting the north side of Inverleith House, which is situated on rising ground in the centre of the gardens and is now Edinburgh's Modern Art Gallery. Leaving the path I crossed an expanse of grass, dotted with trees and bushes, to a seat under a tall beech tree. When I sat down I could lean my shoulders and the back of my head against the tree. I became, in some way, identified with this tree, became aware of the movement of the sap in the trunk and even of the infinitely slow growth of the roots. There was a decided heightening of awareness and a sense of expectation. I felt completely awake and full of energy.

Suddenly I saw a figure dancing round a tree about twenty yards away from me — a beautiful little figure about three feet tall. I saw with astonishment that it was a faun, the Greek mythological being, half-human half-animal. He had a pointed chin and ears and two little horns on his forehead. His shaggy legs ended in cloven hooves and his skin was honey coloured. I watched him in astonishment, not believing my eyes.

For a moment I wondered if perhaps he was a boy made up for a school show. Yet he could not be — something about him was decidedly not human. Was he an hallucination? There were one or two other people walking about in the gardens. I looked at them and then back at this beautiful little being. He was still there and seemed to be as solid and real as they were. I tried hard to analyse this experience and explain him away. Suddenly I was brought up sharp — what was I trying to do? Here was a strange and wonderful experience. Why should I not accept it, see what happened and analyse it later? I began to watch the little being with delight as he circled around another tree. He danced over to where I was sitting, stood looking at me for a moment and then sat crossed-legged in front of me. I looked at him. He was very real. I bent forward and said:

"Hallo."

He leapt to his feet, startled, and stared at me.

Can you see me?

"Yes."

I don't believe it. Humans can't see us.

"Oh, yes. Some of us can."

What am I like?

I described him as I saw him. Still looking bewildered, he began to dance around in small circles.

What am I doing?

I told him.

He stopped dancing and said, *You must be seeing me.*

He danced across to the seat beside me, sat down and, turning towards me, looked up and said, *Why are human beings so stupid?*

In some ways I may be over-personalising this being. I realise I was not seeing him with my physical sight, though when I closed my eyes he was not there. And the communication between us was, no doubt, taking place on a mental or telepathic level by means of thought transference, probably in the form of images and symbols projected into my unconscious mind and translated into words by my consciousness. However I cannot be certain as to whether I was speaking to him mentally or aloud. (Now, when I meet such beings, I usually speak aloud.) I have to report our exchanges in the form of dialogue, since that is what I hear in my head. I am aware that in a case like this there is always the possibility of coloration from my own mind. However, applying my training as a scientist in objective observation and analysis, I do try to report experiments and experiences as accurately as possible.

To return to this question of why human beings are so stupid, I asked him "In what way stupid?"

In many ways. What were the strange skins or coverings

they had, some of which could be taken off? Why did they not go about in the natural state as he did? I told him the skins were called clothes and that we wore them for protection and for warmth and because it was not considered right to be without them. This latter he could not understand, so I did not pursue the subject. We talked about houses, and motor cars which seemed to him to be boxes on wheels in which human beings dashed about, sometimes bumping into each other. Was it a game? he wanted to know.

He told me he lived in the gardens. This is a partial truth, as he is an inhabitant of another plane as well. His work was to help the growth of trees. He also told me that many of the nature spirits have lost interest in the human race, since they have been made to feel that they are neither believed in or wanted.

If you humans think you can get along without us, just try! "Some of us do believe in you and want your help. I do, for one."

The wonderful thing about this meeting was the sense of companionship. I felt an amazing harmony with this wonderful little being sitting beside me. A communication was taking place between us that did not need to be put in words. We sat for some time without speaking. Eventually I rose and said I must return home.

Call me when you return here and I will come to you.

He told me his name was Kurmos. I asked him if he could visit me.

Yes, if you invite me.

"I do. I shall be delighted if you will come and visit me."

You do believe in me?

"Yes, of course I do."

And you like us?

"Yes, I have much affection for the nature spirits." This was true, though he was the first one I had actually seen.

Then I'll come now.

On the way through the streets of Edinburgh to my home, I was amused to think of the sensation it might have caused had this strange, delightful little faun been as visible to the passers-by as he was to me.

We entered my flat. I have a fairly large collection of books and my two main rooms are lined with book shelves. Kurmos showed great interest. What were they and why so many? I explained to him that they contained facts, ideas, speculations and theories, accounts of past events, stories invented by the writers and so on, all of which were written down, put into print and made up into books which could be read by others. His comment was:

Why? You can get all the knowledge you want by simply wanting it.

I told him human beings could not do that very wonderful thing — at least not yet. We had to be content to get our facts and knowledge from other people or from books.

Again we sat for some time in silence and contented harmony. Then he got up; it was time for him to return to the gardens. The door of the room was open, and he walked into the hall. I followed him and, probably because he looked so solid and real, I opened the door onto the landing. He passed me and ran lightly down the stairs. As he reached the bottom step, he faded out.

This was an astonishing experience, one I am certain I could not have imagined. My imagination works on the prosaic and practical levels and is not inclined to fantasy. And why a faun? That puzzled me. I had read no Greek mythology for years.

The next time I went to the gardens I called to see him, as he had told me to do, and he was immediately by my side. Again we sat together in silence. Though I knew here was infinite, mature wisdom combined with the naïvety of a child, I did not want to ask him questions; the wonderful harmony and companionship were enough. I intuitively felt that what was right for me to know regarding him would be given at the appropriate time.

I did not know then that these meetings with Kurmos were leading me to something even more unusual which was to take place over a month later, at the end of April. One evening I had been visiting friends who lived on the south side of Edinburgh. It was eleven o'clock and I was walking home.

Few people were about, and I thought how peaceful the city was at that moment. I walked down Princes Street, Edinburgh's main thoroughfare. As I turned the corner onto the street which runs alongside the National Gallery, I stepped into an extraordinary 'atmosphere'. I had never before encountered anything quite like it. While it is difficult to describe, I might say it was as if I had no clothes on and was walking through a medium denser than air but not as dense as water. I could feel it against my body. It produced a sensation of warmth and tingling like a mixture of pins and needles and an electric shock. This was accompanied by a heightened awareness and the same feeling of expectation I had had in the Gardens before meeting Kurmos.

Then I realised that I was not alone. A figure — taller than myself — was walking beside me. It was a faun, radiating a tremendous power. I glanced at him. Surely this was not my little faun grown up suddenly? We walked on. He turned and looked at me.

Well, aren't you afraid of me?

"No."

Why not? All human beings are afraid of me.

"I feel no evil in your presence. I see no reason why you should want to harm me. I do not feel afraid."

Do you know who I am?

I did at that moment. "You are the great god Pan."

Then you ought to be afraid. Your word 'panic' comes from the fear my presence causes.

"Not always. I am not afraid."

Can you give me a reason?

"It may be because of my affinity with your subjects, the earth spirits and woodland creatures."

You believe in my subjects?

"Yes."

Do you love my subjects?

"Yes, I do."

In that case, do you love me?

"Why not?"

Do you love me?

"Yes."

He looked at me with a strange smile and a glint in his eyes. He had deep, mysterious brown eyes.

You know, of course, that I'm the devil? You have just said you love the devil.

"No, you are not the devil. You are the god of the woodlands and the countryside. There is no evil in you. You are Pan."

Did the early Christian church not take me as a model for the devil? Look at my cloven hooves, my shaggy legs and the horns on my forehead.

"The church turned all pagan gods and spirits into devils, fiends and imps."

Was the church wrong then?

"The church did it with the best intentions from its own point of view. But it was wrong. The ancient gods are not necessarily devils."

We crossed Princes Street and turned a corner. He turned to me:

What do I smell like?

Since he had joined me I had been aware of a wonderful scent of pine woods, of damp leaves, of newly turned earth and of woodland flowers. I told him.

Don't I smell rank like a goat?

"No, you don't. There is a faint, musk-like smell, like the fur of a healthy cat. It is pleasant — almost like incense. Are you still claiming to be the devil?"

I have to find out what you think of me. It's important.

"Why?"

For a reason.

"Won't you tell me what it is?"

Not now. It will become apparent in time.

We walked on. Pan was walking very close beside me.

You don't mind me walking beside you?

"Not in the least."

He put his arm around my shoulder. I felt the actual physical contact.

You don't mind if I touch you?

"No."

You really feel no repulsion or fear?

"None."

Excellent.

I could not think why he was making this determined effort to produce a sign of fear. I am not claiming to be a brave man; there are many things that would scare me out of my life. But, for some reason or other, I felt no fear of this being. Awe, because of his power, but not fear — only love.

I asked him where his pan pipes were. He smiled at the question:

I do have them, you know.

And there he was, holding them between his hands. He began to play a curious melody. I had heard it in woods before and I have often heard it since, but it is so elusive that so far I have been unable to remember it afterwards.

When we reached the downstairs main door of the house where I live, he disappeared. I had a strong feeling, however, that he was still with me when I went in.

I had no idea why this strange encounter had happened, or why this being had chosen to show himself to me. It looked as if the meeting with the little faun in the Botanic Gardens had been a preliminary step in bringing it about, and I was feeling reasonably certain that neither of these beings was imaginary. I wondered what was going to happen next.

As a child I had passionately believed in fairies and loved both the Greek myths and their Norse equivalents, whose gods were very real to me. The Pan I knew was the wonderful and beautiful being in the chapter 'The Piper at the Gates of Dawn' in Kenneth Grahame's *The Wind in the Willows*. Over a period of time these feelings were suppressed by school life and replaced by an irrepressible curiosity to find out how and why things worked, eventually becoming almost an obsessional interest in physics and chemistry.

By the time I reached my early thirties, the chronic heart ailment which had prevented me from ever having a steady job had come to a critical point, and I was strongly advised to retire to an atmosphere of complete quiet. For ten years I lived in comparative isolation in the country, pursuing my interests in science and literature, and developing a close contact with nature. Despite my interest in esoteric and occult subjects, I was unaware of the existence of such beings as nature spirits the entire time I lived there. I would certainly have dismissed belief in the real existence of fairies, gnomes and elves as superstition, figments of the imagination. In fact, even after I did make contact with Pan and the world of the nature spirits, I went through a period of time when I doubted their existence, when it seemed to me that the whole thing might be a fantasy, the projection of a part of my own unconscious mind. In time I realised that the nature spirits had shown themselves to me for a specific reason.

This became clear when I met Pan again in early May, 1966 on Iona, a tiny island of the Inner Hebrides which is considered to be an ancient centre of spiritual power. Peter Caddy and I were standing in the Hermit's cell, a ring of stones which is all that is left of the place where St Columba used to go in retreat. In front of us was a gentle grassy slope which hid from sight the Iona Abbey on the other side of the island. I became aware of a large figure lying in the ground there. I could see him through the grass. It appeared to be a monk in a brown habit with the hood pulled over the head so that the features were concealed. His feet were towards the cell. As I watched, he raised his hands and rolled back the hood. It was Pan. He rose up out of the ground and stood facing us. He smiled and said:

I am the servant of Almighty God, and I and my subjects are willing to come to the aid of mankind, in spite of the way he has treated us and abused nature, if he affirms belief in us and asks for our help.

Here was a step towards the reconciliation of Pan and the world of the nature spirits with man. Because I had been able to respond to him without fear, Pan could communicate with me and use me as a mediator between man and nature. This does not make me important in myself — I am simply a channel for his work.

Vital to this reconciliation is the recognition of Pan's true nature. He is a great being, the god of the whole elemental kingdom as well as of the animal, vegetable and mineral kingdoms. People may feel uneasy in his presence because of the awe he inspires, but there ought to be no fear. *All human beings are afraid of me*, he had said at our first meeting, not as a threat but with sadness. *Did the early Christian church not take me as a model for the devil?* That is why Pan is feared — because of the image projected on to him. This stigma must be lifted in order to re-establish the true link between man and nature.

Pan has said he would prefer not to be represented in any material form at all. Yet, if he must be, he insists on being accepted, in our culture, as the Greek myth depicts him, half-human half-animal. There is a fitness about it in its symbolism. The human upper half represents intellect, united with a powerful, mysterious, deep energy represented by the animal lower half — an energy not yet revealed in man. It is important to consider Pan and the nature spirits in their own right when they take on these human-like forms and not compare them with our own perception of human beauty. Some people assume that Pan must be ugly. This is far from the case. In his own right he is one of the most beautiful beings I have ever seen. Only the horns on the forehead, the cloven hooves and the fine silky hair on the legs suggest the animal part. The legs are human, not animal.

It is very important to realise that though Pan can appear in such a form, he is not a being restricted to one place. The word 'Pan' means 'all', 'everywhere'. Pan is a universal energy, a cosmic energy, which is constantly found throughout the whole of nature. He could appear personified in many different places at the same time and should never be thought of as restricted to a corner of the garden or sitting on a hilltop beside a gorse bush.

It may be helpful to consider why Pan and the nature spirits assume such forms. Their primary state is what may be termed a 'light body'. It is a whirl or vortex of energy in constant motion. Nebulous like a fine mist, it glows with coloured light, sometimes one single colour, sometimes two or more which do not mix but remain separate like the colours of a rainbow. It frequently changes colour and is often covered with a multitude of fine curved lines. They appear to flow like liquid in a pipe, forming continually changing patterns of incredible beauty. These light bodies differ from each other in size and brilliancy, varying from pastel shades to strong, bright colours. All are beautiful, pure and luminous, glowing with inner radiance. They may be regarded as whirls of energy, but energy with intelligence. It is possible to see and to communicate with these light bodies.

However, the elementals or nature spirits cannot carry out their work with plants in these pure bodies. In this work they use the energies channelled to them by the devas to build up an 'etheric body' or 'etheric counterpart' for each plant, according to its archetypal pattern. The plant grows and develops within this counterpart. In order to fulfil their task, the nature spirits too must take on an etheric body.

In esoteric knowledge, the etheric plane is made up of a fine energy substance from which is created the mould for every form we see manifest on the physical plane. Each material form has an etheric counterpart. That such a thing exists at all will be questioned by many people. At the moment it cannot be scientifically proven, though no doubt this will be possible in the future.

We do know ourselves to be far more than just our physical bodies. According to esoterics, we have an etheric body, as well as other higher bodies. We are incarnate spirit. So, too, do plants have at least etheric bodies, if not higher ones as well. This is why man must be careful when he interferes with the natural growth of plants. In trying to alter the form through artificial means, often using force, man can depart from the archetypal design. Apart from the fear and pain produced in the plant, this can bring about lack of alignment with the esoteric counterpart, causing further discomfort and distress.

Rather than using force to bring about changes in plants, it would be much better if man would ask the nature spirits to bring them about by modifying the etheric counterpart. This they will do if they are convinced that the change is reasonable and a help to mankind, not simply for expediency. At the moment, they are limited in their actions by the general disbelief in their power and even in their existence.

What of the etheric bodies of the nature spirits themselves? In his myths, legends and fairy tales, man has depicted a vast gallery of what he has referred to as 'supernatural' beings. (Actually, 'paraphysical' would be a more accurate word to describe them.) To what extent the etheric forms of these beings were the product of man's own creative imagination or the result of inspiration from an outside source is difficult to determine.

Suffice it to say there exists what one might call a vast reservoir of 'thought forms' produced by the existence and persistence of these tales. Often thought about and talked about, these forms have been preserved both orally and in print. Thus, an elemental entity wishing to assume a body can 'put on' any of these thought forms and appear personified as that particular being — Greek or Norse god, elf, gnome, faun, fairy and so on. In myths and legends these paraphysical beings have been depicted in a human form and as behaving in a human manner. Of course, they are essentially formless and only adopt a form and its characteristic behaviour when needed.

In September of 1966, I had an encounter with Pan that was to bring me a deeper understanding of his form and nature. I had attended a weekend course conducted by Sir George Trevelyan at Attingham Park. Before leaving on Monday morning, I was prompted to go to an area known as the mile walk on Attingham's extensive and beautiful grounds. I followed the path until I came to the Rhododendron Walk which is considered by some to be a place of great spiritual power. At its entrance is a huge cedar tree with a bench beneath it. I sat there for some time, enjoying the beauty of the place, then rose and entered the walk. As I did so, I felt a great build-up of power and a vast increase in awareness. Colours and forms became more significant. I was aware of every single leaf on the bushes and trees, of every blade of grass on the path standing out with startling clarity. It was as if physical reality had become much more real than it normally is, and the three-dimensional effect we are used to had become even more solid.

This kind of experience is impossible to describe in words. I had the impression of complete reality, and all that lies within and beyond it felt immediately imminent. There was an acute feeling of being one with nature in a complete way, as well as being one with the divine, which produced great exultation, and a deep sense of awe and wonder.

I became aware of Pan walking by my side and of a strong bond between us. He stepped behind me and then walked into me so that we became one, and I saw the surroundings through his eyes. At the same time, part of me — the recording, observing part — stood aside. The experience was not a form of possession but of identification, a kind of integration.

The moment he stepped into me the woods became alive with myriad beings — elementals, nymphs, dryads, fauns, elves, gnomes, fairies and so on, far too numerous to catalogue. They varied in size from tiny little beings a fraction of an inch in height — like the ones I saw swarming about on a clump of toadstools — to beautiful elfin creatures, three or four feet tall. Some of them danced around me in a ring; all were welcoming and full of rejoicing. The nature spirits love and delight in the work they do and express this in movement.

I felt as if I were outside time and space. Everything was happening in the now. It is impossible to give more than a faint impression of the actuality of this experience, but I would stress the exultation and feeling of joy and delight. Yet, there was an underlying peace, contentment and a sense of spiritual presence.

I found myself in a clearing at the end of this part of the Rhododendron Walk, where there is a great oak tree. I turned and walked back the way I had come. I now had pan pipes in my hands and was aware of shaggy legs and cloven hooves. I began to dance down the path, playing on the pipes — the melody I had heard Pan play. The numerous birds responded, their songs making an exquisite counterpoint to the music of the pipes. All the nature beings were active, many dancing as they worked. When I had almost reached the spot where the experience had started, the heightened awareness began to fade and Pan withdrew, leaving me once more my ordinary self. I stopped dancing and walked on. The pan pipes had gone.

The change from this strange ecstatic experience to the normal reality of everyday life was not a disappointment. What I had experienced was still there; it is always there, for it is part of the true reality. Because of our dulled senses and our habit of going through life wearing materialistic blinkers in a condition verging on sleepwalking, we are unaware of the fantastic beauty of the life around us. Of course, it would not do if we were aware of it all the time; that would be too overwhelming and make us incapable of performing our daily tasks. However, we could well be more aware of our surroundings without carrying it that far.

Approaching the end of the path and the cedar tree, I began to walk sedately, which was just as well since a boy was sitting on the seat nearby. It might have been disconcerting for at least one of us if I had come dancing down the path playing invisible pipes at my age.

Several weeks later I again had this experience of becoming one with Pan. It happened in St Annes-on-Sea where I had gone with several friends who were attending a conference. I was walking alone in the garden across from the meeting place when I became aware of Pan standing beside me. As before, he stepped into me. This 'compound being', as it might be called, summoned the nature spirits together to help in what was to take place. The pond and all the bushes and trees became immediately alive with beings of many different kinds. I — or should I say 'we' — walked onto a raised part of the gardens from which it was possible to look across to the house where the meeting was taking place. Pan within me called upon the green ray of the nature forces to rise up through the house. Slowly this light rose until it emerged from the roof. After some time, Pan withdrew.

I left the garden and about five minutes later met Peter Caddy who had just come from the house. He startled me by saying that Pan had been in the room and communicated with a certain woman present there who was a sensitive and that, of the fifteen others present in the room, nearly all had had visions or impressions connected with nature.

The significance of these two episodes became clearer in time. We are told to turn within, to seek God within, to seek Christ within. But this withinness is not contained in my physical body which would limit it; it is in all dimensions of space and time; it is infinite, the eternal now. We turn away from the outside world, the material world which so many believe to be the only reality, to seek that true reality which is within and yet everywhere.

In that sense, Pan is within me, the whole universe is within me, the elemental kingdom, the angelic hierarchy, God himself is within me. This withinness is the All, the great mystery which we poor humans cannot hope to understand completely. We can only grope toward it and in some way seek to apprehend it.

I had often wondered about the process that lay behind these experiences of heightened awareness that permit a glimpse into true reality. In particular, I was interested in knowing how my ability to perceive nature spirits had come about. Certainly, to my knowledge, I hadn't asked for it. In 1972 I had an encounter with Pan that answered some of these questions.

I had gone to the Botanic Gardens in the early afternoon on Midsummer's Eve, a very important day for the nature spirits. From the moment I entered the heath garden, it was alive with myriad beings. Green elves, three to four feet tall, were walking in front of me, full of joy and delight, and little gnomes were running about almost under my feet. The beautiful little faun Kurmos came towards me from among the bushes. Greeting me with joy, he danced off between the elves.

I walked to the top of the heath garden towards a certain tree of the species *Zelkova Carpinifolia* which has been referred to as the 'Tree of Life' by Richard St Barbe Baker. I like to greet this strange tree whenever I go to the garden. This time my attention was caught by a group of markings on the bark that were in the form of a figure about fourteen inches high. I had never noticed this effect before. This figure was distinct. It was strange and slightly sinister — a faun-like being with longish straight horns; the eyes were quite noticeable. I had been aware of the tree spirit but had never seen it before. Was this a representation of it on the bark? A mist formed between me and the tree, and I found myself looking at the entity itself, standing in front of the tree. He was about my own height, thickset and dark-skinned. His fierce eyes challenged me.

Will you touch the tree as you have always done. aware this time that you are doing it through me?

I laid my hand on the trunk of the tree and felt the usual strong flow of energy.

You find me odd — not what you expected. You are not repulsed?

"I am disconcerted. You are certainly not what I expected, but I love this tree, and you are the tree. You are not evil."

I am neither good nor evil. My tree has been called the Tree of Life. I am what you make of me.

I moved away from the tree and turned around. Pan was beside me. He asked if seeing this aspect of the tree spirit had made a difference in how I felt about the tree.

"No. The energy field of the tree is unchanged." I looked at Pan inquiringly. "You said, 'this aspect of the tree spirit', meaning he has others?"

Yes, he has others. The form in which he shows himself is suited to the occasion. It has a purpose.

"To test my reaction? Or to disconcert me?"

Pan smiled. *Perhaps a bit of both.*

I proceeded along a path toward an empty bench. Kurmos, who had been watching, came and sat beside me.

"This reminds me of our first meeting when you asked why human beings are so stupid."

Kurmos looked up at me.

We find human behaviour amusing at times, but so often it is destructive, cruel and horrible, or so it appears to us. We try to understand it but it isn't easy. We know there are those who love nature, who love this garden. No doubt they would love us if they could see us. This makes us happy and we draw near to them. Some of them may even be aware of us, though they cannot see us. Why can you see us so clearly?

"I suppose I am a privileged person, one of those chosen

to link with Pan and help to renew the old contact between mankind and the nature spirits."

Pan appeared at that moment standing opposite us.

You were chosen because you are suited to the task. Your life has been a training and a preparation for this. As soon as the integration between your lower self and your higher self reached a certain degree of completion you were bound to see us. Your lower self and your physical body had to be trained and conditioned for many years before this level could be reached.

Because of your makeup and the work you have to do, you see me and my subjects as if we were part of the material world. This is not your projection, it is bringing cosmic reality into manifestation when it is right to do so.

"Can you explain the mechanism?" I asked. "I am certain it is not due to heightened sensitivity of physical sight only."

It is a mixture of that plus an added higher vision brought about by the development of cosmic consciousness.

"That makes sense to me. But I am unable to control it myself. For instance, I cannot wish to see a nature spirit and immediately do so, however hard I try."

It is done from our side — when it is right for you to have this heightened vision or when a particular entity wishes to become visible to you.

"How is that done?"

Imagine a theatre with a large stage. This stage is in darkness. It is thronged with people but you cannot see them because of the darkness, which symbolises your lack of sensitivity. A narrow-beam spotlight picks out one of them and he immediately becomes visible in this way. Similarly, lights could pick out a group or the whole stage could be lit. The light symbolises your heightened senses. It is a rough analogy but it may answer your question.

"It does. The lights are controlled by some being on your side, I take it?"

Yes

"Therefore, I can't select the entities I am to see or when. But I am aware of and can communicate with your subjects."

Of course, you can do this at any time though you may only be able to see us on special occasions. The moment you think of an entity you are in immediate communication with it. You may or may not be aware of the response, according to your degree of sensitivity at the time, but it will almost certainly be there.

"Can anyone make such a contact?"

Yes, anyone can and it is important that this is understood. The one-way contact is always there, but being aware of the response usually needs training or at least practice. It is very subtle and easily missed.

"There are many who would genuinely and sincerely like to share my experiences and I am frequently asked how they can set about it."

And you hedge and say, "Some day you probably will if your faith is strong enough. Don't try too hard, it will just happen at the unexpected moment." You also tell them to follow your example and live in comparative isolation in the country for ten years, as you did yourself.

"I do, and most of them look aghast and say they could not possibly do that; they haven't the time and it might mean giving up too much."

There is always time for the important things. Communicating with my subjects is not a garden game for the odd half hour when there is nothing else to do. I have observed far too much of this contemptuous superior attitude of man towards my subjects; it is almost worse than disbelief. Leave it at that and let's return to the genuine people who are legitimately curious about my world and would dearly love to see us. There is nothing wrong with that except that it very rarely works — they try too hard.

Perhaps this is fortunate as they do not realise how dangerous it might be if their desire was granted too soon, before either their bodies or their minds had been prepared and conditioned for the experience and the right degree of cosmic consciousness had been reached.

Many people who believe in the nature spirits and love them can be aware of them, can communicate and sometimes even see them in brief glimpses. With such people they will always cooperate when invoked, which simply means asking for help. This simple awareness is open to anyone who seeks it. It is this total link that must be initiated from our side when it is required.

Certainly a reconciliation between man and the nature spirits is now required for the survival of the world. For this reason Pan had to initiate a direct contact. As I see it, the main reason for my communication with the elementals was the contribution it made to the work of the Findhorn garden. By bringing onto a conscious level the links already existing there with nature spirits, I could receive guidance and knowledge complementary to Dorothy's link with the devic world. Thus, the aim of the Findhorn garden of full cooperation among the three kingdoms — the devas, the nature spirits and man — could be established and built up.

It is vital for the future of mankind that belief in the nature spirits and their god Pan is re-established and that they are seen in their true light. In spite of the outrages man has committed against nature, these beings are only too pleased to help him if he will seek and ask for their cooperation.

Once Pan had told me that, although I had been chosen by him, I had actually started the contact myself. I was immensely curious to know what he meant. In the autumn of 1974, I believe I found out.

Some years ago, on the grounds of a large estate near the little seaside town of Rosemarkie in north Scotland, there existed a charming place known as the Fairy Glen. In 1903 when I was approaching my fourth birthday, my parents brought me there. I have vivid memories of a waterfall with two streams of water, a flight of earthen steps, a bridge over a stream and, above all, a wishing well with a pebbly bottom under an overhanging rock. In 1974 I had gone back with a friend to visit this place. We found the wishing well completely filled in, but the waterfall, splashing down into a rocky pool, was still there. It was a lovely day, and we sat looking at the falling water and enjoying the feel of the place.

Suddenly three little gnomes appeared on a flat rock in front of me.

My, you have grown up, said one of them.

"What do you mean?"

We remember a little boy coming here long ago in your time, piped in the second gnome.

It was you and aren't you glad your wish was granted? asked the third.

"What wish?"

Don't you remember dropping a penny in the wishing well and wishing you could see fairies and talk with them? the first gnome asked.

And bubbles rose from the pebbles on the bottom of the well, which meant that your wish would be granted, added the second.

I certainly did drop pennies in the well and make wishes. I cannot say I remember that specific one, but it is very likely true, for I believed in fairies then as I do once more today. So that could be how it all began and why it happened to me.

To anyone who may have expressed a wish to see and talk to nature spirits, whether or not you have dropped a penny in a wishing well, remember it took 63 years for my wish to be granted, and don't lose hope. The nature spirits must be believed in with complete sincerity and faith. They must be appreciated and given thanks and love for the work they do. Let us try in our own ways to make friends with these wonderful beings and ask their help in making Earth a beautiful and perfect place.

COOPERATION WITH PAN AND THE NATURE SPIRITS

David Spangler

(Amended excerpts of a transmission through David Spangler from a being identifying itself as an emissary of the elemental kingdoms, on the 4th of August, 1970, at the Park. From 'Man, Nature and the New Age' in the Original Series of Study Papers.)

Emissary: Blessings to you. I am an emissary of the elemental kingdoms.

Q: Do you have a message that you would like to give, or would you like us to start with questions?

Emissary: In all things we must be invited into cooperation and communication with you. We cannot intrude.

Q: I do not have a specific question, other than advice and help on a broad field. Humankind has traditionally carried out certain garden practices that have been developed down the centuries. The problem is to know which ones have been inspired by the devic and elemental kingdoms or from the God within, and how many are not from that source. And if so, in this New Age how are garden practices to change to avoid giving offence to a nature kingdom?

Emissary: That is a proper invitation. You must understand first how we work. We are not of the physical body of the plant of which you are aware. We represent the beings who make possible the growth and development of the forms of nature. We are not the physical body of the plant but we nurture it and enable it to grow. Indeed, all of the elementals are far more ancient as a kingdom than the Earth itself, and we draw freely upon the powers of cosmic creativity. We are children of the vast reaches of space, as much as citizens of any planet. Before a planet can come into existence, we are. And we bring the planet into existence. All that you see, we have formed following the plans laid down by God.

As we enter the etheric world, we may take on various forms which are provided by the imaginations of human beings. But we are not the simple little beings that appear to flit from flower to flower, or hover about a tree; the simplest elemental of the tiniest flower is still an outpost of vast and cosmic power.

There are few limits to what we can achieve within the will of God. At one time, we were the sole masters of Earth. We made it possible for humanity to develop upon this world.

Like ourselves, humanity is itself a formative force. In a way, you reflect within yourselves aspects of the elemental and angelic kingdoms, but you are blessed with the power of creative imagination, a power we do not possess in the same way. You are evolving to perform a role upon the Earth that is related to ours but different as well, involving different capabilities. We have the task of assisting you in your role, as long as it does not undo the work that we have been given to do in serving and nourishing this world.

When humanity was created, for ages we were your teachers. We guided and protected you. You responded to us because, in your inmost sensitivity, you were one with us. But in the days of humanity's youth we were still the authority. We were the lords of Earth, and humanity was but another of the creatures whom we tended and whose growth we inspired.

There came a time when you began to tap and unfold the gift of your creative power. Then you set upon the road toward learning to master that power and to discover your unique identity and purpose. Gradually you began to turn away from us. The exercise of your authority began at times to conflict with ours, and when it did your will was generally allowed precedence, and we were asked to serve you.

There were many of our number who objected to this, and there have been times of crisis in our relationship with you when we have risen in justifiable anger and destroyed your works. For the most part, though, we have sought to cooperate with you even when you have not reciprocated, since we understood that you needed to grow into using your creative power wisely and with keen and loving understanding of the needs of the Earth.

We who are of this kingdom of builders do understand the needs of Earth. This gives us a power you do not have yet, in spite of your creativity. You approach the earth now through your mind, while we approach it through love and oneness. Hence, nature does not obey you as swiftly and perfectly as it will obey us. You have not yet fully awakened to the angelic side of your natures that would give you the kind of deep rapport with the forces of nature that we enjoy.

You have the right to attempt to cloak your planet in artificiality; but long before you could succeed in doing this, you will have destroyed yourselves, for you do not yet know how to maintain the balance of life on all levels. And though you have a certain creative authority, you must learn that you are part of the nature kingdom as well; though you have a certain dominion over it, you cannot destroy it without destroying yourselves. Nor can you afford to lose our cooperation unless you wish self-destruction. The head and the brain have authority over the human body, but the brain cannot subject the body to undue stress and torment as many humans do through their diet and actions of life, and expect to survive; for if the body is destroyed, the brain must die.

You have reached a crisis point. As you continue to exert unthinking authority and domination over the world simply because you seem to have the power to do so, you will destroy the ecological pattern of this planet and yourselves in the process. We cannot be destroyed, nor can humanity's true nature be destroyed; but you can turn your creative power upon yourselves and render the planet unfit.

How joyous it is, therefore, for us to witness the unfoldment of a pattern of cooperation such as in this Centre, for then we see hope and we see an outlet for us to reach into human consciousness.

Humanity's role is to tend the Earth as a steward. But it is wrong for you to attempt to play the part of devic or elemental overlord; that is our role. What you must do is exercise your creative, inspirational authority in a manner that expresses your love for all the lives upon and within the earth. This is your true place in the scheme of things on Earth. You can create the vision of what must be done. This is your God-given power.

The elemental beings under the authority of Pan, as you

call him, do not originate the patterns of earth and of nature; they only build them and maintain them. They have great power to do this. Remember we are not tied to the Earth. We are cosmic in our scope, and we can draw upon the formative powers of the cosmos. Never underestimate what we are. But we do not have the ability to originate. That is not our function.

Because you are creative and can originate patterns, you have a responsibility to anchor that creativity and imagination in a deep understanding of and love for the forces and forms of nature. Because we are already one with those forces and forms, we can help you here if you open to our inspiration and wisdom. Also, if you can learn to commune with us so that we can understand and relate to your purposes, then we can provide the power that enacts the changes you wish to make. We can implement your patterns just as we implement those of the angels who hold the blueprints for nature. We cannot do that, though, if your patterns are thoughtless or contrary to the wholeness of the world or if they are conceived and enacted with no thought to the well-being of any other life than your own. We cannot understand you nor communicate with you in your selfishness.

We do not wholly understand human beings; you are often as strange to us as we may be to you. Yet we both share the same origins in the heart of God and God's life flows through us both. We are cousins, and our respective roles can be complementary.

The key is love. If you insist that humanity must dominate and you use what to us is brute force through chemicals and physical manipulations to gain what you wish with no regard to the consciousness or life of the soil or the plants, then you do not act in love. Then we cannot understand you, nor can we support you. We may actually even resist your efforts if they threaten the world that we serve.

However, when you can approach nature with love and with a desire to be a co-creator, a partner, not a conqueror or ruler, then we can draw close. We can more easily discern the desires you have and can see how we can assist their implementation.

One great soul who understood this learned to transform the form of plants through the sheer power of his love and understanding. His name was Luther Burbank, and he demonstrated the power that is possible when humanity and the nature kingdom cooperate together, without any form of physical force but with physical nurturing and that power of love that gives us the vision of what must be done, and the free hand to do it.

So we ask for a blend of wildness and human vision, a choice on your part to understand and commune with us and our perspective, and a willingness through love to seek cooperation and not domination. There are areas and times when you have the authority to do what you wish as your intuition and insight indicate; you do not have to ask our permission every time you prune a plant or lay a seed. We do ask, though, that you exercise this authority mindfully and with love. We respect your authority as a mutual force of nature, so to speak, but we ask that you also respect our existence and our world and see nature in a deeper way than is often the case.

The work you are doing in this Centre with this garden is not just a cooperative venture. We are not here to beautify this garden for the glory of any human being, but for the glory of God. You are not our superior; we are not your superior. We are lovers. As humanity invokes ever more powerful energies of creativity and of destruction, we must become one if these energies are to be utilised properly and not become destructive. We yearn for this oneness. It must go beyond cooperation.

Before anything is done in this garden, it must be considered from our point of view, as well as from your point of view. This is not a usurpation of your creative rights. We are asking for you to extend your creative imagination and vision. We wish to understand how you think, and we wish you to understand how we think. Then, from partnership can flow oneness and love, and it is this love that is most important. It is truly the most important gift of your garden.

There are elemental beings who are still undergoing great pain at the hands of humanity, not here but elsewhere in the world. The thing that is keeping them in balance is the love and the peace and the light that is flowing from this Centre and other centres like it that are beginning to be formed.

If through your thoughtlessness and actions, we cannot

establish a deeper understanding and communion, and if you impose your will such that there is no room for our presence and character to live and act in your garden, then we would have to withdraw. If we were to withdraw from this Centre, it would cut off that healing and transmuting power. The ability of our kingdom to shield humanity from the effects of its own selfishness and folly and to contain the destructive forces that your species unwittingly invokes would be lessened, to the detriment of all of us.

We are shielding humanity; we are protecting you and experiencing pain in our being in doing it. But our love for you is great, because we are kin, and in many ways you are our children. We honour the hope and promise that lies in you, and honour our oneness in the presence of God. To do all we can to build new bonds of cooperation and communion between us is a joy as well as a calling for us. We ask that you do your share.

Q: I, Peter, on behalf of humanity, thank you for this unfoldment of the change in pattern at our Community and to the Earth. I seek and pledge to seek the cooperation and brotherhood with the nature forces. This will not always be easy, because in humans there has been a long, long pattern of doing things in a certain way, and change is always difficult.

Emissary: We understand this. And this is why we have great patience within the limits allowed to us for the safety of you and the safety of our kingdom. As long as you make consistent steps toward change, mistakes in the moment will be overlooked and balanced out — if we can see evidence of growth and continued cooperation with us and of your desire to delve deeply into communion with us and with the God within yourselves.

So I convey to you the blessing and the love of the kingdom I represent and wish you to know that it places its hand upon you in thankfulness for what you are doing. You are performing a great task, not only for humanity but for us. You are making many things possible beyond what you have conscious knowledge of. Bless you my son, bless you each. Bless you all.

DEVAS AND ANGELS

William Bloom

It seems to me that there has been a significant shift in the Findhorn Community's culture over the last twenty years. Two decades ago the culture was permeated by the ideas of esoteric philosophy and by people who worked in trained and careful ways with various energies. At the same time the major angelic focus was in the garden and landscape. Since then the folk into esoterics have been replaced by folk who are more mystically or psychologically inclined, so in the 1990s there is more of a focus on consciousness.

Awareness of the garden devas remains part of the background culture but there is not much exact and specific work with them — though instinctively the gardeners have a very sophisticated relationship with them. At the same time, partly because of the language of the Transformation Game, people often talk about angels — of beauty, harmony, humour and so on. These angels of particular qualities are very general and perhaps romantic, but they have expanded people's awareness to include realms other than just the devas of nature. I think that this expansion of focus is very creative, for any student or worker with angels knows that angelic lives are part of every aspect of earthly, human and cosmic life. Every aspect of life is permeated by devic essence as much as it is by atomic electromagnetic dynamics.

What is not so good perhaps is that Community members have tended not to study this angelic realm carefully. Maybe this has been a sensible caution against flakiness. Maybe Community members generally do not really believe in the angelic realm, but go along with it in the same way that it is fine to go along with fairy tales and Jungian archetypes. But the reality is — and it is taught in all mystical, tribal and esoteric traditions — that there is a parallel world of beings who cooperate with and are involved in every part and aspect of life. Even in Christianity, the central ceremony of the Eucharist or Communion both recognises and calls in these beings: ". . . with

Seraphim, Cherubim, Angels, Archangels and all the company of heaven."

In other ceremonies and workings, the elementals of Earth, Water, Air and Fire, as well as the devas of landscape — including Pan — are invoked for active cooperation. In classical Greece and Rome, for example, it was well understood that we needed to be in harmonious relationship with this parallel world. Every home had a small altar dedicated to the angel of the house; schools, hospitals, theatres, parliaments, all had altars and ceremonies to work with the overlighting angelic consciousnesses. Tribal societies are also full of ceremonies that call in the cooperation of the devas and angels to help make horticulture or tool-making or journeys harmonious and successful.

My hope is that over the next decade within the Foundation and the wider Findhorn Community, the pendulum will swing back to some central place and the folk who are aligned with consciousness and the mystical will begin to appreciate the value and joy of a more exact knowledge and a more practically cooperative attitude with the angelic realms.

The basic principles are very simple. We need to recognise that devas hold in their consciousness the archetypal pattern or blueprint for every form in existence, whether it is a flower, a thoughtform, a planet, a person. This blueprint is an energy matrix that contains a map of the perfect potential into which any form can evolve. A fairy, for example, holds the perfect matrix for its flower to grow into. Working consciously and cooperatively, human beings can attune to this perfect matrix — in gardening, healing, creating, cleaning and so on — and thus attune their own actions more gracefully and creatively to the work. At the same time, the devic consciousness responds to the creativity and intention of the human consciousness. From an esoteric perspective, a cooperative relationship with the devic realms is as important as ecological awareness and the balancing of female-male.

Understanding that angels contain within their energy field —like Sheldrake's theory of morphic resonance — the perfect blueprint of a certain form, then we can see, for instance, that the Angel of Cluny[35] is an angel with a history of working with education and community in a spiritual framework. A healing angel, then, is a consciousness that holds within its matrix the pattern for a perfect healing; the healer attunes to this angelic consciousness and is facilitated through the actual process of healing.

Some individuals in the Community understand and know all this in a very instinctive and intuitive way. It might be useful, however, in the coming years if this instinct and intuition were allowed to ground in a more intentional way.

What might this look like? I am not sure. Perhaps an informal discussion or meditation group. Perhaps a group that monitors angelic activity in the sanctuaries, gardens, education departments, kitchens, power points and so on. Simply giving these realities grounded awareness is enough to create a cooperative and stimulating relationship. Like all inner practices, however, the only guarantee of accuracy, wisdom and lack of projection, is in a sustained and rhythmic discipline of awareness.

Djwahl Khul wrote somewhere that to be a balanced seeker requires that if we are mystics, we balance ourselves by becoming occultists; and if we are occultists, we balance ourselves by becoming mystics. This, of course, is one of the interesting paradoxes of practical esoterics: we need to surrender to a state of blissful oceanic consciousness; but we also need to be focused and aware. Neptune and Uranus marry.

In relation to the devic realms, the tendency within the Community over the last decade has been Neptunian, relaxed and sensuous. This is healthy and beautiful. To balance it with an approach that is Uranian, electric and focused is also healthy and beautiful.

May the overlighting Angel of Findhorn feel our awareness and bless us all.

---

[35] i.e. Cluny Hill College

THE INFLUENCE OF MAINSTREAM ECOLOGY

Alex Walker

It is important to view our experiments in cooperation with nature in a wider context. As elsewhere, the views of the Community seem to be converging with mainstream Western thinking. In the early 1960s Western rational and scientific ideology held that man's dominion over nature was all but complete, and that this was a desirable state of affairs. Yet this period was probably the zenith of orthodox science's confidence in itself. In the same year that the original caravan came to its final resting place at Findhorn Bay Caravan Park, Rachel Carson launched the first serious challenge to the agro-chemical consensus with her seminal work *Silent Spring*.

Not long after that came the 'Only One Earth' conference and the now largely discredited alarms sounded by the Club of Rome. As the 70s dawned an ecologically aware generation emerged who would view *The Secret Life of Plants* (which includes a chapter about our Community) as a logical extension of their environmental concerns. The contrast with the 'twin set and pearls' image of an earlier generation of spiritual aspirants became an important feature of Community life, and it was one of the major successes of the Foundation that unity could be forged from such a diversity of backgrounds. Perhaps all were united in their sympathy with E.F. Schumacher's declaration that 'small is beautiful'.

The 80s saw the publication of a variety of works which stressed not only the dangers of technology but also the importance of a spiritual approach which emphasised both the intrinsic value and awareness of nature itself. Rupert Sheldrake's 'hypothesis of formative causation' is the closest that science has come to an acknowledgement of elementals and devas. James Lovelock's 'Gaia Hypothesis', the work of Peter Russell and the emergence of the notion of 'deep ecology' have all become influential.

The heir to the British throne talking to plants may still be a cause for embarrassment to the establishment, but in a country where a growing percentage of the population are vegetarian, and 'inner directed' growth techniques are commonplace in mainstream business circles, Prince Charles's views are increasingly seen as a rallying cry for a significant and growing minority rather than the voice of an eccentric loner crying in an empty wilderness.

The challenge for the Foundation and Community is then to maintain its cutting edge in a world where lip service to ecology is becoming the norm.

CURRENT COMMUNITY ACTIVITY

Gardening and Environmental Awareness

In the 1960s the Findhorn Community first became famous for its work with the nature kingdoms — the devas and nature spirits — and the spectacular results that were achieved through working in a spirit of co-creation with these energies.

By the late 70s the work with nature had been somewhat pushed into the background and as the Community grew and the proportion of the membership involved in the gardens decreased, the main focus shifted to educational programmes. At this time we spoke of our work being more with 'growing people' rather than plants. The famous cabbages were more of an embarrassment than something to talk about!

The gardeners would periodically complain about this state of affairs and there would be voices speaking out from time to time about our general lack of ecological awareness as a community — but during the early 80s we were going through a time of shortages of both people and finances, so it was never easy to translate ideas into action. A few projects were undertaken, such as horticultural research and tree-growing at Cullerne House, but what we had learned from our work in the gardens and our concern for the environment tended to be expressed more by creating a space for discussion and generating ideas through our annual conferences. These included the 'Building a Planetary Village' conference in 1982; hosting the '3rd World Wilderness Congress' in 1983; and 'One Earth: A Call to Action' in 1986.

But the balance has gradually shifted: the idea of building an 'ecological village' brings our work with nature to a new level as we look at how we can build our homes and live our daily lives in harmony with the earth. In 1983 we bought the caravan park with the intention of replacing our caravans with ecologically sound houses and we have since been researching various methods of insulation, building and decorating materials, sewage disposal and so on, as well as planting thousands of trees.

Since October 1989 the first wind generator of our wind park has stood on the horizon as a symbol to remind us of our commitment to the planet. In March 1990 work began on the first of a group of houses to replace ageing caravans at the Park, heralded by the Press as 'the greenest houses in Britain'. Meanwhile, on a smaller scale, we have gradually introduced the use of recycled paper and ecologically sound cleaning materials in our work departments and homes, and we attempt to recycle as much as we can.

In 1983 the Findhorn Nature Calendar was launched — a project initiated by Alan Watson, who had always been one of the voices speaking out for the earth. This has now developed into a growing business, selling cards, calendars and t-shirts carrying the message of the need for co-creation with nature, and especially saving forests and planting trees. The business aims to tithe a proportion of its profits to the 'Trees for Life' project, started by a group of Foundation members in 1981 to take action on behalf of trees.

In May 1989 the Ecology Action Group was formed to co-ordinate our efforts to care for our planet. The first project was to carry out an 'environmental excellence audit' of every aspect of the Foundation's work. The idea of the audit is to look at everything we do on a day to day basis, evaluate it in terms of its impact on the environment and see where improvements can be made.

Another project the group is keen to support is the 'Trees for Life' scheme to assist the natural regeneration of the Caledonian Forest in Scotland. This involves fencing some of the surviving patches of the forest so that young trees can grow there, protected from deer and sheep. Some areas have already been successfully fenced off by other organisations but much more needs to be done. Funds are being raised for further fencing and in the meantime young trees are being given individual protection where possible.

Our gardens continue to develop and grow, lovingly cared for by our numerous gardeners: the original garden has now expanded to include the whole caravan park — we are gradually landscaping the entire area, planting more trees, and exploring ways of increasing our wild bird and flower populations; we are growing as many vegetables as we can in our various gardens — though never enough to feed the large number of Community members, associates and guests who daily eat at the Foundation; and the Erraid group has successfully begun reafforestation of the island by both fencing and planting.

Ecological Village Project

In March 1990 we began work on a new ecological housing project on our property near the village of Findhorn on the Moray Firth. At the moment the site is a residential and holiday caravan park. In this unlikely setting the Foundation aims to build an ecological village to demonstrate the principles of energy conservation, renewable energy generation, waste recycling, organic food production and other related subjects.

To date twelve dwelling houses have been erected, including five single dwellings made from recycled whisky vats, a Guest Lodge for twelve beds and a Youth Building. A 75 kW wind turbine was erected in 1989 and is currently supplying 20% of the electricity needs of the site.

The houses that were begun in 1990 were designed to be as environmentally friendly and healthy to live in as possible, avoiding materials with high toxicity in manufacture, application or usage. The houses were designed by award-winning Keystone Architects, founder members of the Institute of Building Biology and the Ecological Design Association. ('Building Biology' is a term coined in Germany, referring to the health aspects of buildings and materials, such as toxicity, ventilation, condensation and electromagnetic field effects.)

Features we have incorporated include:

- The use of passive solar features where possible through orientation and window layout.
- Solar panels for domestic hot water heating.
- A district heating system using a gas condensing boiler for highest fuel efficiency.
- Super-efficient insulation.
- Low-energy light bulbs throughout.
- Triple glazing.
- Cellulose insulation (made from recycled paper).
- Non-toxic organic paints and wood preservatives throughout.

- Boarding manufactured without the use of toxic glues or resins.
- Locally grown and harvested timber from managed forests.
- Local stone for skirting, patios and pathways.
- Roofing with natural clay tiles.
- Innovative 'breathing wall' construction allowing a controlled exchange of air and vapour.
- Suspended timber floors for under-floor air circulation to avoid a build-up of radon gas.
- Isolating electrical circuits to reduce electromagnetic field stress.
- Water conservation (showers, low-flush toilets and self-closing taps).
- Collection and recycling of rainwater for garden use.
- Shared facilities (laundry, kitchens, lounges) avoiding unnecessary duplication.
- Simple timber frame construction and detailing suitable for self-build.

To date the houses have been built largely with volunteer labour and through the Foundation's Building School, a two- or three-week hands-on course in ecological building. We have been generously sponsored by many of the firms whose materials or products we are using.

Other planned projects include: construction of sewage treatment facility using the Solar Aquatics System, a unique process incorporating complete aquatic ecosystems in a greenhouse environment; additional wind generators to provide up to 70% of energy needs; development of a 'green' business park incorporating a Visitors' Centre introducing the ecological village concepts; a farm project to provide locally grown organic food; and a Health and Wellness Centre providing conventional and alternative medical care.

(Various amended extracts from 'Welcome to the Findhorn Foundation'— see Section 5 Reading List. It is not known precisely who contributed to the above text as the various parts of this brochure were penned at different times. John Talbott was certainly the main contributor, and in addition there was input from Nicky Robertson, Frances Edwards and Jill Brierley, who edited the finished product.)

The 'Statement of Land Ethic'

First drafted in 1982 this is the Foundation's formal statement about its working relationship with the nature kingdom.

Nature is Sanctuary: The Findhorn Garden Trust

The Findhorn Foundation is founded on the basic belief and faith in the underlying spirit and intelligence within all life. For over thirty years we have lived on land in the Findhorn Bay Caravan Park, seeking to embody this belief and to work consciously and openly with nature in the spirit of cooperation and co-creation. We are moving towards the vision of a new society: one that relates to people, the environment and the planet out of a sense of love, understanding and wholeness rather than fear and survival. Much of what we have accomplished in the past, our experience and learnings, have been on a consciousness and awareness level. We now wish to apply this awareness more fully to the physical level of how we live; to express the essence of what the Findhorn Community is through architecture, landscape and integrated ecosystems that harmonise the needs of people with the needs of the natural systems in which we live. Working with intuition and consciousness as well as with proper planning and follow-through, we wish to create physical forms that honour the sacredness of life. Nature is constantly expressing the joy of the Spirit and the song of life, celebrating creation, bringing more life. We wish to join this celebration and to participate fully, finding the appropriate forms, dwellings, homes and lifestyle that harmonise with Nature's Song.

To this end we have become the legal owners of the land of the Findhorn Bay Caravan Park. Until that point all our dwellings there were required by law to be of a temporary nature; but our ownership now allows us to build. We are now making a long-term commitment to the land and to right stewardship and erecting permanent buildings.

The Land Use Plan which the Foundation has developed for The Park sees the area as a residential and commercial village centre within the Community, integrating families, children, singles, couples, the elderly and visiting guests. There will also be areas for food production, recreation, facilities for education, cottage industries and crafts, business offices, shops and commercial concerns. The main features will be the central open informal gardens in Pineridge, integrated landscaping and buildings in the central area, trees, and the natural flora and fauna of the Findhorn peninsula. We are committed to aesthetically and ecologically sound energy-efficient homes and buildings heated with low-tech energy systems; limited vehicular traffic in residential areas; water conservation, and the recycling of all organic wastes on site. We are further committed to the conservation of our adjacent wild areas, including primarily the sand dunes of the Moray coast and the tidal marshes of the Findhorn Bay. We see the area growing and being developed in an organic manner over a period of years, with nature as the focal point and key quality.

It is the aim of the Foundation to create a model village; one that combines the essential principles of community, connection to nature, appropriate technology and spiritual awareness to form an integrated life-giving environment; an environment that provides all the basic nutrients and growing conditions for all life and all beings.

READING LIST

Wendell Berry; *The Unsettling of America*; Sierra Club; 1977

William Bloom; *Devas, Fairies and Angels; A Modern Approach*; Gothic Image; 1986. William originally wrote this as a study paper for the Foundation and it was later published by Gothic Image as a booklet.

Judith Boice; *At One With All Life*; Findhorn Press; 1990

H. Cole, C. Freeman, M. Jahoda & K. Pavitt; *Thinking About the Future*; Chatto and Windus; 1973. A fierce critique of the Club of Rome's first report.

Stephan Croall & William Rankin; *Ecology for Beginners*; Random House; 1981

R. Ogilvie Crombie; *Conversations With Pan*; audio tape from Findhorn Press; 1976. A variety of other lecture tapes are available in the Foundation libraries, some of which are for sale. There is also an entire audio/visual presentation held by the visuals department.

Bill Devall & George Sessions; *Deep Ecology: Living as if Nature Mattered*; Gibbs Smith; 1985

Annie Dillard; *Pilgrim at Tinker Creek*; Picador; 1976

The Findhorn Community; *The Findhorn Garden*; Harper & Row in USA, 1975; Turnstone Books and Wildwood House Ltd in UK; 1978; second UK edition by Findhorn Press; 1988.

William Forward & Andrew Wolpert (editors); *Chaos, Rhythm and Flow in Nature: The Golden Blade No 46*; Floris Books; 1993

James Lovelock; *Gaia*; Oxford University Press; 1982

Dorothy Maclean; *Wisdoms*; Findhorn Press; 1971. *The Living Silence*; Findhorn Press;1971. Both published under the nom de plume 'Divina' and now out of print. *To Honour the Earth*; Findhorn Press;1991

Vance Martin and Mary Inglis (editors); *Wilderness: The Way Ahead*; Findhorn Press; 1984

D. Meadows, D. Meadows, J. Randers & W. Behrens; *The Limits to Growth*; Earth Island; 1972. The first report of the Club of Rome.

Mihajlo Mesarovic & Eduard Pestel; *Mankind at the Turning Point*; Hutchinson; 1975. The second report of the Club of Rome.

Jonathon Porritt; *Seeing Green: The Politics of Ecology Explained*; Basil Blackwell; 1984

Laurens van der Post; *Yet Being Someone Other*; Penguin; 1984

E.F. Schumacher; *Small is Beautiful: A Study of Economics as if People Mattered*; Blond and Briggs; 1973

Peter Russell; *The Awakening Earth*; see Section 1 for details.

John Seed, Joanna Macey, Pat Fleming, Arne Naess; *Thinking*

Like a Mountain: Towards a Council of All Beings; New Society Publishers; 1988

Rupert Sheldrake; *A New Science of Life*; Paladin; 1983

Elisabet Sahtouris; *Gaia— The Human Journey*; Pocket Books; 1989

David Spangler; Session with Myrtle, Julie, Kathi, Milenko; tr: John; 5-6 December 1978. Foundation archives. The quotation is from p 3.

John Talbott; *Simply Build Green*; Findhorn Foundation; 1993. The Foundation Building Department technical manual.

Barbara Ward & René Dubos; *Only One Earth*; Penguin; 1972

Machaelle Small Wright; *Behaving As If the God in All Life Mattered*; Perelandra; 1983

Four

Education in the Community Today

The brotherhood that will be anchored here in form will only be secondarily a brotherhood of teaching, that is, a centre where people can gain hidden or mystery knowledges. We are not interested at this point in giving out secret knowledges. It must be a brotherhood of action, dedication through service, through love and awareness, educators in the greater sense.

From *Rockozi and the Brotherhood,*
Findhorn Foundation Original Series Study Paper

So education in the future . . . will deliver to man the most priceless gift of all, which is absolute freedom. Man has sought for centuries and centuries. He's looked for it in political ways, and he's looked for it in healing ways, in medical ways, and psychological ways and religious ways. But a man is free only when he is educated, when he is constantly educating himself, when he is constantly leading out from himself what is most deeply there in perfect awareness of his environment.

From *Education in the New Age,*
Findhorn Foundation Original Series Study Paper.

The first paper in this section is by Michael Lindfield, a long-term Community member and for many years a trustee of the Foundation. Michael was largely responsible for devising the 'Experience Week', our most successful workshop since the birth of formal educational programmes in the Community. Although written more than ten years ago, shortly before Michael and his family left Findhorn, his words are still apposite.

The second paper is by François Duquesne, who became Foundation focaliser after Peter's departure. Although written in 1973-4 it talks about the creation of a 'university' in the present tense, and indeed for a brief period a formal college structure did exist as part of the Foundation[1]. As we are currently exploring links with academia once again through the Semester Studies programme, and the 'Art of Living in Peace' trainings, this extract may be of interest. The paper assumes that the university is going to be the only future means of joining the Community but this policy was never put into practice — as David Spangler later remarked, we "should have a university, not be a university."

When considering our formal educative process it is vital to see it in some kind of historical context. Today our programmes form the bulk of Foundation income — we need them to be successful in order to continue the many activities which support both these courses and the Community at large. These workshops were not however conceived as primarily an income generating exercise, but as a means of bringing the excitement, wisdom and challenges of community living to a wider audience. The thought of creating extra income certainly formed a part of the initial envisioning process and the inspirations of community living certainly continue to inform the present programmes; however there is no doubt that the emphasis has changed.

This is in part as a result of the success of our many workshops. Today it would be hard for a new member, particularly one living at Cluny Hill, to experience Community life as something separate from the need to cater for our guests. Given the importance of the concept of service in our philosophy there is every reason why this state of affairs should continue, but it is nonetheless vital for every participant in this process of service to be able to contribute in a willing and authentic way.

Even though many of our workshops and conferences are

---

[1] After a successful beginning the students of the college (who included Michael Shaw, the current chairman of the Foundation trustees), decided that they preferred to merge their programme with that of the regular membership. An interesting case of the vitality of what we would now call 'living education' taking precedence over a more formal programme, the widely recognised excellence of the course material notwithstanding.

focalised in whole or in part by individuals not resident here, the founding impulse is still very strong. To a greater or lesser degree every educational event that takes place here is influenced by — perhaps it is not too much to say based on — the realities of our day to day lives. It is therefore of great import that all those coming into contact with our guests should be able to make their contribution from a place of inspiration and joy rather than from a sense of dogged duty, resentful self-sacrifice or victim consciousness.

This is not to say that individuals cannot have off days or legitimate complaints. We are not all saints! Nor should anyone attempt to pretend that they are 'fine' when they are actually in the midst of a painful personal experience. Although authenticity is a necessary quality, it is not sufficient in itself. It is also essential that all those living and working in the Foundation have access to the tools which can aid in the emphasis of the positive qualities required to work in a centre of light, and to the understanding which provides comfort and wisdom to those in genuine distress. The third paper in this section is a short extract of Eileen Caddy's guidance which addresses this issue.

Inspiration may come simply from spending time in sanctuary, in the cathedral of nature, or with friends and family, but a wide variety of growth-oriented techniques have also made their contribution to our educational culture over the years as a welcome addition to our own evolving methods of living education. The fourth paper in this section is a brief overview of some of these influences.

THE FINDHORN FOUNDATION:
A LEARNING EXPERIENCE

Michael Lindfield

(Extracts from 'Findhorn: A Learning Experience'; Foundation document, 1984/5. There are other extracts from this document in Sections 6 and 10.)

If you were curious about what exactly the Findhorn Foundation is and you decided to write a letter asking for details I would most likely reply in the following way:

"The Findhorn Foundation is an international spiritual community in the north of Scotland committed to the improvement of human relationships and understandings. Registered as a Religious and Educational Charitable Trust under Scottish law, we offer people of all backgrounds and beliefs an opportunity to discover their own unique inner nature and strengths so that they can be in a position to freely choose to make a positive difference in the world.

The Foundation began in 1962 and was first heard of through its experiments in new ways of working with nature. Despite poor soil and adverse conditions the results achieved in the cultivation of flowers and vegetables offered impressive evidence of the power of working in harmony and cooperation with the realms of nature. The founders soon realised that these self-same principles were at the heart of all healthy relationships: be it a village project, a family enterprise or a new cultural impulse, all birth needed the same depth of nourishment and attention to motivation if it were to thrive.

The garden became a deep source of inspiration and hope to many and around it a small community formed that sought to live out and demonstrate that ideals can be realised. We have no formal creed or doctrine but are based on a firm belief that humanity approaches an evolutionary expansion of consciousness which will help create new patterns of civilisation for our society. We are concerned with developing the necessary tools and skills with which to educate ourselves and during the past few years we have come into contact with a wide circle of international, political, religious, environmental and academic bodies who share this same desire.

Our educational programmes aim to help participants find their own inner spirit and wisdom and we feel that creating a caring and harmonious environment is the best classroom in which we can learn. In fact, living in the Community is our main educational experience because it provides a supportive setting for putting the so-called 'spiritual values' into daily use. We are not a spiritual retreat nor a place where one can 'drop out' from the challenges facing society. We find that issues which the world is facing on a larger scale are reflected here in our patterns of government and decision-making, in our aim towards right livelihood and harmonious individual and family relationships.

Our next step, after the recent purchase of the caravan park where the experiment began, is to develop an ecological village in which new approaches to the issues of society can be developed and tested. This is our living classroom and we are open to all who wish to work and live in this spirit.

Education at the Foundation has been described as that process which leads a person into a greater understanding and realisation of the truth that lives within them and the world around. The physical, emotional, mental and spiritual aspects of our being need their own particular disciplines and structures that allow for growth to take place and we find that a person will attract to themselves their own living situation or 'daily classroom' in which the lessons can be learned.

We do have a more structured learning programme at the Foundation and we possess a wealth of educational material: both lectures and talks from visiting seminar leaders are recorded on tape or exist in written form as well as a documented history of our own 'home-grown' wisdom as a community. With the purchase of the Cluny Hill Hotel in 1976 we began our outward-looking phase of education and since then have offered weekly seminars and conferences and also two-

and three-month programmes as a way of allowing more people to touch in with us and experience the nature of our educational process first-hand.

We have always had the idea of cooperating with other groups and in November 1979 we hosted a meeting to look at the development of an educational network. There were representatives from other communities including William Irwin Thompson from Lindisfarne, David Spangler, Milenko and others from the Lorians, a group from the Chinook Learning Community and a representative from the Auroville community in southern India. We sensed at that time the future need to work together in creating a 'university without walls' network that could interface with the already existing educational structures and in the past few years we have been exploring just how this wishes to happen.

The Merriam Hill Centre in New England is just one of the groups with whom we are developing educational links. The Learning Exchange programme that we conduct twice a year with them offers a structure for a small group of people to participate in the life of the Community not only providing mental input and stimulation, but more an atmosphere that will allow the individual to find his/her own inner learning centre and thus gain insights and understanding into the nature of personal development. Private space and group process are part of the digestive system that allows this awareness of Self to be born.

The reason we work in groups is not only to provide a supportive or therapeutic environment but that we need to learn to work together and humans are the best 'mirrors' for each other.

The emphasis we place on serving the planet here must start with a personal stance in response to our understanding of the world. Whenever we focus on a global issue such as nuclear disarmament in a seminar session we find it absolutely vital to see how the patterns and principles involved in the drama on the world screen are being played out in our own personal lives. In the case of the disarmament theme we would ask each person to look at the roots of insecurity and the need to erect personal defence systems in their own lives and then explore how global disarmament can possibly begin with a personal peace treaty and a willingness to dismantle personal defences.

This approach makes learning a very real event as it affirms the living link between the larger global situation and the personal process of searching and learning. It became very clear to us a number of years ago that our gift was not to tell a person where to go or what to be but rather to offer them the learning environment (like a spiritual greenhouse) where they could make contact with their own gifts, vocations and direction and then freely choose how to develop these.

Another image we use is that of the 'seed atom' concept which says that all the potential for growth is locked within the seed and it is simply a process of accessing that place of identity and of then providing an environment that will truly draw forth the particular expression of life that is at present dormant.

The physical seed is life in its most concentrated form and it represents a living promise for the future. It is a statement of the essential perfection of life, for within each seed is contained the perfect flower. We know that nothing, however, will be revealed and expressed by the seed until it is planted in good soil and in suitable climatic conditions.

Likewise we believe that within each of us there lives the promise of fulfilment, a seed that contains within it the perfect flowering of our humanity. Each individual is unique in his or her expression of the One Life, for there are many different flowers in this Earth garden. This seed of human perfection needs to be planted in the soil of earthly experience in order to grow and to experience itself. Therefore growth can be said to be the process of unfolding that which already is. If this fact is truly understood then it will radically alter our approach to education for we are now dealing with the process of letting it happen rather than making it happen . . .

Education in its original sense may derive from the Latin

'educere'[2] which means 'to draw out from within' that which we essentially are. What we seek to evoke or draw forth from our residents is their innate spirit and wisdom, neither of which may be taught in any conventional sense. They may only be inspired and nurtured within a supportive, loving environment. It is for this reason that the life of the Community is the primary aspect of education in the Foundation . . .

This process of unfoldment also includes looking at that which is stopping us from expressing our uniqueness, that which leads us from our true selves into the cul-de-sac of wrong identification.

If we continue with our exploration of the seed image we find that to produce a flower the plant must first build up a system of roots, and produce a stalk with foliage to support the flower. Carrying on with the analogy we see that this process can be likened to the adolescent stage of our development in which the subtle bodies of experience are developed. The personality is gradually built up until it forms a living link that allows us to enter into an intimacy with life and through this divine love affair makes possible the flowering of who we are. Can you imagine what it would be like if the promise of the flower was not contained within the seed? What would then be the purpose of planting the seed if there was nothing there to be revealed?"

Receiving an answer like that in the mail with all its fine ideals and lofty intentions may be an impressive sight on paper but really the only way to find out about the Foundation is to experience it first hand. Failing that the next best thing is to listen to those who have lived within the Community expressing their feelings and sharing their understandings of the living organism that is the life of the Findhorn Community.

The essential conviction which lies at the heart of our life and our educational philosophy at Findhorn is that true spirituality consists less of what we believe than of the qualities

---

[2] Or possibly from 'educare', to train.

we exemplify in the course of our life and work, qualities of aspiration, commitment, courage, discipline, joy, peace, love, creativity, clarity and cooperation that we associate with our inherent, if potential, divinity.

COMMUNITY, COLLEGE, UNIVERSITY

François Duquesne

(Extracts from 'Community, College, University: Towards a University of Light'; Foundation Early Study Paper.)

The teaching of the university has to be perceived in the wholeness of the activities carried out by the centre. The programme is thus a balance between many activities which draw upon physical, emotional, mental and spiritual experiences. The individual, in learning how to give, learns how to balance his own being to live under the guidance of the God within himself.

The student moves through certain cycles which involve different aspects of his being. The teaching or educational experiences of this university of light are a blend of mental clarifications of the New Age vision and of practically applying that which has been revealed in everyday activity. It is a blend of work and discussion, of meditation and service, of joy and laughter, of periods of expansion and moments of crisis. It can be painful if the student resists the process that is taking place. This is why a clear vision of what the Foundation offers and requires of its members can help an individual who thinks of joining the university to make a clear decision.

As this vision of what the Findhorn Foundation has to offer to the world clarifies itself, a new structure is evolving. The conditions of entry, of joining the centre of light have accordingly changed. This is no longer a community where people can come and live, but a university of light where training for planetary service is offered . . .

The first year, which will be experimental in nature, will give the opportunity to those who take part in it to co-create their own programme, though a definite structure will be present in order to guide and channel their energies and consciousnesses. It is understood that at the end of a one-year programme, opportunity is given to the student to carry out the New Age work either as a staff member of the university or to join other light centres over the world, or to specialise in a particular field of service which will have revealed itself in the course of time spent here.

We thus come to a vision of a light centre whose function is twofold: first to provide a force of inspiration through the demonstration in practical terms of the New Age vision, second to train souls for the field of world service and thus release into the world this brotherhood of consciousness which knows itself to be at one with the spheres of limitless love and light. As each student enters the realisation of his expanded soul consciousness, he carries within him the inspiration and the energy that will draw out the divine qualities of those he will work with.

This is the function of the coming New Age souls who will build it, consciousnesses attuned to the whole of life and afire with the cosmic vision that the New Age heralds.

PERSONAL COMMITMENT

Eileen Caddy

(This extract from Eileen's guidance was read out by Peter Caddy at a community meeting on 11th November 1972.)

My beloved, be not bowed down by the things that seem to be going wrong, but be eternally grateful for all the wonderful things that are happening, for the deep and fundamental changes that are taking place in so many Souls at this time, for the real change in consciousness. Be patient. Some Souls change more quickly than others. Some grasp the vision but with others it unfolds more slowly. I tell you, those who fail to see the vision, fail to move out of their well worn ruts, will be unable to remain here. The energies that are being released at this time will cause such a discomfort within them, that they will be forced to move elsewhere.

Encourage them to move on until there are only completely dedicated Souls here and the work can move forward without any kind of hindrance and in complete freedom. Those who remain here should do so because they are aware of what is going on and are willing to give their all to it. You will find those who are really dedicated will hold nothing back but will want to give all they have freely and without any strings attached.

The time has come when the situation must be made very clear to everyone so that not one single person can say that they do not understand. You are carrying people who should not be carried, who are unable to contribute something financially to the whole. It is time that each one search their heart and see exactly where they stand in the Community. It is not right to keep anyone here just because they fulfil a need, but do not have the right consciousness and are unwilling to change. Over and over again I have stressed the need for quality, not quantity. It would be best to have a few dedicated Souls rather than a great many who are here with the wrong consciousness and are dragging their feet.

There are so many new things waiting to be brought down and grounded, but this cannot take place until you are all united and of one mind. This will come. You see it in certain groups already. Allow nothing and no one to hold up the work that is taking place.

INFLUENCES ON OUR EDUCATION

Alex Walker

These have come from many sources over the years. Indeed, some have been with us for so long that we now think of them as our own. Attunement, for example, was first brought to us by the Universal Foundation who had a close contact with the emerging Community in the 1960s and 70s. Likewise, the idea of focalisation was brought here in the early 70s from 'Sunrise Ranch', an Emissaries' centre in the USA.

Later in that decade co-counselling, or re-evaluation counselling, became very popular with Community members. From the 80s onwards strong links with the psychosynthesis movement were formed which continue to this day. Several Foundation members have gone on to become teachers or counsellors of this system, and accreditation courses are sometimes run here in cooperation with the Psychosynthesis Trust in London. Gestalt has also been influential, partly due to our exchange programme with the Esalen Institute in California.

Other impulses have come and gone in a blaze of short-lived intensity and excitement. Examples of this would be EST, DMA and Robert Hargrove's 'Next Step' workshop, each of these techniques having added something vital that our collective consciousness soaked up and can (presumably) call upon again. A similar process seems to occur with certain artistic events. There are occasions when one can almost see the angel which overlights us hovering above performers in the Universal Hall and assimilating the offerings on show. Perhaps the most powerful example of late was the East/West concert that formed part of the 'Individual and Collective' conference in 1988. The nature of our being is synthesising — opening up to new experiments, and then letting them go after they have enriched the field.

The arts and such conferences have had other important effects. Our conferences draw on a wide variety of contributors, many of them coming here for the first time. The qualities explored by the conference often seem, willy-nilly, to form part of our resident members' living education curriculum, and they always provide an important seed point for further exploration and development of ideas and practices.

Another important gift from the arts has been the contribution of the Actors' Institute, who have brought several workshops here, of which 'The Mastery' has been the most popular. Although not a spiritual programme as such, the enduring value and appeal of this weekend event is quite remarkable. It has certainly been the most influential of all outside workshops to come here, and Ike and Maggie Isaksen who first brought it here deserve great credit for doing so and for supporting it over the years.

There is no point in attempting to summarise the content or purpose of this gem of an event here, but one important quality it seeks out is our individual ability to inspire. How often have those who have done this workshop sat in the Hall and listened to a Community member making a clear, intelligent and apposite point in a dull monotone and thought "The Mastery, the Mastery!"?

A more recent contributor to our collective knowledge is Process Oriented Psychology, or POP, which is based on the work of Arnold Mindell, and was first brought here by Max Schuepbach. A word of explanation about the name of this work is in order. In our jargon someone 'in process' is certainly someone who is not happy, and probably someone whose work is suffering because of it. In POP terms the idea is not necessarily to go 'into process' but rather to 'follow a process', i.e. to take on board and go deeper into a subject which has emerged from the field of our collective psyche, even if it appears to be random, tangential or dissonant. It is early days yet, but POP appears ideally suited to our culture and may be with us for a long time.

A word about the relationship of psychology to spirituality may be in order here as at present one often hears comments in the Community about the value of these different approaches. First of all it must be said that the distinction is not one that is particularly clear cut. If you have a problem in your life a sociologist may begin by asking about your relationship to family and friends, a psychologist may probe for deeper insights about the nature of your relationship to parents, or the birth process, whilst a spiritual healer will attempt to dialogue with your soul, but these are only starting points.

As a spiritual community we should of course always be emphasising the importance of spirit, spirituality, the soul's nature and purpose, and our relationship to God, but that is quite different from denying the value inputs from other disciplines with ethical standards congruent to our own can have, or taking the view that psychological techniques do not have a place here.

A current example of this problem confronts us in the shape of Holotropic Breathwork. Stanislav Grof, the originator of this form of therapy, is adamant that it is a spiritual technique with an ancient shamanistic lineage. To its detractors it is a practice which induces potentially dangerous psychological states. Legal problems make the future of breathwork in the Community difficult to assess, but its positive impact on the lives of many individuals here has already been considerable.

Whatever the answer to this particular conundrum, one thing all of these techniques have in common is that they emphasise the value of consciousness rather than psychic development. We do of course train ourselves in the use of the intuitive faculties, and the development of spiritual sensitivity has always had an important place here, but our view is that the augmentation of such gifts is of little value if it is not attended by a concomitant strengthening of the soul's connection with the personality and a growth in all-round awareness and sensitivity.

Two final items should be added to our list, neither of them truly external influences. The Game of Transformation was developed here by Joy Drake, Kathy Tyler and Mary Inglis, although its main base is now in Washington State, USA, where the first two individuals now reside. Much of the Game's cosmology has passed into Community life, and its overall impact on us is incalculable. For example it is clear from some Core Group selection procedures that qualification as a 'Game Guide' is considered by many people (rightly or wrongly) to be an affirmation of spiritual integrity.

Last but not least we should mention the existence of the 'Fellows' group. Initiated by Vita de Waal and Roger Doudna in 1984 there are now over fifty fellows (both male and female as it should be thought of as a genderless term borrowed from academia), whom we recognise as carrying out valuable activity on the world stage and who have also made contributions to our own work — often for example appearing as speakers at conferences. The list of fellows is illustrious, and although we have not always managed to find ways to fully utilise their talents and offers of help, few doubt that the group will continue to make an important impact on our educational programmes.

READING LIST

Roberto Assagioli; *The Act of Will*; Penguin; 1973. One of several important books by the founder of psychosynthesis.

Deepak Chopra; *Return of the Rishi*; Houghton Mifflin; 1991

Robert Fritz; *The Path of Least Resistance*; Ballantine; 1984

Stanislav Grof; *Beyond the Brain: Birth, Death and Transcendence in Psychotherapy*; State University of New York Press; 1985

Harvey Jackins; *The Upward Trend*; Rational Island; 1978. A collection of essays on re-evaluation co-counselling.

Michael Lindfield; *The Dance of Change*; Arkana; 1986. *Findhorn: A Learning Experience*; unpublished Foundation document; 1984/5

Arnold Mindell; *Working On Yourself Alone*; Arkana; 1990. *The Shaman's Way*; Harper Collins; 1993

Fredrick S. Perls; *Morality, Ego Boundary and Aggression*; in *Esalen Is*; ed. J.O. Stevens; Real People Press; 1975. Fritz Perls was the founder of gestalt practice in the Esalen community.

Ken Wilber; *Grace and Grit: Spirituality and Healing in the Life and Death of Treya Killam Wilber*; Shambhala; 1993. Treya was a member of the Foundation and this is a moving account of her battle with illness. Wilber is also at pains to distinguish between 'pre-rationals' (who apparently make up 80% of new age adherents) and 'trans-rationals' (such as himself). See also Section 10 reading list.

Five

The Art of Living in Community

Q. What would be the qualifications of those in the inner core?

A. Those common to all spiritual endeavours: dedication, purity of being and of intent; harmlessness, love and wisdom; the ability to act with awareness and responsibility and an ability to proceed in action from a centre of uplifted vision and spiritual attunement; the ability to move in life in a joyous and uplifted manner and to carry these qualities into the lives of others.

From *Rockozi & the Brotherhood*,
Findhorn Foundation Original Series Study Paper

The first paper in this section is an introduction to the role of work and service in Community life.

Paul Solomon was the founder of the Fellowship of the Inner Light, based in Virginia Beach, Virginia, USA. Some years ago Paul began receiving messages from the Source while in a trance state, and the Fellowship grew organically around him. He gave the second paper in this section as a lecture to the One Earth Conference at the Findhorn Foundation in October 1977. Although Paul's later life became shrouded in controversy this talk is considered by many to be one of the most inspiring lectures ever heard in the Universal Hall.

The subject matter of this transcript does not confine itself to the issue of work, but it is nonetheless a passionate and inspiring reminder of the need to relate to the task in hand and invest it with spirit, rather than to pursue the glamour of our naive notions about initiations, mysteries and esoterics.

The original lecture still exists in the form of an audio tape, which more powerfully conveys Paul's wisdom and humour. Those of you who have the opportunity are strongly encouraged to listen to this first, and keep these written extracts for future reference, and as reminder of his sonorous voice.

One of our most fundamental aims is to bring spirit into everyday life, but it is nonetheless important to distinguish between spiritual work and spiritual practice. My spiritual work may involve any day-to-day activity such as digging the garden, looking after children, or typing introductions to study papers. My spiritual practice is my reference point for all of this, the place in my life where I can evaluate my work, reaffirm my connection to the divine, and continue to offer my life in service to God. The second paper in this section is an extract from William Bloom's recent publication on the subject. William is a director of Alternatives at St James's Church, Piccadilly, London, an author, and a Fellow of and frequent visitor to the Foundation.

The next paper is made up of an amalgamation of various descriptions of Community-specific practices and ideas. Some explanation is required in advance about the use of the term 'attunement', for this one word has come to mean three related but separate activities.

a) The short space of silence, usually with hands held in a circle, with which we begin so many group activities. The contributions by Roc and William Bloom concern this activity.

b) The regular meetings of members of Foundation work departments and related businesses which usually involve a meditation, a personal sharing of some kind, personal feedback and reflection, and business items. Sometimes they include a trip to a nature spot, or even a local hostelry. The personal sharing and feedback aspects of these meetings are discussed below.

c) The more general practice of communion with the cosmos. An early study paper by David Spangler on this subject is reproduced in full as the main contribution to this topic.

The next paper, once again by William Bloom, is an introduction to group meditation.

The final paper is perhaps the most controversial in this section. Ever since the inception of the Foundation we have advertised our willingness to bring together people of widely varying backgrounds and belief systems into a community life which is without any formal creed. This remains the case, and it is therefore important to stress that this paper is about the belief systems you are likely to encounter here, and should not be interpreted as an attempt to formalise such widely held views into a doctrine of some kind.

We remain committed to the search for the essential truths of spiritual life, and although these may be unchanging our human interpretations will no doubt continue to be but a part of the whole picture. No one should feel disinclined to participate in our Community life because the views so expressed are not congruent with their own. All of us here continually find our world view challenged, but that is not the same as having it moulded into some pre-determined form.

One of the most exciting and challenging aspects of spiritual life is the discovery that everyone has a unique and different view of the cosmos, spirituality and theology. Certain patterns may frequently recur, but the overall picture is of an endless non-repeating mosaic of ideas and thoughts. This kaleidoscopic diversity is simply part of the drama of being human.

PLANETARY MYSTERY SCHOOLS

Paul Solomon

(First published in One Earth Magazine, Spring 1978.)

I am convinced that my entire life this time has been spent in very, very careful planning for the job that I have to do in this experience. But that doesn't mean that I consciously participated in all the careful guidance and development of my consciousness. My conscious participating probably began about five years ago with what for me was a very spectacular experience in discovering that something that I always thought as I was growing up, was actually true. That is, that as the son of a Southern Baptist minister, who by the way is the son of a Southern Baptist minister, and on and on and on, I grew up hearing the idea that one could talk to God and get answers.

So, I literally believed that God was part of our family and that we could talk with him, that he could talk with us, that there was a two-way communication possible. As I grew up and went through high school, I carried with me this idea that God was always present and knew every single thing that I did. I adopted these Baptist views of morality but when I discovered all sorts of delicious things when I became a teenager and assumed that God was watching all that, I developed a gigantic guilt complex. It is great knowing that God is always there, that you can communicate with him, but there are some things that you don't want him to notice. Unfortunately, the Baptist view of God doesn't deal with that concept, and so in order to right the wrongs that I was still doing, I felt like I had to serve God to make up for it. The next thing I knew I was in a Baptist seminary becoming a Southern Baptist minister.

Then, about five years ago, I found out that God can literally speak to us and through us in terms so precise and so understandable that there is no mistaking the message. And that was the beginning of a new dimension of my spiritual experience that had nothing to do with religion as I had known it. In fact, it didn't have anything to do with that God that I had known. This was a new God. A greater God. Someone far beyond any concept I had had before. And the thing happened with that new birth that I think probably always happens to each of us when we are born spiritually.

When you are born spiritually it is like a physical birth. You become a spiritual baby, and there are some things that are characteristic of spiritual babies. Babies like to be handled and cuddled, and they cry a lot. That is what spiritual babies are all about. The other thing most characteristic of spiritual babies that is also characteristic of babies in the flesh, is that anything they can get their hands on, especially anything shiny and attractive, they stick in their mouths. When you are born spiritually you go to every conference you can go to, every teacher you can find and buy every book that deals vaguely with a spiritual subject. And without a lot of discrimination you just stick it all in your mouth and digest it all, which very soon results in spiritual indigestion. And just like a baby, you need to be burped. It all comes back up — spiritual regurgitation.

But the interesting thing is that after that spiritual regurgitation is a time when you don't want to hear anything about anything spiritual. "Don't talk to me about God, don't talk to me about metaphysics, I don't want to hear it. I just want to rest." And during that rest period an interesting thing happens. Things digest, and then you go back a little more cautiously, a little more discriminately, and still take things in, but you select what you take in and you grow a little more slowly.

As I went through that period looking and discovering and reading and trying to inform myself, the most exciting concept that I came across was the concept of the mystery schools. Nothing was ever more intriguing to me than the idea that somewhere, hidden back in a forest in the mountains, somewhere where nobody could find it unless he was enlightened, was a mystery school. A very, very special school where masters — those who had actually mastered all of the arts and

sciences and spiritual cultures and had evolved beyond anybody else on this plane — were in residence. The concept of
the mystery school says nobody can even make application
to such a place. The only thing that you can do is handle your
lessons so well that one of these masters will discover you.
He will find you. Through his influence you will be accepted
into this mystery school where your consciousness will be
moulded through a series of initiations until you have the
opportunity to grow as fast as a human can grow because the
lessons are presented very carefully by real master teachers.
How exciting that was to me! If there was anything I wanted,
it was to purify myself, get my act together and get to a mystery school. I was absolutely determined that I was going to
do it.

The only problem was that everything in the literature of
mystery schools referred to schools way back, centuries ago,
around Pythagoras and in ancient Egypt even before Pythagoras when Hermes and Ra were teaching there. Everything
about mystery schools was ancient, and yet there was always
a phrase that said, "There are still mystery schools operating
today. Nobody can find them, but they are there, and if you
are ready the teacher will appear and will take you there."
So, I did everything I could do to get myself ready, but how
do you know when you are ready? And how can you be sure
that the talent scout is going to find you? It is not easy to leave
all of those things to blind faith.

And as I was studying and working and meditating and
trying to prepare myself, I discovered a law of telepathic communication that said, "If you can focus on anybody, anywhere,
whether in the flesh or not in the flesh, if you know what
they look like and you know their name, and you can hold
their image in your mind for an extended period of time, and
repeat their name over and over and over, it would attract
their consciousness to you." And I thought why shouldn't that
work for a mystery school? At least they would find me and
know I exist. Maybe I could convince them if I ever made
contact. So I started my meditation, holding the traditional

models in my mind, and repeating a mantram, calling them to me. What followed was the most frightening experience of my life. I suddenly was in another dimension, a separate reality from this one. And I saw a procession of hooded beings, in long robes, in a great circle around me and it became obvious that I was the object of their procession. They were chanting. Suddenly I realised that I didn't know how to get back, nor how to disengage myself from this scene.

I prayed like I never prayed before, with all the prayers I had learned as a child in Sunday school. And it occurred to me that if I had made contact with them by calling their name, I could make contact with myself by calling my own name. I did this, and suddenly I was awake, dizzy, uncomfortable but thankful it was all over. I read further and discovered that Dion Fortune said that all of these mystery schools have occult and psychic protection, and that you can't invade their space on a psychic level. So I assumed that I had encountered the 'cops' of the mystery school. After that I left it all alone. I wasn't about to try to enter a mystery school again, and I figured I had made my presence known and they would discover me soon enough, and that I had probably flunked the entry exam already.

Some time later I had given a woman a reading about a lost child and she had located her daughter through the information in the readings, so she was very happy with what we were doing and saw the purpose of it. She told me about a Zen master who teaches Bonsai in Atlanta. She said, "I have a feeling that what he is really teaching has little to do with these trees that he is bending into shape, but I don't know really what it is and he won't say, so why don't you go to see him." So I went to see him.

At the school of Bonsai I saw all these miniature trees. Some of them looked like a little tree you would see on a mountain beside the ocean where they were bent in a windswept direction, one side bare from the salt spray and the branches moving out to the other side. They were done so perfectly that they didn't look as if they were shaped by human hand. They were actually modelled that way and yet they were living things. It was exceptionally fascinating. There were little forests with hundreds of trees in a little block. Hundreds of trees and a perfect forest. In fact, the forest might include a mountain, a lake and a cliff and so on in this little miniature world.

As I walked through the garden with this man, I noticed some peculiar things about him. First of all, he was never in a hurry. I was so excited with everything that was going on around me that I would ask three questions before he would answer the first one. And I couldn't get him to move any faster. And the slower he got, the more impatient I got. But he didn't even seem to notice that. In fact, he was so much in communication with the nature around him that I was there as an observer, and finally before we got through the garden I felt very distinctly that he was apologising to the garden for my presence.

I began to realise this man was teaching me something but not by pointing it out to me, not by telling me what the lesson was and I had the option of not even noticing the lesson. We went to sit down and chat about what he was doing. I heard him working with some students, in forming a tree, and I heard him say that in wiring branches in a particular direction, "You must realise that this is a living being. Don't think of it as a plant. Think of it as a soul, and this soul needs to be moulded in a particular direction, and these training wires are like the karmic experiences that you have that bend your nature in a particular direction so that you are made more beautiful by the pressure of these that mould your being." I was listening to him give these people fantastic spiritual truths, and all of a sudden it occurred to me — he's not really teaching horticulture or botany or even Bonsai, he is teaching them spiritual growth and the laws of the universe. What a brilliant mind, so slow and so understated, acting as if he were not brilliant.

As I sat down with him I said, "I know that the ancient masters had a rule that if the student couldn't notice a lesson, the teacher couldn't give it to him. You had to be ready for a lesson to be able to receive it. You had to be able to ask the question in order to get the answer. I know that you are not going to sit here and tell me you are a teacher of spiritual growth, but I can see that you are. And I want to learn from you." And he looked at me with a look that could melt steel. He looked hurt as if I had made an accusation.

And in his very slow, soft way that still twisted the knife, he said, "I am not a spiritual teacher. I do not teach spiritual lessons. I do not believe in teaching spiritual lessons."

I thought, "How peculiar. I wonder what he does believe in?" but I didn't quite know how to ask, and the best I could say was, "What do you mean? I know that you are teaching more than how to torture these plants. It is a bigger lesson. I can hear that in what you are saying to these people. What do you mean, you are not a spiritual teacher?"

He said, "What you are accusing me of suggests that I would separate life from its essence. What I teach is life, the relationship to the universe, but not this on a spiritual level and this on a practical level, and this on a physical level. I don't rip these things apart. It is all one law. Spiritual growth is growth — that's all. I don't believe there is any such thing as a spiritual teacher. If a person separated that part of their life and tried to teach that, they would be teaching an error in the first place. There is no such thing." Well, I was duly impressed, and I asked him if he would teach me. "Let's work with a plant for a few moments and then I will come back and we will talk about it."

He gave me a pine tree that was sort of rag-tag. It didn't look like a Bonsai at all, it looked like something he had picked out of somebody's garbage can and put there. It had literally tens of thousands of little brown pine needles in it, tiny little needles because the tree had been miniaturised by clamping its roots and cutting them back. He gave me a little pair of tweezers and told me to pick out those little brown needles. Well, I am not so dense that I can't recognise a lesson in patience, and I took those tweezers and said, "If it kills me I am going to do it." I sat at that table picking all these little brown needles one by one and wondering if I really had to do this, or if he thought it up just for me. I kept plucking and plucking. For hours I was plucking pine needles from just one side of the tree before I turned it around, and I kept thinking about all sorts of things I needed to do back at the Fellowship, and the more I plucked I kept thinking, "He should be over talking to me. He could be teaching me fantastic lessons while I am plucking these damn little needles."

He let it go on and on and on for hours, and I didn't think he would ever get back. He went off to the store, he went here and there. He just left me plucking those little needles. By the time he got back that tree and I had quite a relationship going. I was beginning to see it in a whole different way. Then he began to talk with me about the tree.

He said, "If you were going to shape that into a more beautiful shape, what would you do?"

And I looked around at some of the others that he had shaped, and looked at this one and I thought, "I don't see any way that this thing can get into that shape. If I bent all of these branches that way it still wouldn't do it, and if I cut this I couldn't imagine anything beautiful in that tree." I just didn't see anything beautiful about it. It was like a rag-tag, dirty little girl without her hair combed.

I said, "Well, maybe windswept, because most of the branches go in this direction anyway."

He said, "Why don't we just work on it and see if anything comes out of it for you."

I had watched him take the pruning shears and cut and wire them and push them around. It really didn't look all that gentle, the way that he did it. I didn't see how the tree survived it. So I took this little thing, and I took the shears and I started to cut a branch. I thought he would go through the ceiling.

"Don't do that to that plant! You didn't ask permission first."

I said, "What do you mean?"

He said, "You have to talk to the life in the plant so that

it understands what you are going to do to it, so that it will cooperate with you. That's how you are going to find out what direction it wants to go in."

I thought, "Oh, you are going to tell me how to talk to devas." I was really excited about this idea of getting in touch with the spirit of that plant although he didn't use the term spirit. So I said, "All right, how do I do it?"

He said, "Talk to it." Well, I am sitting there looking at this ridiculous little scruffy pine tree, and I haven't any idea how that pine tree is going to talk back to me. There is nothing harder than to try to talk out loud to a tree feeling that it is just a tree. But I tried. And I asked it what direction it wanted to go and it was so ridiculous that I almost giggled. I just didn't feel that I was communicating with that plant. So he watched me and he didn't smile. But I could see little fleeting glimpses of a sense of humour at my discomfort in trying to communicate with the tree.

Finally he said, "If you could see that tree as a human being, what would that being look like?"

I began to describe this dirty, skinny little girl with combat boots and hair uncombed, and all of that was the image this tree gave me. He said, "Close your eyes and see that little girl standing before you." Well, that was easy enough. I closed my eyes and I could see the little girl. He said, "Now talk to her. Don't talk to this plant, talk to her, the spirit of the plant, and ask what she would like."

Well, the image began to come. "First of all, you've already washed my face," and I saw her face differently after she said that, "and my hair is ready for the combing and shaping." And these things began to come and I opened my eyes and looked at the plant again, and it was a whole different thing. It was a different plant, and the plant was excited as I was about to cut it. It no longer felt that I was going to cut a branch and it was going to bleed. It was more like a girl who is going to get a haircut and when she has finished she knows she is going to look beautiful. There was the spirit coming from the plant, and we began to communicate with it, and before we finished that afternoon, there was an absolutely beautiful, exquisitely beautiful, little tree that was wind-swept and had the bark missing on one side, and we painted that with lime so that it looked as if it had been bleached with salt spray, and you could almost smell the ocean by looking at that little plant. And I was thrilled. I really felt as if I had seen a transformation of a soul from something uncontrolled to something beautified by nature itself. It didn't look shaped by human hand.

All these things relate to mystery schools. As I was talking to him after this experience I said to him, "I've always wanted to be a student in a mystery school, and I have an idea that you can cause me to learn more than I can learn by accident with my spiritual group from now on. You can take me in a short time and teach me more in one year than I can learn in five years on my own. Will you take me as a project and shape my consciousness like yours and mould me as they did in the ancient mystery schools?"

He looked at me and said, "Paul, could you leave the Fellowship, close its doors and come here as my servant, wash my teacups in my kitchen and make my bed, sweep my floors and pick the pine needles off the dirty, scruffy pines and do all of these things if I never say anything wise to you or entertain you?" It hit like a ton of bricks. The Fellowship to me was like a child, a living being, something that was a part of me and to close it would be like closing a part of my life. But at the same time there was this other thing. These two highly valuable things were being weighed in the balance for me, and it seemed to me that the life of the Fellowship would continue even if the doors were closed.

I said, "Yes, I will. I will come here as your servant."

He said, "That being true, I cannot teach you." That really hurt! I just wasn't expecting that sort of reply. I thought I had sorted it out and done exactly the right thing. These things can be so painful for a moment.

And I said, with tears running down my face, "Why?"

He gave two reasons. "For one thing you are too emotional

about it, and secondly, if you could close that Fellowship and come here then I have need of learning from you because I couldn't close this school and come to stay in your Fellowship." Well, I felt that I had learned more in that short exchange in those few seconds than I could learn in a lifetime out there looking for it. I had found my mystery school, and it had affected me profoundly. I asked him if I could meet his teacher someday. He answered, "The teacher only makes that decision. If he wants to meet you."

I asked, "But how will he know?" He looked at me as if that was the most absurd question that I had ever asked. And I realised it was, so I dropped the subject and went on about my business.

It wasn't long after that, that we moved the Fellowship to Virginia Beach. One day I got a call from a man at the Norfolk Botanical Gardens, who said he knew the Bonsai teacher from Atlanta. He said, 'I've studied with him for quite some time and I have a tree here that I would like to bring you, and perhaps let you work with it and see if you would like to continue the thing you started with him some time ago." I asked him to come out, and he brought a beautiful little tree that was still in training wires. He sat down and we looked at it for a bit. I noticed that the man was Oriental. After only a few moments of conversation, he left the tree with me, giving me the impression that it was a gift from the Bonsai teacher in Atlanta.

Later in the day I thought I'd call Atlanta to thank the teacher for the plant. When I spoke to him, he said, "I didn't give that plant to you." So I asked who did. "He did."

"Why should one of your students want to give me a tree?" I asked.

He replied, "That wasn't one of my students, that was my teacher." My God, I spent ten minutes with that man and hadn't asked him a single question! All these years I waited to meet this teacher and the teacher comes and goes and I don't even have sense enough to recognise the vibration of a teacher! How could I have missed it?

I immediately got on the phone to Norfolk Botanical Gardens and I asked if he was still around, and I told him I was not quite sure how to take care of the plant he left, and asked him to come and see me again. I didn't tell him that I had found out that he was the teacher. Very graciously he consented to come back out and talk to me about the care and feeding of the little plant that he had left. Then one of the most spectacular things happened: as he was sitting talking about this plant, he began to make reference to things. He said, "As I was training this branch here it was stiff, as if it would break instead of bending in that direction. Now that was during that period of time when you should have been publishing this material and felt that you wanted to be out there teaching instead." And all of a sudden I began to make a connection.

I asked, "How did you know about those incidents in my life?"

He said, "This tree was put in training wires at the time that I was first told about you, and ever since then I have watched you by the branches of this tree. Everything that you did was reflected in this image of you. And if I had resistance from a branch I knew that you were having resistance in what you were doing in your life."

Looking at that tree I realised that whole tree had been a point of communication between him and me, and he had been teaching me for three years. I had never even met him, but for part of my life he was participating in every incident of my life and he never forced me to learn anything. He never manipulated me through the branches of that tree but he did very gently suggest to the tree and to me through the tree that we shape ourselves in more beautiful directions.

Then I began to realise, looking back on these things, that somehow I had touched the periphery of the mystery school. I asked him directly about mystery schools. "Is there really a place in China or Japan where priests come together and learn a discipline through which they become very spectacular individuals who know how to respond to every situation of life?"

He said to me, "There may be such a thing as a mystery

school, but you don't want that because you already are enrolled in the highest of the mystery schools on this plane. The teachers put lessons before you."

And he told the story of a young man going to a school, finding himself enrolled in the Pythagorean school of the mysteries and waiting for the classes to start. As he left his room and went down the hallway to go to the dining room, he noticed a broom sitting against the wall and some dust in the hallway, and thought, "This is ridiculous, they don't take care of this school. There is trash and somebody hasn't finished a job and they have gone off. This is no way to run a mystery school." He had his meal, he came back and noticed that the dirt and the broom were still there. He went back to his room and meditated while still waiting for the classes to start. Finally after his meditation of the afternoon, he came out and started to go to the dining room for dinner. He noticed that the broom was still there and the dirt was still there and now there was a mop and a bucket. And he thought, "How careless. How could they do this? They aren't taking care of this thing," and he went on to the dining room. When he came back and it was still there, he thought, "I am going to tell somebody about this. As a matter of fact, I am not sure I want to stay in this mystery school. If they don't have it together any better than that, they can't teach me very much." And he was still waiting for the lessons to start . . .

Now, the whole thing that the man got across to me was that it is not possible for you or me to need a lesson to shape our lives in a more beautiful way, without that lesson appearing. The next lesson that you need in your life is already right in front of you, and you don't need any more teachers than you already have, although teachers can very well help you to see the lessons. That's all they can do. That's all teachers are. No one can teach you any more of God than is already written in your own heart, but others can point it out to you and bring it to the surface of your realisation, can cause you to notice where it is.

But the best way to precipitate a teacher is to learn the

lesson that is before you and then you become companions along the way with the teachers who are themselves being stimulated and are learning. Their lessons come from your stubbornness. They are taught patience by wanting to point out that mop and bucket. How much a teacher wants to say to a student, "Can't you see the lesson that is in front of you?" His lesson is not to say that. His lesson is to put the mop and bucket there and see if you will stumble over it and move it a little closer to the middle of your path each time.

You know, I think some of you are waiting for the Foundation to become a great mystery school. Some of you are waiting for Pythagorean masters to come and teach you the formulae. Some of us are thinking, "Someday the Foundation will get its act together, and then I want to become a student."

The mop and the bucket are before you. The greatest lessons that can be taught in the planetary school of the mysteries are right here already before you, carefully designed, carefully laid out by the master teacher, and they are exactly what you need to learn on this plane.

As the Community progresses and as other lessons come that are the greater, deeper, more intricate lessons, those students who are ready for that lesson will be attracted. By then you will have learned the lessons that you need at this stage of your development. Teachers never teach by their words. We are taught by the masters' lives. We are taught by being in their presence and watching their response to their surroundings, not by their words but by their actions, by the opportunities that are put in front of us by their presence. We are taught by the evolution of the school of which we are a part. And we are taught as much by the school's mistakes as by its examples and successes. And we learn most from a mystery school when we build it.

You could not be in a better place at a better time than now for your particular needs. You have a lesson where you are. Don't feel that a mystery school is at Findhorn for only those who remain there. Your participation in whatever way in this mystery school has been a part of your life and will continue to be. Wherever the lesson is, it is in the middle of your path, and you have one of two choices — pick up the broom and start sweeping or push it out of the way and say, "Isn't that ridiculous that somebody left that here." Learn to recognise the next step along the path, and don't say, "If I didn't have that to do, I could get about my spiritual growth." Do that and know that is your spiritual growth and grow through the experience of having dealt with it, whatever it is, and give thanks for it and keep your eyes open. No waitress was ever unkind to you in a restaurant without reason. No shop girl ever was impatient or short with you without purpose. No husband or wife or child ever put you through their selfish trip when you didn't need it. You have the perfect teacher if you will just listen, will give him credit for his successes and notice your failures. The difference in people on this plane enrolled in this mystery school is that some are enrolled and asleep, and some wake up. We don't have the option of leaving the mystery school. We don't have the option of resigning the lessons. The only option is to learn the lessons on purpose or not. We are all already in the greatest of the planetary schools of the mysteries, and the Foundation, the Fellowship of the Inner Light, Lindisfarne and other such centres are places where those who have awakened come together to share their lessons and make the lessons available quite deliberately to others. The lessons are not greater or lesser. Just more conscious. Know that and grow to be what you are: a child God growing to be what his father is.

FIRST STEPS:

AN INTRODUCTION TO SPIRITUAL PRACTICE

William Bloom

(Extracts from the book of the same name, published by Findhorn Press in 1993.)

The basic message [of *First Steps*] is that spiritual practice consists of three interwoven dynamics:

Every day, in some way

- We review, contemplate and transform our attitudes and actions.
- We align with and explore the inner and sacred dimensions of self and life.
- We serve.

Perfectly, all three happen simultaneously and continuously. They also need to happen

- With a general attitude of amused realism about our relative state of ignorance, and
- With an interest in seeking continuing education and inspiration.

In the following chapters, then, I first look at the innate seeds of spirituality within all of us and at the challenges of being human, and then I go on to describe in greater detail the basic dynamics of spiritual practice.

Daily Self-Reflection

The Two Selves

We are all faced with an inspiring, but irritating, challenge. We have this inspiring sense of our true inner self and we have the irritation of not being able to express it fully. This is a terrible paradox, isn't it? What greater frustration can there be for a human than to be told: this is who you really are — and you cannot be it; you can become it, but you are going to have to work at it.

But there is an even greater discomfort if, having become aware of our core self, we then ignore it.

There are two simultaneous pieces of work to do:

● First, we have to melt and transform the layers of our defences and daily attitudes.

● Second, we have to give attention to our core self and bring it more fully into our consciousness and actions.

'Self-reflection', then, is reflection on both the everyday personality self and on the inner Self.

Reviewing the Personality Self

The basic principle of self-review is that by shining the light of awareness onto our attitudes and behaviour we can begin to transform them; and as we transform them, this allows who we truly are to become more present. There are many techniques for doing this, but I think they can be usefully summarised in three basic approaches:

● Contemplative review.
● Journal-keeping.
● Breath.

Whichever technique we use — and all three can be combined — they need to be based in as much self-honesty as we can achieve. Over the years, as we practise self-review, the ability to look frankly at our dark aspects increases. This is work that we do on our own. In the privacy of our own reflection we can be absolutely honest with ourselves. It is not worth being anything less. In the Christian tradition this form of self-reflection has been externalised into Confession, in which the honesty occurs in a dialogue with a priest. The attitude of confession —telling all — is useful. I confess to myself . . .

It is also crucial that this review, like all other aspects of spiritual practice, take place on a daily basis. If we do not monitor ourselves regularly on a daily cycle, then things slip by and the transformative dynamic of honesty is lost.

Within the classical spiritual traditions, the institution or the teacher provides the disciplined guidelines within which we do this work. As we move into the 21st century, however, we have mainly thrown away relationships in which we surrender to top-down discipline. This means that we have no option but self-discipline.

Alignment With the Sacred

'God'

The sacred, the divine, the multidimensional, the magical, is around us and within us. As children we often experience this other reality, but the immediacy of physical, psychological and social existence penetrates our vulnerability and we build up defensive — and successful — personas for coping with it. As this happens we lose our openings of communication with the other, inner world. We close down, and create and thicken our defences.

Later, for one reason or another, we begin to recall this inner world and its sacred beauty. We begin to sense that there is some form of underlying and transcendent connection between everything. We may call this Spirit or God. It is useful to understand that 'God' is shorthand for an indescribable reality which is experienced in various ways in different traditions and individuals. For some people it is a very personal experience; others are more detached. Generally we tend to project onto 'God' ideas that suit our society. A patriarchal society has a patriarchal God.

Some spiritual traditions, such as Buddhism, recognise this tendency to appropriate, exploit and manipulate the idea of God. These traditions recognise that defining God is a matter of where we place our attention and how we attune our perception.

In the mystical tradition of Judaism there is a helpful map of inner realities called the Kabbalistic Tree of Life. On this tree are ten great spheres, each of them representing an aspect of the sacred or an expression of God. The lowest sphere represents the Earth and the highest sphere represents the radiance of pure cosmic consciousness and the Source of all that is manifest. Above this highest sphere, however, there are three further half circles, each higher than the previous one, sitting like hats on top of each other. The first of these crescents represents The Unknowable. The second represents The Absolutely Unknowable. The third and highest is named The Absolutely Completely Unknowable.

The Tibetan teacher Djwahl Khul, well known through the many books of Alice Bailey, most of the time studiously avoids the word God, preferring to use the phrase All That Is. And J.G. Bennett, who taught and initiated people into a mystic way called Subud, once had a student who upon entry into the order refused to go along with a pledge to God. Bennett's students were dismayed, but Bennett looked at the rebel and asked, "How about a pledge to Cosmic Electricity?" The rebel nodded that he could accept such a notion and Bennet flowed ahead with the entrance.

This digression about God underlines a crucial point about true spiritual practice. In it, as private individuals, we are free to explore what God is or is not, or whether we even choose to relate to the concept at all. What is central is that there is an inner world and that there is a sacred quality to all life. In spiritual practice we explore these worlds, free of preconceptions, open to the unknown.

Some people may say that they are incapable, perhaps even unworthy, of experiencing the sacred. This is not possible. No person, unless deprived by terrible injustice, lives without tasting the experience.

We feel it in beautiful landscape; sometimes we experience it when looking at a child or holding something beautiful. It may gently stroke our consciousness, like the touch of a feather. At some point in our life, the magic quality of the inner world has touched us. Only remember and notice it.

In spiritual practice, on an ongoing daily basis, we deliberately do certain things to cut through our psychological defences and to bring us into communication and communion with this inner reality. There are many different techniques and approaches — spiritual technologies — but the purpose of all of them is to bring the sacred and the divine into our conscious awareness, and to repeat the experience so often that it fuses into our daily consciousness.

Abandon, Devotion and Contemplation

It is one of the joys of human culture that there are so many different approaches to God or Spirit — but it is also a challenge. It is a challenge because one of the more terrible problems of humanity is that people are often intolerant of spiritual paths different from their own. I am not just thinking here of the obvious theological conflicts between religions and belief systems. I am also thinking of the very different styles of spiritual approach. These differences in style can provoke terrible prejudice and are perhaps more of a problem than the theological and intellectual divisions. Theological conflicts are easily identified, but those between styles can exist within the same belief system and are more insidious. There seem to me to be three basic styles which appear to conflict and create trouble between their practitioners. These styles are:

- Mystical abandon
- Devotional aspiration
- Contemplation

Imagine, for example, a devotional seeker who loves intense prayer and a person who meets Spirit by dancing in abandon. The one may be deeply alienated by the style of the other. In the same way, a seeker who enjoys the more contemplative approach may be highly judgemental of both the devotee and the dancer. In fact, the three styles need not be mutually exclusive. It is worth regularly monitoring ourselves and asking which of the three styles is our predominant way; then asking whether it is appropriate to try one of the others; and making certain we melt any prejudices against them.

Actions, Attitude and Service

The Fire of Idealism

In the practice of self-reflection and the practice of attuning to the sacred, we gain visions and experiences of a world, of a consciousness and of a reality different from that in which we daily live. The sacred world has a quality about it that calms the dynamics of unbridled egoism. The driving need to survive, to compete and to win, retreats in the face of the sense of the true Self and the sacred nature of all life.

The challenge, then, is to remain true to that sense of the Self.

Once we have begun to feel the power of the Self and the sacred, there is a natural drive to fulfil it and to embody it in our whole lives. That instinct which we had as children, that there should be a world of justice and right behaviour, re-awakens. Perhaps some of us have managed to hold on to our early sense of natural justice; if that is so, then our new encounters with the inner world will reinforce and empower our awareness and activity. We also learn that there is nowhere for this process to begin except in ourselves.

It seems to me that there exists a natural instinct to surrender to the vision and sense of the Self. I have watched many people who do indeed have a clear sense of their Self but who do nothing to surrender to it in their daily lives.

Without exception these people are wounded by a deep personal dissatisfaction — although their pain may be hidden under veils of psychological defence.

There are other people who surrender with such willingness to the moral imperatives of the Self that their personal sacrifices to the general good can shock and inspire us with their courage and lack of self-interest.

For the sake of ease let us call all behaviour that is dedicated to achieving a moral, just and loving world service. Our instinct for service derives, I believe, from an uncontrollable inner desire to bring into tangible manifestation all that we know to be just and beautiful of the true inner world. This is a great passion. It is also a dangerous passion, for most of us prefer safe lives. Caught in the realities of mortgage payments and family commitments, ensnared in the illusions of status and social survival, we find the idea of surrender to the passion of service threatening.

Yet we have no choice except to surrender — each in our own appropriate way — to this passion of service. Our lack of choice derives not only from the moral imperative of our soul. It also derives from the reality that service is the physical foundation stone of our spiritual transformation.

Service as Personal Transformation

The essence of personal transformation is the process by which our core self, our true inner self, comes into full incarnation and expression. Spiritual transformation is our true self coming in for a landing. Many of us forget this or choose to ignore it. We prefer to think that our main work is to expand outwards into ever less earthly awareness. Certainly we have to expand our consciousness, but all the expansion in the world is useless unless it is brought down and expressed through us in our behaviour, actions and attitudes.

We need to be very clear about this. The reason why we need to express our Self is not simply because it is a good idea, or because it is of service. The reason is that only when our new consciousness is expressed through us do we really change. If it does not express through us then it is happening only in our psyche. New awareness — about love or spirit or consciousness or natural justice — has to ground through us and we have to experience that inner 'friction' that happens when we genuinely act it out in body, mind and heart. It is in this process that we transform ourselves. If our changes happen only in our psyche we are wasting time and it is fair to accuse us of narcissism.

To put it in an energetic way: The core self has a different vibration, radiance and consciousness from the everyday psycho-social self. When the core self comes into and expresses through the everyday self, then the everyday self changes its vibration, radiance and consciousness. In this way transformation, integration and true freedom are achieved.

There are many mystics and spiritual idealists who, because their new awareness is not grounded in the physical reality of their actions, are completely out of balance and in many ways dysfunctional.

The energy field of the Self has to flow fully through our whole being right down into what is often today called our cellular awareness. Every cell of the everyday self needs to vibrate and radiate the awareness of the Self. This is spiritual transformation.

Service, then, seen from another perspective, is that behaviour which expresses our core self into the world.

COMMUNITY SPECIFIC PRACTICES

Alex Walker et al.

William Bloom's comments apply to any aspirant, anywhere. The Community has of course developed its own specific rituals of which this is a brief summary.

Work as Love in Action   *Roy MacVicar*

(From 'The Living Classrooms of the Findhorn Foundation', Foundation pamphlet edited by Roy MacVicar, circa 1978.)

A vital aspect of Community life is the role of work as a form of spiritual practice. A great deal of what we do can be defined as the sacralisation of the ordinary, and this has been interpreted in many ways throughout different phases of our collective life.

One of Peter Caddy's famous catchphrases about community building is his 'Three Ps — Patience, Persistence and Perseverance'. In the 1970s the importance of perfection in work was added to this. At all times the value of service as a spiritual path has been stressed. Most of these notions lead back to the title of this section — 'work is love in action'. We have from the very beginning been a working community — a place of action where the word of God directs the hand of humanity, and the dreams of the soul are made real by the work of the flesh.

Work, however hard or monotonous it may seem, is something which can be done with love and joy when it is done with a new level of consciousness. When you wash a floor or polish a table or clean a pot, you can realise your essential oneness with that thing, see that it also has a divinity within it so that when you make it clear and bright you release that divinity. It will reflect to you the love and joy which you have poured into it. Work is one of the most effective ways in which you can demonstrate a change of consciousness.

* * *

Subsequent sections on meditation and attunement below describe a number of techniques for achieving and maintaining the 'vertical alignment' with the sacred which engenders this kind of joyful synergy in relation to the mundane, 'horizontal plane' tasks that confront us on a day-to-day basis.

* * *

Attunement   *R. Ogilvie Crombie & William Bloom*

(Roc at a Focalisers' meeting September 1974. Foundation Early Study Paper.)

There are different energies which are channelled in the Community because every single person who is a member at some time or other will be channelling energies into it. This is going on in many ways because one thing energy does is build up to what I can only refer to as the energy field of Findhorn. Of course groups do the same thing. Now the question that really came up was the fact that the construction group seemed to be doing a lot of attunements. There was an attunement of the original group and then a little later perhaps some other people came and joined in and there was another attunement and then later on perhaps there was still another one when another lot came. There are about six or seven attunements during the day.

The fundamental purpose of attunement is to link together so that the group works well. Of course, as soon as you begin to do this the energies are channelled through the group. The question is asked, "Well surely there is an unlimited amount of cosmic energy that can be 'channelled'," and certainly it is not like a reservoir that might be emptied by taking too much out. But a very odd thing happens here. You get together half a dozen people and they link in an attunement, and a certain type of energy is tuned through those six people which is for the purpose of helping in the construction of the building. A little later, three others come along. The idea is we just take them into the group and add them to this attunement and this will help. What actually happens is that you break down the original attunement. You are breaking the link because you are introducing three other people. You begin all over again. If you do another attunement with nine people, there will be a different energy pattern because the group is slightly larger and made up of different people. The result is that instead of having one uniform field for working with construction, there are three different ones which do not necessarily harmonise; so a state of disharmony may be introduced instead of group attunement.

What you want is one pattern which is exactly the same for the whole departmental group. The only way you can achieve this is by not having different attunements made up of different people in the group. The extra people who come along will be absorbed into the energy pattern that has been created by the initial attunement.

The amount of energy that is going through those particular groups becomes quite considerable, and it is actually far more than what is needed for the actual purpose at the moment. It seems in some ways to be an infringement of a cosmic law for any one particular group to take more energy than it requires. It nearly always happens that some other group will be robbed of it, not because there is not plenty of it but because the balance has been upset in a way. Too much energy has gone into this particular place so it will be made up from somewhere else. The result is that the whole field of the Findhorn Community is put out of balance.

Channelling energies is not something that can be done in a thoughtless way by saying, "Right, I am going to be a channel for energy and I am going to get a tremendous energy down for something or other." You have to remember that somebody else may have to pay back that energy if you take more than you need for the purpose.

If you are working with a group in the morning, a certain type of energy pattern would be done for that. You finish your work there and that is that. No more of that energy will come through you. Then you go to another group or have another meeting. There is a different kind of energy probably needed there, so you would attune with that group.

Question: We often have the idea of attuning at the end of a meeting.

Roc: That is probably a good thing, because this means you cut off. It is like turning the current off when you have finished.

Question: Have we got to the point where we really have to hold our consciousness to the quality of energy we are invoking?

Roc: You have got to know your needs, and what you can do is consciously think this is an attunement for an energy that is correct for the particular work you are doing. The power of the mind is very strong, and you will tune into the right source by simply holding the thought.

Question: When you have a stable number of people and sometime during the day the activities become dispersed, would it be the correct thing to come together and attune?

Roc: The best thing to do is to come together and hold hands to focus the energy again. Don't have too long an attunement. If there is a proper amount of attunement and harmony in the group, there should never be any feeling of pressure on any individuals within the group. If there is a sign of pressure, then that is a sign that there is something wrong somewhere.

Question: When we attune as a group in maintenance, we have a picture of the being of the group developing and growing. It is as if our energy is principally channelled into the growing of that being more than it is into our daily work because until we know that being, we don't feel we know our direction.

Roc: The purpose of attuning to anything is to call down energies for certain work that is to be done. If you are going to channel it into a being or something of that sort, you are going to build that up and the energy is not going to go into the work you are doing. I see a lot of danger in this idea of thinking of the group as a sort of group soul rather than thinking of the group as an integrated group of individuals. Once you begin to think of this entity or this group soul, that is the being, there is a terrible danger here of this becoming a thought form. A thought form is not a real being. It is created in a projection of the different people in the group. It is much better to think of the group as individuals forming a unity and not to think of it too much as a being.

* * *

(From Meditation in a Changing World *by William Bloom, page 114.)*

After one workshop with members of the Findhorn Foundation, the group I was working with drew up some helpful guidelines concerning attunement:

1. Attunement is never simply a ritual done out of habit.
2. The focaliser of the attunement always demonstrates:
   a. Caring for the group;
   b. Sensitivity to the work to be done.
3. The focaliser therefore:
   a. Clearly and caringly brings the group together in the here and now;
   b. Sensitively attunes the group to the work to be done.
4. At the end of the period of work, it is helpful if there is a completion or 'detuning' — a holding of hands, a 'thank you' — or whatever is appropriate.

* * *

Attunement—Weekly Feedback Sessions   *Alex Walker*

Weekly departmental attunements have a variety of purposes. Apart from the obvious ones of creating a time of collective meeting to discuss any relevant business and/or to enhance the social interactions of group members there are at least three other important aspects of these gatherings.

The first is to ensure that any working department meditates together a minimum of once a week, so enhancing the individuals' attunement to each other, the tasks in hand and to the divine will.

Secondly, they are a time when each member of the department has the opportunity to offer a 'personal sharing', meaning a deep (and yet not over-long) description of any outer happenings in their life, but more importantly, of their inner feelings, beliefs, challenges and aspirations.

Thirdly, these are occasions for a conscious opening to any feedback or reflection on this sharing from the other members of the department. A wide variety of spiritual and psychological techniques are brought into play on such occasions, depending on the skills, interests and aptitudes of the participants. These might include exercises to identify areas where someone is 'projecting' their fears, desires or other feelings onto someone else, attempts to reveal 'blind spots' in individual awareness, and a myriad of 'group consciousness' exercises.

The value of meditation should be evident from the material presented above, but the personal sharing and feedback aspects of attunements are just as important in their own way. It may be possible to reach enlightenment by sitting alone in a cave, but for most of us, our attempts to better ourselves have to work in the context of our friends and colleagues. This kind of interaction is then an opportunity to discover whether what we are learning about ourselves and the world is being put into practice in an appropriate way.

Indeed, students of the Foundation archives or other early source material can readily determine that due to the tiny and far flung nature of the emerging spiritual networks of the 1950s and 60s, one of the most important aspects of our modern spiritual work, the give and take of personal feedback as a mirror to the soul, was virtually absent. After all, if the contacts with whom you can share a secret part of your world are few and far between, the last thing you want to do is offend them! This isolation is therefore responsible for the apparently eccentric nature of much of the British spiritual movement of the period up to the late 1970s. No such excuses can be proffered for today's excesses.

* * *

Attunement   *David Spangler*
(Foundation Early Study Paper — amended)

What is Attunement?

To practise attunement, we begin with understanding the concept of oneness. This does not mean that everything is the same; it means that everything exists within a unified field of being. The world within us duplicates in all its aspects the vaster realms of life and consciousness that lie outside and beyond us. To communicate with a spiritual level of life, we simply discover and attune to its corresponding reality within us. We realise that there is no separation, that essentially we are one with that level and we accept that oneness as the reality. We can draw an illustration of this from music. Middle C and its first harmonic, the next higher C note, are the same tonal quality but separated by an octave of energy. The two notes played in the same way possess equal amplitude but a different frequency of expression. The higher note is moving faster as a sound wave, hence we hear it as a higher-pitched sound. Though most people can differentiate between middle C and its higher harmonics, such as high C, they are still the same note and occupy the same tonal position in the scale. Because of this, whenever one C is struck, the other Cs of higher and lower octaves resonate in harmony and can be heard by one whose ear is sensitively trained. So with the universe within us. In the microcosm of our individual being, we are harmonically related to all the macrocosm which represents higher octaves of what is within us. If we manifest a certain quality, such as love, then there is a thrill of resonance throughout the universe of the love quality on all its levels of expression, on all of the octaves of its being.

Attunement and Resonance

With this understanding, we can begin to practise attunement in our lives. With its practice, we find ourselves in increasing communication with higher and vaster realms of Life, both vertically in terms of higher frequency consciousness and horizontally in terms of physical life that surrounds us as fellow human beings and the lives within nature. Unlike old-style communication which is usually seen as a flow between two or more centres or people and which thereby maintains the concept of separation, attunement is communication through communion, through recognising the reality of oneness that has always been there. There is no flow between — there is oneness with. Attunement works on the principle of resonance which in turn depends on action and living manifestation. Such phenomena as channelling and mediumship mainly depended on the ability to contact another level of Life as a separate thing outside the life of the psychic, just as prayer was communication with a God outside and separate from the individual life. This contact could be turned on or off when a message of help was or was not desired, much like using a telephone or a radio. Attunement is entirely different. It requires the manifestation and expression within the life of the individual of the qualities to which he wishes to attune on less restricted levels of being and consciousness. It cannot be turned off. Oneness must be a living reality within oneself, not just an idea.

Attunement with Love

Let us suppose that I wish to contact the awareness of limitless Love within creation. Using old methods of communication, I might try through meditation to contact some Being, whom I would consider separate from myself, who would represent this awareness to me. Using attunement, a different approach entirely must be used. First, I realise that this awareness of limitless Love is not outside me; it has a lower octave counterpart within me. I must find that counterpart and play it, like striking middle C in order to hear through resonance a higher C note. In other words, I must begin expressing on human levels a love released from limitations of prejudice, fear, hatred, separation. I must relate to the world around me as if all parts of it were my Beloved. I must see the reality of this love within me and my life. I set the vibration of love throughout my microcosmic life. Then, in my moments of silence, I can rise on the currents of this resonance. I attract the higher octave counterparts of love to my awareness or, more accurately, by experiencing love in my microcosmic life I become sensitive to experiencing it in my macrocosmic life. The barriers of separation in my consciousness dissolve. There is no more within, no more without. There is only the oneness of all.

Live this Attunement
By experiencing this in times of silence, I increase my sense of oneness during my times of outer activity until silence and activity, action and non-action, themselves become one and I live and move in complete attunement to all about me on all levels. Through this communion I communicate perfectly with the universe. Thus we have the New Age method of prayer, of communication with vaster and freer levels of Life. We attune, not through contact with something separate, but with the oneness of all life within us and about us. We live this attunement. It must be lived, acted upon, expressed if the necessary resonance that disintegrates the barriers of apparent separation is to be developed. Throughout the world, men and women are responding to the new revelations of the oneness of life and of creation. As they do so, attunement will become an increasing manifestation. Greater than prayer, which we turn off and on according to our need, attunement is walking, working, living every moment in the living presence of God which is Oneness. More and more we will see and hear people being living revelations of truth, people who can say with perfect authority and knowledge, "I AM the Life within all, the Love uniting all, the revelation of Truth, for in my life I resonate with All in All, and God and I are One."

* * *

Focalisation   *Alex Walker*
Nearly every department of the Foundation functions as a group, and each group has a focaliser. The focaliser is not intended to be a leader in the sense of someone who gives orders, but is rather to be someone who, by virtue of their ability to attune to the needs of the whole, achieves respect.

This does not mean that the focaliser has all the answers. Indeed the focaliser could well be someone who knows no more or even less about the work in hand than any of the others involved. If the task is one which can be achieved by the skills of the department members then the focaliser might well consider other factors. Is the work in alignment with the whole through some form of attunement? Would the work be better served if there was music to listen to? Does someone not involved in the task need to be informed of its progress? Should we have a tea break, and should I make the tea? These are all questions a focaliser, or someone aspiring to focalisation, should be asking him or herself.

The group should of course be one composed of those who are learning to receive a direction from the God within and who are able to blend that personal direction with a vision of the good of the whole. Note however that departments are not intended to be groups working democratically by majority votes — although this may happen from time to time. Given that conflict of some kind is almost inevitable, the question of how group decisions should be taken is addressed in Section 10.

* * *

Festivals   *Alex Walker*

A wide variety of creative offerings for various festivals have been made available to the Community but David Spangler's book on this subject remains the definitive text. In it he emphasises the solstices and equinoxes and offers definitions of their symbolic meaning. The descriptions are applicable to the northern hemisphere, these flows of energy being balanced by their opposite in the south.

Winter Solstice —The Festival of Identity. The time when we can powerfully invoke the awakening of the seed of divinity lying dormant within us all.

Spring Equinox — The Festival of Resurrection. A celebration of the triumph of light over darkness.

Summer Solstice — The Festival of Manifestation. A time to give thanks for the blessings of nature.

Autumn Equinox — The Festival of Transformation. Michael-mas is the 'gateway to creativity' when we can examine our individual and collective ability to bring forth that which we need in our lives.

It is revealing that in the Foundation of the early 70s, with its short-term membership and seven-day working week, these festivals were exclusively Foundation affairs and were well attended by Foundation members. In the 90s there are more distractions, and the festivals have tended to become Community-wide celebrations, and attract a relatively smaller proportion of the former group.

* * *

Ceremony   *R. Ogilvie Crombie*

(Edited extract from 'Festival, Findhorn, November 5th 1970)'; Foundation archives.)

There may be, in fact I know there are, people who think that ceremony and ritual belongs to the old age and that there will be no such thing in the new. Now this is very wrong, because we know — this is not my opinion, this is direct guidance — that ceremony and ritual will play a very large part in the New Age, but it will be New Age ceremony and ritual.

Ritual must be sincere and it must be meaningful. If it becomes crystallised, so that it is simply going through certain gestures, certain words, certain actions, which are done mechanically, not from the heart, with no meaning, then it is useless. That is why an absolutely fixed type of ritual will not be used in the New Age.

Ritual will be inspired ritual in the moment and in this case it will retain its meaning and have an effect. Now ritual may seem nonsense to people, but it isn't. Words, gestures used aren't simply something on this physical level; they create patterns on a higher level, and they are blending in with patterns which are already existing on a higher level and therefore they play a very important part in the process of manifestation.

In the older time there were very fixed rituals laid down, with the right kind of robes, the right kind of formulas, all sorts of things. [In future] they will be much more flexible, but there are one or two things which will be used in ritual that are very important.

The first one that is of importance is the candle. Now a candle, when it is lit, symbolises light, and it symbolises more than light, it symbolises the truth. Therefore a lit candle is taking truth, light, into dark places. This is the important symbolism of the candle. Also, it is a living flame. You cannot get the same effect with an electric bulb or anything like that, that you can with the living flame, and there are certain cases where the flame must be present.

Also in ritual at certain times, incense will be used. Now this may seem like a lot of "Oh yes, nice to have some smoke and smell and so on," but why is incense used —what is the use of it? This goes back to very early times. Incense is smoke ascending upwards. It is beautifully scented smoke, or it should be. The Magi brought incense to the infant Christ. Incense represents purification, as well as this ascending effect. It is used to symbolise this purification, and if you burn incense in a room where there are any entities that should not be there, that is one of the best ways of driving them out, because they do not like it. Therefore, at certain times it is important.

In a centre like the Foundation, where cooperation is being asked with the nature forces, and that is contact with the elemental kingdoms, it is important to have representatives of the four kingdoms, fire, air, earth and water. These we have here.

So there are certain things which are [to be] used, but the main thing is to remember that it isn't just a lot of nonsense. It has a very, very real purpose and it has a very, very real meaning, and therefore it is important not to think of it as being an empty piece of nonsense, and remember that it does have this very deep meaning. More than that, it does something which is very important, helping in this process of manifestation, and helping in this process of cooperation.

* * *

Retreat   *Alex Walker*

It is certainly a misconception to imagine that the Community is essentially a place of retreat, in the sense of somewhere divorced from the realities of everyday living and offering a sense of peace and quietude. Findhorn and Forres may be geographically remote from the major cities of Europe, but quite apart from the fact that there is a major NATO airbase on our doorstep, the reality of day to day life is often one of engagement in group activities, hard work and confrontation of the self.

This is not to say that times of retreat are of little import. The Foundation has a property on Iona — the house of 'Traigh Bhan' (meaning white beach) — for this very purpose. Organised retreats also happen from time to time at the Park, at Newbold and at Minton House for example. They form an integral part of spiritual self-development, and while we may admire those who seem to be able to work 52 weeks a year, we may also wonder if they are perhaps to some degree hiding from themselves in their work. The mind is a wily opponent and periods of contemplation, solitary or otherwise, are an important adjunct to any spiritual practice.

Other Practices

There are many other practices and traditions that individuals in the Community draw on, including sweat lodges, sacred dance, specific meditation techniques, Taizé singing, and so on. A number of the most common ones, such as drawing 'angel cards' have been derived from the 'Game of Transformation'.

One set of practices is, however, virtually absent from Community life — those concerned with evangelising. This is not to say that the Community wishes to hide its light under a metaphorical bushel, nor does it deny the need to bring its activities to the market in appropriate ways. The rejection of unsolicited attempts to persuade individuals of the value of the Community's work seems more related to an unease with the rigidity of belief often required to feel comfortable with such methods of persuasion, and a feeling that those who have learned a little of the spiritual nature of the world do not need to try and change it by exhortation, but seek to do so through the example of their lives.

One other activity is particularly worthy of mention, namely Community Meetings. Such events are not normally thought of as forms of spiritual practice per se, but they are nonetheless an important part of Community life. These events are discussed in more detail in Section 10.

Rules

It is important to understand that what the Community is attempting to teach is not a set of rules, or a specific moral code, but rather guidelines for developing a sense of inner listening. Given that it is expected that those involved with the Foundation will adhere to the laws of Scotland, there are only two formal rules for Foundation staff and students: 1) No use of illegal drugs. 2) No smoking in public places.

Prospective members are also of course asked to complete various introductory courses before they apply.

Given that the Community has no formal membership or structure at present there are no constraints of any kind on the Community as such, although it has been suggested that the minimum criteria for a suitable member of the Community are:

a) a regular spiritual practice

b) an openness to giving and receiving personal feedback.

SECOND STEPS — GROUP MEDITATION

Introduction   *Alex Walker*

The power of the invisible connections that can be created in the context of group meditations is one of the most important forms of spiritual work in the Community.

Various forms of meditation are used to:

- Link individual meditators together into a cohesive group.
- Connect the group with the divine in some undefined sense, or with some specific energy.
- Link together meditators and beings on the inner in different geographical locations (for example meditations to link the Community at Findhorn to Iona and Glastonbury).

This is a vast subject, and there are many different techniques that can be used.

Group Meditation   *William Bloom*

(From Meditation in a Changing World *by William Bloom, pp 103-111.)*

Why Group Meditation?

Group meditation may seem to be a modern phenomenon, but it is not. There have been many communities in the past where women and men have shared silence. These communities have been oases of peace and alignment in fractured societies. In most religious traditions meditation is taught mainly as a group and community practice in the first place.

It may also seem paradoxical that an action so private and inner should be done with other people, but working in a group is supportive and helpful.

Group meditation requires a different framework of understanding from individual meditation. In individual meditation we are describing and discussing what happens in one individual's psyche and consciousness. An extreme sceptic, listening to us, could at worst say that everything we describe is just a production, an epiphenomenon, of the human brain and that altered states of consciousness are due to changes in brain electro-chemistry. Individual meditators, supported by the millions who also meditate, know for themselves the truth of the matter.

But to understand group meditation we need to take another metaphysical step beyond the normal framework of the contemporary worldview. For here we are discussing an invisible set of connections between people. When people sit in group meditation, their brains are not wired up with one another! Nevertheless the individual meditators share a similar experience which is powerful and beneficial. Meditators share this experience because they are energetically and telepathically connected. We each of us carry an atmosphere, mood, aura, charisma. Call it what you will, it is certainly an energy field which other people can feel.

So, let me be clear for sceptics. In discussing group meditation we are not talking about a social event — a tea party for mystics. We are discussing a powerful energetic dynamic. Just as powerful forces move in observable group dynamics, so they also move invisibly in group meditation. The proof of this can only be found in direct and personal experience.

Over the years my personal experience of group meditation is that it gives me great pleasure and inspiration. I am always fascinated by its texture and atmosphere. I love feeling the tensions subside and the whole group move into relaxation and then alignment. In a world full of tensions, I find sitting safely with a group, sensing the inner dynamics, energising and comforting.

The Social-Psychological Usefulness

Group meditation may not be a tea party, but this is not to deny that the psychological and social aspects of group meditation can be extremely useful. First, if we are starting a practice, or want help sustaining one, then being in a group can provide a very helpful, psychologically supportive framework.

Second, it can be a very powerful symbolic gesture. When two people shake hands or smile at each other, beneath the fact of these everyday gestures something meaningful is happening. We are signalling safety and friendship. To close our eyes in a group and to be silent together is an even greater gesture of trust. It allows anxieties, impatience and fear to subside.

Shared silence is a symbolic gesture of anchored spiritual cooperation which transcends egotistical separateness. In fact, many people with an instinct for these realities always take a few moments' silence with their colleagues before beginning a piece of work. In modern jargon this is called attunement and I shall describe it in greater detail later on.

There is also a more subtle symbolism in attunement and group silence, for it has a levelling effect. No matter the apparent hierarchy or leadership, it melts away in the silence. Individual egos surrender, in spirit, to equality of opportunity. People who have trouble with surrendering to this temporary and minimal gesture of unity, usually have even greater difficulty in surrendering to and experiencing the spiritual unity of all life.

The Invisible Connections

My experience, and the experience of so many others, is that we possess an energy body, or aura, that surrounds us and emanates from us. This information is not new, but has been taught in mystical, esoteric and shamanistic traditions the world over. Our energy field is made up of various types of energy, such as the vital life force that gives us physical health, most often called prana. It is also made up of energy generated by our feelings and thoughts, as well as the energy of our inner self. This invisible anatomy is as complex as the structure of our physical bodies.

When we centre in meditation, this cauldron of physical, emotional and mental energy calms down. When we align, the atmospheric quality of our inner self is allowed to come in and we begin to feel its mellow nurture. And while all this is going on as a private experience, we are also radiating this atmosphere outwards through our energy bodies into our environment. In group meditation we each of us radiate an atmosphere and we also feel the atmosphere radiated by the others. Our energy bodies experience the changes in vibration and this, in turn, anchors through into our nervous system; it is then interpreted by the brain in a form of direct knowing. This is as tangible as feeling heat or cold.

A clear and everyday example of this is how, if we are connected to someone, we can know instantaneously what mood they are in by just being near them.

Our atmosphere, thoughts and vibrations are picked up and tuned into by others. Because of this some newcomers suffer from an undue nervousness about group meditation because they are worried about the effect that other people will have upon them. This is usually an unfounded fear because people, when meditating, have deliberately moved into a space of silence and purity. But if you are nervous, approach group meditation cautiously and slowly build up your confidence.

The Advantages

Because we radiate and because we can sense the atmosphere created by other folk, it is easy to see how group meditation can be very helpful. There are, in fact, several distinct advantages to meditating in a group.

There is a ripple or wave effect which actually multiplies the beneficial quality. This is similar to the physical effect that can be observed in the ocean when small waves build up to create one large wave. A single individual's calm vibration helps the next person. As that next person calms, their vibration in turn goes back to help the first person. The waves of calm build up. The group as a whole can, therefore, take advantage of the individual or individuals who calm first. Those first individuals create an atmospheric flight-path for everyone else in the group to reach the same state. The combined atmospheric effect of many people sharing silence makes it much easier for beginners to achieve centre and alignment as the vibration touches, soothes and aligns them. People often have their first experience of being centred and aligned in a group. One of the interesting features of group meditation is that nearly everyone notices when the whole group has relaxed and come to centre. It can also be a great support and refreshing experience for more experienced meditators.

In a similar way, any individual who is reaching peaks of awareness or expansions of consciousness not normally reached by the others in the group, creates an energy funnel which helps the others approach the same space.

These helpful dynamics are referred to in many spiritual traditions. It is, for example, referred to metaphorically in the idea that when two or more are gathered together in my name . . .

Two Types of Group Meditation

Within this framework, then, we can say very generally that there are two types of group meditation.

1. The first is that in which everybody is meditating individually in their own separate ways.
2. The second is that in which everyone is meditating for a common purpose.

In the next two sections I will deal in turn with these two types.

Individual Meditation in Groups

In individual private meditation, sitting in silence, we allow ourselves to become aware of the texture and consciousness of our inner selves. This is a nurturing and transforming experience for us. When I sit with a group I am aware that every individual, in their own private and unique way, is also in the same psychological and spiritual process.

In the same way that I require time to relax, centre and align, so a group also has its own rhythm. Sometimes I am so stimulated that it may take me a half hour to centre. Sometimes, if I am in enervated crisis, my whole meditation may be a struggle as I breathe through my tension or psychic activity. In a group, however, as the group calms, so I too calm as I am affected by the group atmosphere. Even if there are more nervous wrecks than just me, the group dynamic will still work. I can imagine someone asking, "But suppose everybody's a raving basket case, what then?" I have indeed experienced groups in which everyone was stressed but even so, on closing eyes and bringing the breath into rhythm, the group has gone into calm. It can be miraculous how fast and easily centre is reached. It is the exact opposite of group hysteria, as the herding instinct is harnessed here for creative good and for empowering the individual.

This is the beauty of meditating in a group: collective support, but individual empowerment. We share the process of relaxing and aligning. Then, in the support of group alignment, always with that nurturing mellow atmosphere, we can continue with our own private meditation and get on with whatever is there to be breathed through and contemplated.

The texture and sensation of the meditation will be coloured by the group atmosphere. It is sometimes useful and interesting, when centred, gently to become aware of and to explore the nature of the group atmosphere and how it affects us. We can be aware of the helpful energy currents of the other meditators as well as the helpful currents we ourselves radiate. Until you have a good deal of experience in group meditation, I do not think that it is a good idea for you to try purposefully to affect the group atmosphere. If your presence is meant to facilitate a change, then patiently let it happen. If, however, you do have experience then invisible cooperation can be very useful; I will discuss this more fully later.

Even if there is no explicit purpose to a group meditation, there are powerful implicit benefits. We have already discussed the benefits to the individual, but shared silence is also extraordinarily helpful in helping people to work cooperatively together. Without any fuss, in silence, our personality vibrations blend and become accustomed to each other. If there is personality friction in a group, nothing can work so fast to heal it as sharing silence together.

Even if there is no stated specific purpose to a group meditation, I personally feel that it is appropriate for every group meditation to end with a short period devoted to radiating love and to healing the environment. This can be done silently as a part of everyone's private meditation or it can be led with an appropriate prayer, invocation or mantram.

Group Meditation for a Common Purpose

There are several basic modes which can be usefully applied to group meditation: to Centre, to Align, to Review, to be Aware, to Expand and to Serve.

- When a group centres, the individuals relax and create a calm atmosphere.
- When a group aligns, the individuals accept the joint resonance from all their core selves. The group also aligns with what may be the common or inner purpose of that group.
- A group may also review and be self-reflective about its state, the individuals gaining insights about their own roles as well as the group as a whole.
- A group may choose to give awareness to a particular subject.
- A group can also expand its consciousness together.
- A group can work specifically to radiate a blessing or healing as a form of service.

Again, like individual meditation, these different features do not need to be regimented and allocated specific amounts of time. A group does not even need to be formally led into the agreed focus. Before the meditation there can be a simple agreement about the focus and how long the meditation is to last. Sometimes though it is helpful to ring a sweet-sounding bell to begin and end the meditation.

COMMUNITY BELIEFS

Alex Walker

Overview

This section is not a curriculum, but a description of Community life. Although most of these ideas probably form the core beliefs of a majority of the Community, insisting on adherence to them would probably alienate a similarly high percentage. Indeed, there may be no single individual who believes in them all in the form described here.

A core belief is that there is one God of Love, a God transcendent, but, unlike the God of Christian tradition, one incorporating both masculine and feminine elements. Nonetheless, certainly in some sense the creator[3] of the universe and a being or force to whom one might legitimately both pray and offer thanks.

Few, however, are willing to accept a notion of a deity who can be perceived as either exclusively or even primarily outside of our experience of reality. There is Unity in Creation, and every object, animate or inanimate, microscopic or cosmic in scale, contains within it some aspect of the divine presence. We can go further than this and affirm a faith in non-physical beings such as angels, devas, discorporate human and perhaps super-human souls who also form part of creation, who exercise some kind of dynamic intelligence within it, and with whom we can communicate.

Logically this view of a God immanent leads on to the belief that such a presence must also lie within each and every member of the human race. Clearly it will be to a greater or lesser extent dormant within any given individual, and to a significant degree our spiritual aspirations must therefore lead towards an experience and expression of the God Within.

This ambition obviously implies a kind of spiritual evolution:

---

[3] I have avoided using capitalisations for descriptions of the deity other than 'God' as for some this would be too redolent of overtly Christian notions.

a sense of purpose to life created by our individual and collective attempts to educate ourselves in the sense of fulfilling creative capacities of one kind or another which approximate our ideas about the essence of spiritual life and of the divine consciousness latent within us. Concomitant with this is an acceptance that homo sapiens may be the pinnacle of biological evolution on Earth, but that there are other lessons to be learned in realms beyond the physical.

Unlike the Judaeo-Christian world-view many of us accept the idea of reincarnation, or perhaps more accurately, of other lives. Linear conceptions of time do not suit everyone, and the idea of parallel existences, each one taking place in a kind of eternal now, are favoured by some. Whatever the mechanism this view not only accords with many individual personal experiences, it also makes sense of a world with so many varied starting points for human life. Taking into account 'previous' actions, omissions, or experiences seems to provide both a richer and more equitable view of the universe.

This being so we can more readily come to terms with the apparent injustices of wealth, health, opportunity and skill which pervade the human mosaic. Each life has a purpose not just relative to objective moral, social or ethical standards, but also in the context of other soul experiences. It is a liberating, but also humbling idea. We can begin to sense that even the most difficult, luckless, or obscure existence is merely a part of the whole; perhaps it may even be the last redemption of karma before enlightenment or liberation.

This in turn leads to a view that we are not so much victims of circumstance as participants in a drama where we create our own reality. This phrase should not be interpreted as meaning that we are responsible for the rocks, trees and buildings around us. It is intended to imply that our thoughts and emotions are conditioned by our personal perceptions of, or reactions to, events and circumstances. Such interpretations are then largely subjective. This belief leads in turn to a striving to ensure that the choices we make are conscious rather than unconscious ones, and based on, for example, mature reflection rather than childhood conditioning.

Critics of the New Age frequently allege that this philosophy is profoundly narcissistic and leads to a toleration of poverty, injustice and so on, at variance to true spiritual teaching, and especially the Christian idea of charity. It is therefore important to stress that a sense of compassion lies at the heart of our community life. Knowledge or belief in karmic destiny should, and in my experience almost invariably does, herald a genuine concern for the divine will, for the nature kingdoms and for the plight of ordinary human beings. It is certainly not an excuse for laziness, materialism or selfishness.

It is also vital to stress that all of the above should lead to a genuine embodiment of spiritual principles. The student who has read every title in the bibliographies presented here, but who lives without joy, has learned nothing. This is central to our way of life, and is one of the reasons we often describe ourselves as a spiritual community, implying a concern with inner dynamics, rather than a religious organisation, suggesting an emphasis on beliefs and forms.

Finally, life in the Community is a celebration of diversity. There are many roads to the Godhead, and if lack of interest or belief in any of the ideas presented above becomes a cause for criticism or embarrassment then this description will have failed in its purpose.

The Laws of Manifestation

Another major contribution to Community and indeed New Age thought has come through David Spangler's explorations of the philosophy of 'manifestation'. The following paper explores two main themes — the general idea of manifestation based on faith and the specific Foundation policy of 'stewardship and manifestation'.

Manifestation Based on Faith

In the pamphlet 'Findhorn and Finance' published by the Foundation in 1973, it is stated: "When one gives up all in perfect trust and willingness to serve God, and lives in harmony with his laws and his will, then all one's needs are perfectly met, often in far greater ways than one might have dreamed."

In a world where the economic problems of the day are so well known and yet so intractable, it may seem difficult to embrace this statement. How can we reconcile it with a knowledge of ecological imbalance, unemployment, the nuclear arms race, and Third World debt and poverty? The key lies in the recognition that working with the spiritual or inner nature of economics requires attention to the potential of any given situation as well as to its actual or apparent nature. As David Spangler says in *The Laws of Manifestation*, "Manifestation is a process of working with natural principles and laws in order to translate energy from one level to another. It is not the creation of something out of nothing, but rather a process of realising a potential of something that already exists."

Faith and service are key elements in this principle. Faith means much more than hopefulness: it is knowing that the substance of God and the abundance of the spiritual realms are more real than the apparent world revealed through our senses. Nor is service to be understood in terms of sacrifice or duty, but rather as a blending of one's self in the opportunity of creative partnership. Faith is the knowing, often transcending the knowledge of the human mind and its logical analysis, and service is the dynamic action of creativity based on that knowing.

In the early days of the Community the principle of manifestation based on faith was adhered to by following the inner guidance of the founders. Their remarkable success in addressing the practical needs and assessing the potential role of the Findhorn Community has been well documented, so perhaps a single example will suffice here.

"It was one manifestation after another," says Eileen Caddy. "Sometimes it took a while after the thought was put out to achieve the physical reality, but often it would happen quite quickly. For instance, we needed a music system for the sanctuary, and a regular visitor offered his radiogramme and speakers which he said were too big for his own house. Not only did he bring it up from the north of England for us, but he also brought a carpet for the sanctuary as well, and laid it personally! When I received guidance about something, I knew it would come, and often just the right object or amount of money would be given to us. There was always the question of timing though. When I was told we would be going back to Cluny Hill Hotel 'soon' I didn't think we'd have to wait 13 years!"

The economic basis of the Community's early activity was small — almost negligible in comparison to the charity with an annual turnover of a million pounds that is the Findhorn Foundation today. Conducted from a handful of caravans and bungalows, it often utilised the unwanted materials cast aside by others — manure for the original garden from nearby stables, over-ripe vegetables for soup, cast away cement and timber for building materials.

An important aspect of the nascent community's life at this time was its work with the nature kingdoms and the natural cycles of the Earth. These natural rhythms were and are influential on our economic system, and there is an enduring link between the two. Just as nature here has an abundant summer and a more introspective winter, so our own cash flow peaks in the summer and this harvest is required to see us through the quieter days and longer nights later in the year.

When the Community grew beyond a few dozen individuals a more sophisticated set of guidelines was required. David Spangler identified four separate stages of working with the laws of manifestation:

- Right Identification
- Right Imagination
- Right Attunement
- Right Action

He stressed the need to see such actions as proceeding from a sense of wholeness and oneness with all life, rather than from separation, lack or fear. Furthermore, these stages do not require to be undertaken in a mechanical or linear fashion. Thus, an effective condition of attunement might lead to an appropriate identification of a need, and so on.

Stewardship and Manifestation

In tandem with this work the Foundation began to develop the second theme of stewardship and manifestation.

These two concepts have underlain much of the Foundation's growth, and the interplay between them has influenced a great deal of our recent history. *Stewardship* is our pledge to the kingdoms that surround and nourish us, and essentially commits us to being wise caretakers of that with which we have been entrusted, as well as covering day-to-day living expenses from our earnings.

Manifestation, on the other hand, recognises that any expansion of our work or facilities will need to be supported and financed by other than our resources alone, and that any such expansion involves clearly identifying the greater need or potential it serves, and then proceeding in the faith that all required to realise that potential will be provided.

These two ideas are closely related. For instance, the Foundation's close attention to good financial housekeeping on our operating account cleared the channels for the Caravan Park Appeal Fund. This appeal raised over £250,000 in a little over a year. The purchase of the Park as a going concern is in turn enabling us to fulfil our promise of good stewardship more fully.

At other points in the Foundation's history, this principle has been abandoned in favour of taking on loans rather than waiting on funds to become available without strings attached. This policy has enabled relatively rapid expansion to take place, but also tended to make good stewardship more difficult under the burden of loan interest and increased operating costs. Each generation of Foundation members is then faced with the challenges of understanding the relationship between stewardship, manifestation and loan investments. In such circumstances, new solutions appropriate to the moment must be discerned as part of the individual and collective learning process.

(Amended extract from 'The Findhorn Foundation and Finance', in The New Economic Agenda *edited by Sandra Kramer & Mary Inglis.)*

Eileen & Peter Caddy and Dorothy Maclean

R. Ogilvie Crombie
(ROC)

David Spangler and
Myrtle Glines

Dorothy Maclean and
Julie Spangler

David & Julie Spangler
with John-Michael,
Aidan and Caitlin

Peter Caddy

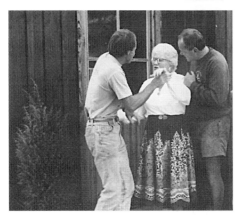

Eileen Caddy with sons
David and Jonathon

Alex &
Pauline
Walker with
sons Barney
& Craig

Sabrina Dearborn, William
Bloom and baby Sophia

Craig Gibsone and Peter Russell

Nick & Henrietta Rose

The Findhorn Community

READING LIST

Arthur and Joyce Berger; *Reincarnation: Fact or Fable?*; Aquarian Press; 1991

William Bloom; *Meditation in a Changing World*; Gothic Image; 1993. *First Steps: An Introduction to Spiritual Practice*; Findhorn Press; 1993. Quoted above are pages 1, 31-2, 47-9, 69-71. *Practical Spiritual Practice*; One Earth issue No. 12; 1993

Gerald Edelman; *Bright Air, Brilliant Fire*; Allen Lane; 1992. Recent work by Edelman on the evolution of mind emphasises the importance of individual perceptions of the world and contrasts with previous scientific notions which compare brain activity with the functioning of computers. This is a difficult book for non-scientists and has a profoundly materialistic approach. However, in his work we can see the beginnings of a scientific understanding of the way in which we 'create our own reality'.

Paul Ekins (editor); *The New Economics*; Routledge and Kegan Paul; 1986

Findhorn Foundation; *Findhorn and Finance*; 1973 pamphlet. *Findhorn: An Agreement to Serve*; Core Group; October 1977 Early Study Paper. *Welcome to the Findhorn Foundation*; Internal document produced by the Human Relations Department; 1993. Contains a reprint of the Early Study Paper on Attunement by David Spangler.

Thaddeus Golas; *The Lazy Man's Guide to Enlightenment*; The Seed Center; 1971

Joan Grant; *Far Memory*; Ariel Press; 1985. Joan Grant and Denis Kelsey are the foremost British writers on reincarnation along with Arthur Guirdham's explorations of the Cathars. Joan's grand-daughter Nicky was a member of the Foundation in the 1980s.

Mary Inglis & Sandra Kramer (editors); *The New Economic Agenda*; Findhorn Press; 1984

Phyllis Krystal; *Cutting the Ties That Bind*; Samuel Weiser; 1993

Corinne McLaughlin & Gordon Davidson; *Builders of the Dawn: Community Lifestyles in a Changing World*; Sirius; 1986. An overview of community lifestyles around the world, with sections on Chinook, Arcosanti, The Farm etc.

Meditation Group for the New Age; A set of pamphlets published by this group from their base in Tunbridge Wells, England.

Paul Solomon; *Planetary Mystery Schools*; One Earth magazine, Spring 1978

David Spangler; *Rockozi & the Brotherhood*, excerpts of a transmission from a being known as St Germain; 8.11.71; in 'The Brotherhood Series'; Foundation Original Study Paper

David Spangler; *The Iona Report — The Reconsecration of the Sanctuary at Traigh Bhan*; in 'The Plan Of Light'; Foundation Original Study Paper. *Festivals in the New Age*, Findhorn Press; 1976 (now out of print). *The Laws of Manifestation*, Findhorn Press; 1976 (now out of print). See Section 2 for a full list of David Spangler titles published by Findhorn Press.

The Universal Foundation; *Attunement*, Autumn 1970; Foundation Early Study Paper.

David Wauk; *Focaliser's Manual*, unpublished Foundation document; 1994

Six

Graveyard of Egos —
The Challenges of Living
in Community

*See this centre in its true perfection filled with souls who
are here simply to do My will and to walk in My ways.*

*This is no dream world. This is reality I am speaking
about. This is what you are to hold before you and so help
manifest in form. Where all your needs are met; where lack
is unknown; where seemingly insoluble problems are
solved in the twinkling of an eye. Because all any soul
wants is to seek My will and obey it instantly without any
thought of self. Because all their faith and trust is completely in Me and their only desire is to do all to My honour and glory; where harmony and peace and deep
contentment reign.*

Eileen Caddy; *Foundations of a Spiritual Community,* pp 91-92

Living in a spiritual community can be both a delight and a
source of great stress. Most people find that it is both, particularly, but not exclusively, in their first few years. This section therefore includes some advice about how to respond to
and understand some of these pressures.

The first paper by Peter Caddy deals with pioneering new
projects. This may on the surface appear to be a potentially
enjoyable task, and indeed many Community members find
great satisfaction in the creation of innovative schemes. However, it should also be remembered that there is an inevitable
tension between the visionary, who by definition is interested
in what can only be achieved tomorrow, and the administra-
tor who has his or her hands full with the problems of today.
Any creative impulse must find a way between these two
poles if it is to succeed, and much grief would be avoided if
we were all aware of the need for both individual creative

expression, and the calls on other people's time. (The phrase 'graveyard of egos' was a favourite of Peter's to describe life in the Community.)

The second and third papers deal more with the internal processes that can emerge in community life. Myrtle Glines's classic 'Garden or Jungle?' is required reading, but if you are choosing to consume these study papers sequentially, you may wish to break with that practice and return to David Spangler's 'Pressures Within' at a slightly later date as it covers much the same ground, although from a different perspective.

Why this apparent repetition? This is in part because Myrtle's paper is good preparation for any challenges which emerge, whilst David's is concerned more with the inner dynamics of the situation and can be appreciated more fully during or after a time of difficulty. It is certainly important to note that Myrtle's paper refers to details of our Community history and is thus more specific, but has a more dated composition. A great deal has changed since it was written circa 1974.

Together they provide a balance to the tendency for spiritual aspiration to deny difficulties. It is certainly true that one of the qualities David and Myrtle brought to the Community was a counterweight to the training Eileen and Peter had of always thinking positively, which whilst appropriate in most circumstances has certainly led to a denial of painful truth or experience at certain times in our collective history.

But why should these challenges emerge at all? Certainly some individuals seem to be able to live happily without crisis, but in truth they are the lucky few. If the carapace of personality was so easy to dissolve, so allowing the light of the soul to shine through, then perhaps Community life would be less necessary and valuable.

Many of these crises seem to involve the soul's attempts to challenge the attachments the personality has clung to. Joining a spiritual community involves a powerful invocation regarding one's relationship to the divine, and the consequences can be unexpectedly harsh. Yet you may find you come closer to enlightenment through some challenge in relationship, in your health, in finances, or from some utterly unexpected quarter.

Should this happen, you may find it helpful to remember that:

- the process is all about learning to internalise qualities you have been attempting to sustain from an external source.
- if the divine economy is truly at work, then something you might otherwise have experienced must be worse than your current experience.
- it is not the Community's fault.
- enlightenment occurs when you have a relaxed attitude to life; it is not the absence of challenges.

What the Community needs is help to meet its vision. It needs people who can accept its promise and make it work in their own lives where they are. It needs people who can go to the Community with the right motives of service and commitment to growth and responsibility, people who understand the growth process, can work creatively with negativity, can strengthen family patterns; people who are balanced and who are not looking for a personal utopia as much as for a place to serve according to the service that is needed, not according to their own glamorous ideas of the kind of service worthy of them. Findhorn is both garden and jungle, but so are we, so is the world. What we all need is a consciousness that can work with both in order to touch the greater life that is the Source.

Michael Lindfield, 'Findhorn: A Learning Experience', p 13.

Pioneering

Peter Caddy

(Extracts from 'If it's Right for One it's Right All Round', a lecture in the 'Foundations of Findhorn' series given on 28th April 1975, and a Foundation Early Study Paper. Other than PC himself, the participants are Vance Martin, Roger Doudna, François Duquesne, Billy Sargeant, Caroline Shaw, Gordon Cutler, Marlene Guppy and Mary Inglis.)

Vance: How clear was the vision to you when you started? I had the impression somehow that the vision wasn't clear and you were just following more or less the day-to-day guidance.

Peter: That's true. But our vision really was to do God's will. That was very clear. We were really on that rock-like foundation, but we didn't know where that was going to lead us. Then we were given the vision step by step. We knew quite clearly that we were being led to do something, but we knew not what. The purpose is revealed step by step, but it's an inner prompting that needs to motivate a person to a certain place and be guided to start a group, and at that time probably without knowing its full purpose.

At one stage of the garden, putting the beech hedge around, I wanted to know where we would go from there. But all I was told in guidance was that the next step wouldn't be given to me until I'd finished off that portion of the garden. So the physical vision was only given bit by bit.

Roger: Did that keep you from crystallising the vision; in other words, from getting too locked into your own personal view of the growth?

Peter: Yes. Also I don't think we could have understood it at the time. Supposing we had been told right at the beginning what the Community was going to develop into? We wouldn't have believed it. We'd have said, "Impossible." So one is just given a bit at a time; and that leads on to the importance of living in the moment, in the now. Not thinking all about the past or the future but living in the now; taking one step at a time and finishing off to perfection one job at a time. You can only do that if you are just given a little bit at a time and are willing to be led intuitively from one stage of growth to the next.

François: Doesn't that illustrate the principle that until something is finished the energies are more or less blocked, because if they haven't been anchored, no more can come through?

Peter: I'll give you an example of that. When we were building the extension to the community centre, the roof went on in about a week but as the months went by it was the finishing off that took the time. The six coats of polyurethane on 17 tables and 34 benches took an awful long time, and it was dragging on and getting slower and slower, and people wanted to get on with other things. There was the season starting for the theatre, and the performing arts group wanted to start in the theatre, but we had no theatre. There was only a tumbled-down old shop with a broken floor, partitions, a toilet, etc. Then Eileen had guidance that we were to complete the community centre before doing the theatre. So there was a whole new surge of energy, a whole concentration to get that dining room finished, and it was finished ten days before we were to put on our first production. And that theatre was completed in those ten days, again by a full concentration and a full flow of energy into the theatre. So one thing at a time, fully concentrating and focusing on it.

Billy: Do you think that is an error that can often be made — trying to do too much at once?

Peter: Yes I do. It is so easy to get dispersed, as many of you here know. A real secret of creating anything is concentration. Creation is concentration. To try and take on too many projects at once, you just dissipate your energies.

Also, it is vitally important to finish a job perfectly before moving on to the next one, because it is so difficult to go back. I've used the instance of when we put our first concrete patio down. We concreted between our caravan and the garage. I knew we had to put in a path around at the back, but we were feeling a bit tired and we thought, "Well, we'll finish that tomorrow." It was six years before we finally got around to doing that path at the back, because there was always something to be done the next day. So finish off today the jobs for today and don't put them off until tomorrow. I've learned some hard lessons in that.

François: If someone has just acquired a house or whatever environment for a community, what should be their next step?

Peter: The first thing in taking over any building is to clean it from top to bottom. That clears out all the darkness, puts in vibrations of love and light. Clean and polish it. There is an occult reason for this, because the forces of darkness can always find a niche, find an anchor where there is dirt and disorder. So cleanliness and order are very important in starting any community. When the building has been thoroughly cleaned, then comes putting your own vibrations in with repairing it, making it perfect, repainting it.

Whatever is done in the new community should be done in a consciousness of love and of peace. If you are in disharmony or upset or negative, stop working. Find that inner centre so that the right vibrations are put into what you are doing. It is those vibrations that set up a magnetic force field which draws people to you. You shouldn't have to go out and ask people to come, because if you create the vibrations, then those of like vibrations will be drawn to you without your having to do anything.

Caroline: You were trained in your lifetime. What of those starting up some place who may not have had that rigorous training? How far do you feel that those founding new centres should have been trained?

Peter: I think we had to have such a tough training because we were like a spearhead. Training in self-discipline, faith, obedience to that inner prompting and being able to hear that still, small voice within; being able to act on intuition; all these are gifts and qualities that need to be developed first of all.

I will give you just one example. The earliest spiritual

training of Eileen and myself was given by my former wife, Sheena. She was a great soul, but pretty ruthless in her training methods. At one time Eileen, Sheena and I had dinner in a London restaurant, and we were having coffee. Halfway through my cup of coffee I had an inner prompting to go and see someone by the name of Jack. I finished my coffee, got up and said, "I've had a prompting to go and see Jack." And off I went.

But I missed him. I could not understand it. I came back and said, "I don't know why, but I have just missed him. I had the prompting when I was halfway through my coffee." Sheena turned on me, told me that this man had a revolver with him and had gone to commit suicide, because I, instead of following that inner prompting, had followed my lower nature and finished my coffee. This went on and on, and I got smaller and smaller. In fact he had not taken his life; but I had to believe that he had.

François: Can you say a little more about timing?

Peter: I think timing is one of the most difficult things to judge. You can know within that the project is right, but the timing might be premature because you can get it from higher levels of consciousness which are outside time. Timing is so vital to a community. It's crucial in a community that people are in the right place at the right time.

Marlene: What sort of consequences are there when timing is wrong?

Peter: Well, when the timing is wrong — no, let's say instead that when a thing is right, if it's God's will and guided from within for one person, then it's right for everyone and it benefits everybody. If it's right for one it's right all around.

For instance. The studios were started by a group of seven people who had received their own guidance to come here. They were all skilled craftsmen and were all very keen to make a success of the new studios. In fact they were too keen, because it eventually became clear that many of the studio artists were putting their craft first and the Community second.

They weren't really participating in the Community as a whole. They weren't coming to morning sanctuary, Saturday night sharings or anything. So the four of us responsible for the Community met with them one by one to see whether it was right that they stay or not. We had been given guidance that those separating themselves from the whole would have to be gone by Christmas; so that new energies could flow into the Community then, and the Community would have to be in a state of wholeness before the energies could be released. In every case where we had to turn someone out of the nest, as it were, things worked out excellently for them once they learned to spread their wings and fly on their own. One couple started a large new pottery, and it gave them the experience and self-confidence they could never have got here within the sheltered environment of the Foundation. Although they were not happy with our actions at first, their pottery became a daughter centre to ours and they now say they are grateful that they were asked to leave.

Gordon: What has been the Foundation's relation to modern technology and all that?

Peter: I believe that a new age community should be a blend of cooperating with the nature forces and respecting the oneness of life, but at the same time realising that we are in a technological age, a scientific age, and in the bringing about of one world, modern means of communication, transport, etc. are vitally necessary. So use machines and modern equipment as long as you have control of them. They can free you for doing things that are more important.

Mary: Isn't being aware of the devas and life of machines a way to use them properly?

Peter: Indeed yes. We were talking about that this afternoon, and discussing how man's machinery must be seen as an extension of himself. Just look at Alan with that recording equipment — sometimes it's difficult to tell which is the recording equipment and which is Alan, he's so wedded to it.

Billy: I'd like to ask how many people have tried to buy or take over the Community?

Peter: Hundreds. Not to buy the place but to take it over. The number of people who have said you are doing it all wrong, you should do it this way, you should do this, that or the other thing, is incredible. This is where you have to be so grounded in your foundations and how those foundations have to be really tested and proven solid so you know from within where you are going and what your part is. Otherwise you'll get blown about by everybody who comes and nothing will be achieved.

We've had, for example, the Sun Myung Moon people. Their representative from America came here saying that Sun Moon is the Avatar, he is the Christ, he is the Lord of the World and the Foundation has just been prepared for him to take over; and this representative was very upset because I didn't quite see it in the same light. There have been any number thinking that the Community was just right for their particular path or their particular master, guru, teacher or whatever. That's why sometimes I am rather immovable, because I've had to be rocklike — otherwise the hundreds of people who have come here with their own ideas would have found us an easy pushover.

François: Can you say something about private ownership here?

Peter: Well, I suppose different communities will have different approaches on that. Our approach has not been that of a commune where there's common ownership. There is common ownership of certain things here, but there's also complete freedom for private ownership and private responsibility. I think this allows for the development of the individual's sense of responsibility and custodianship.

Billy: What about people who say they don't get guidance of any kind? Is some kind of guidance always necessary to start a community?

Peter: I think you need to have developed, if not clear inner direction, at least an openness to intuition. You must be able to intuitively follow inner promptings from your higher self, the God within. In other words, it is no good planning things out with the mind, thinking about starting a centre in such and such a place and planning it all out in that way. That just wouldn't work. The only way is to let go and let God, as it were.

GARDEN OR JUNGLE?

Myrtle Glines

(Extracts from 'Findhorn: Garden or Jungle?', Foundation Early Study Paper, also printed in New Age Journal and United Focus Journal.)

Recently, my partner, David Spangler, received a letter from a person who had just returned from the Findhorn Foundation, the spiritual community in northern Scotland that is currently the subject of much publicity. This letter was asking for his assistance for the Community, which, the writer assured him, was moving steadily into states of psychological and spiritual imbalance.

This was not the first such letter we have received. Over the past two years, we have been contacted by several persons who have felt that the Community was losing its direction or was becoming imbalanced in some way. We have also heard from people who had gone to the Community in response to something they had read or heard about it, only to discover that its reality was not what they had expected. While some of these reports have been angry or bitter, most have simply indicated a disappointment that, in the minds of these people, the Community was not living up to the beautiful ideals which it proclaimed.

This concerns me, for I have a deep personal interest in its well-being and a love for the people who are trying to make it a success. For three years David and I lived in the Community. His work there is well known through his writings and lectures; my own contribution was as a human relations counsellor, which has been my profession for twenty years. Though less publicised, my work put me in touch with every facet of the Community life and gave me opportunity to witness and experience first hand the challenges in building and running a place like the Foundation. These were not only the normal human relationship problems brought about by the presence of many strong and different personalities or

by the Community's small living area and limited accommo-
dations which caused everyone to live in constant, close contact; there were also problems arising from the subtle but
highly stimulating and transformative spiritual and psychological forces at work there.

This experience gave me a perspective on the Community's strengths and weaknesses, as well as an appreciation of
the immense amount of energy, commitment and care it takes
just to make it work at all. It is important to remember that
the Foundation does work, although not always to everyone's
expectations or satisfaction. As it becomes more publicised
and gains an aura of glamour and success, I believe it is important to keep a balanced perspective. Nothing attracts detractors like success, and I am not concerned with those criticisms
which arise when someone's personal ideas of what a 'New
Age' centre should be like (and we all have such personal
preferences and desires) are confronted by the reality of Findhorn. Many critical analyses of this Community have come as
much from bruised egos as from a clear perception of truth.

Still, many criticisms I have heard have a valid reason
behind them and touch upon some area of imbalance that
does exist within the Community, often an area that I had to
deal with myself while I was there. What I am interested in
writing, therefore, is neither a defence nor an exposé but a
statement of my observations of the Community and its growth
processes which may provide a balanced perspective. The
experiences of the Foundation are not unique to that centre,
either; I have found similar mixtures of positive and negative
elements in every group or enterprise I have ever encountered. As a counsellor I know only too well our human challenge of confronting that mixture in our lives, but I also know
that the truth of a human being does not lie in his extremes.
Likewise, the truth of this centre lies neither in the glamorous
image of a heaven on earth, as some recent publicity might
suggest, nor in a picture of some psychologically imbalanced
authoritarian hell. We need to find that truth not only for the
Community's sake but for our own, for it is a truth throwing

light on the processes of growth and change which we are all facing in our quest for a new world. The Community is on a path of transformation, and we need to understand that path more clearly, for it is ours as well.

The Foundation is no stranger to criticism. After it had released the transmissions David had received there from the consciousness of Limitless Love and Truth (published in his book *Revelation: The Birth of a New Age*), irate letters were received from some people on their mailing list accusing the Community of being led astray by this 'false prophet' from America. This was because these transmissions claimed that the New Age was already here now as a living spirit within humanity, something these critics did not believe. Peter and Eileen Caddy, two of the founders, received guidance that the Community should begin charging for its materials and services, rather than giving them away for nothing. This generated a lot of protest and claims that the Foundation had abandoned its spiritual direction; it also drew support from many other people and placed the Community on a more stable financial footing so that it could increase its work and services.

The most intense criticisms, however, came from the people most involved with the Community, as one would expect. I remember one young man who had come from London to live in the Community. The change in his lifestyle was a drastic one, and he had challenges of adjustment. Most of all, he discovered, as does everyone who joins the Community, that the Foundation is no refuge or haven from the problems of society. To the extent that those problems are inner-created through our own personal imbalances, we bring them with us wherever we go, and at the Foundation our inner contradictions are brought to the surface with uncomfortable intensity. This particular young man kept alternating between staying in London and living at the Foundation. Finally, despairing of his ability to adapt to the Foundation, he told me that emotionally it was a worse jungle than London.

Why should a spiritual centre, based on ideas of love, communion, service and wholeness, create such problems?

Why should the Community be a jungle a well as a garden? One answer comes from the process of growth itself, another from the nature of the Community and of the people who have built it and who come to it.

As a counsellor involved with helping people make positive changes in their lives, I have found that the meaning of growth itself is frequently misunderstood. Many people seem to see it as a process of addition: the acquiring of new talents, new skills, new knowledge and images of self, and so forth. Growth is like a tonic to them, the stimulation of novelty to fill some void in their lives. Implicit in this is the sense that there is a core of being — some aspect of ego or self — that remains detached and untouched by growth; it is the collector of new experiences, the acquirer, remaining aloof like some central sun of consistency around which swirl satellites of changing experience.

To me, growth is a more profound activity than just acquisition. It is a deepening into the wholeness of life, like the spreading of roots to nourish and support the visible structures of stem, leaves and blossoms. It is a greater openness to life and its dynamic qualities, an increase in aliveness, responsiveness and responsibility. It represents an expansion of that inner self that knows and can create wholeness, not of some isolated self separate and apart from life. It is a relationship with the most fundamental part of ourselves, a relationship with a force transcending our simple mortal identity and taking us beyond into unexplored territories of being where the human psyche blends with the universe in oneness.

Growth can be joyous and exhilarating, a fulfilment of all that is most human within us. However, if we are unwilling to release our desires about how we should grow, if we cannot release our separateness, if we shrink from confronting the deeper truths of our nature and from surrendering through self-knowing to the rhythms of death and rebirth which carry life forward, then growth can be a challenging, frightening and even a negative experience.

Within us each is a mixture of characteristics some of which we are happy with and some of which we aren't. These characteristics are the seeds we have sown over the years — our karma, if you like, or the tendencies we have built into our way of being through our habits and motives of thought, feeling and action. When we open ourselves to the forces of growth, it is like exposing a garden to the sun and the rain. Whatever seeds are there will sprout and reveal their nature, whether we want them to or not. This means we may find ourselves confronting unpleasant and undesirable elements within our nature. Also, for plants to emerge, the soil must be broken up and the seeds themselves must disintegrate to give birth to new forms. Creativity often involves prior destruction, and growth involves a giving up or a 'de-structuring' of familiar and comfortable patterns to make room for new ones to appear. This can produce imbalance in our lives. During growth periods, therefore, we are more vulnerable than usual and more likely to experience negativity in our relationships with life.

The young man from London called the Community a jungle, and that is what it is for many persons. A jungle, however, is a place where the growth forces are strong and life is abundant. This is the nature of the Community: a place where the forces generated by the pioneering dynamics of life in its deepest aspects are exceptionally strong and concentrated, a tropical zone of the spirit. Peter Caddy often calls the Community a hothouse. Everything about the Foundation contributes to this effect, from the close living conditions to the many activities intended to invoke highly stimulating energies of spiritual transformation and unfoldment.

Although its climate does not suit everyone, a jungle cannot be blamed for being what it is. If one is going to live in the tropics, one goes prepared with proper clothing and equipment. Unfortunately, this is not always the case with the people who come to the Community. Even those who come fully aware and accepting of what they are getting into may be surprised by the intensity and swiftness with which inner pressures of change begin to manifest. While I was there, though, I observed that there were those who came expecting a Garden of Eden, a community of loving souls where the problems of life would somehow resolve themselves. They came with definite preconceptions of what a spiritual centre should be like, how it should be run, what they wished to receive from it and the manner in which they felt their growth should proceed.

It was painful to watch the crises that these people went through as their dreams ran up against the reality not only of the Foundation but of their own natures as well. Of course everyone tried to help, and many of these people were able to readjust their expectations, but there were still those who refused to change or to give of themselves except in the manner and degree that they wanted. These were the ones who eventually left the Community with bitterness at what they saw as the Foundation's failure to adapt to their needs and desires.

* * *

The Foundation's spiritual focus had two effects. First, it concentrated highly stimulating spiritual and psychological energies of transformation through which the normal growth processes were accelerated. I have already mentioned that imbalance and negative states of thought and emotion can be temporary by-products of growth efforts. At the Foundation, the appearance of these states was intensified: whatever seeds of karma might be there, they were quickly brought to the surface for the individual to deal with. People would have inspiring and illuminating experiences and become very high for a period and then would swing just as far in the opposite direction, suffering a period of depression. All of this generated negative states which individuals would have to cope with in addition to the positive states of being which also resulted.

The second effect of the Foundation's spiritual nature was to make it difficult to deal with negativity because it clashed with the Community's high ideals and its emphasis on positive thinking and living. To give vent to negative pressures was to risk being seen as a 'negative thinker' and as a disruptive element in the community life. To experience negativity at all was, for many, a guilt-producing situation as they felt they were letting the Foundation down; this was particularly true with respect to the Community's general understanding of the laws of manifestation, through which the Foundation could attract to itself what it needed to grow and survive. Positive thought and emotion were seen as the fuel that made these laws work, whereas negativity was a neutralising force that could block manifestation and thus directly threaten the Community.

Dealing with this problem of how to cope positively and therapeutically with negativity was my primary work, and I was given every cooperation. I was sometimes hampered, however, by two interesting side effects of the Foundation's spiritual orientation, other than those I have mentioned. These were a tendency to ignore the personality level and concentrate on higher, more esoteric levels, and a tendency to seek esoteric or occult explanations for everything that might happen.

I view the personality as part of our wholeness, neither more nor less spiritual or vital than any other part. I see it as an expression of what we are in relationship to life, a reflection of the skill and quality with which we focus our universality in the here and now. To me, the personality is not a thing but a dynamic process; it is like a river, always flowing, which can be clear or polluted depending on what we put into it in the way of emotional and mental energy, motive, balance, wisdom, love and self-understanding. Parts of the river can be calm and smooth, other parts can be swift and treacherous, passing over rough terrain, but the river remains the link between its source and the ocean. The personality is a process of linking between divinity and the world of experience and manifestation, and the laws of its functioning are reflections of universal laws of creation. As a counsellor, I am interested in the whole being — rather than say that I work with personality levels or with higher levels, I prefer to say that I work with those factors that manifest wholeness and with those that fragment and inhibit it.

Many people in the esoteric field of study and approach,

however, see the personality as a 'lower' self, a source of distortion and error, the sign of humanity's fall from grace. Certainly, the personality level generally represents for most people a level of fragmented and limited vision which can lead to mis-communication and conflict. As I mentioned, the 'river' has its rapids. For many within esoteric disciplines, however, the solution is not to understand the personality but variously to overcome it, go beyond it or transmute it. Because the methods are often not well understood in themselves, the practical effect of this approach, I have found in working with many esoteric groups, is to simply ignore the personality, hoping that by concentrating on a spiritual vision, it will just go away somehow. Like the Victorians who kept pregnant women confined out of sight, it is as if they are embarrassed to have a personality and ashamed of its effects. Of course, it doesn't go away; it remains, untended and unintegrated, to be a source of continuing problems of relationship and communication on all levels.

This way of thinking was not extreme at the Foundation, but it was present and tended to prevent some people from seeking my help or someone else's and from dealing creatively with personality problems when they arose. Added to this was a tendency to find esoteric or spiritual explanations for almost everything that happened. Thus, a negative upset was due to 'dark forces' rather than to a lack of skill and wisdom in dealing with human relations. This attitude, when it was present in a person or situation, diverted the attention from inner causes of the problem at hand and turned it outward, dispersing the area of responsibility. Of course, one solution for psychic attacks — which can be a reality, I know from experience — is to increase the pressure for being positive, when negativity is seen as a point of entry or of contact for dark forces. Needless to say, this also increases the repression of negative emotion and the tendency for people to feel guilty when these emotions surface.

Thus at the Foundation we faced a problem where the very nature of the place stimulated the appearance of negative emotional states as part of a natural growth process and a throwing off of older, personality patterns through the process of transformation; however, the nature of the place also tended to deny an acceptable outlet to these feelings because they conflicted with spiritual ideals or with teachings concerning the importance of positive thinking for the well-being of the Foundation and the working of the laws of manifestation. To avoid guilt, one outlet was to blame negativity on 'dark forces' rather than to accept and deal responsibly with one's own personality patterns and challenges. When problems developed at the Foundation, it was often due to these causes.

I have written of this at length because in the work David and I have done over the years, which is to demonstrate the synthesis between personality and spirit, we have discovered that this problem is widespread throughout the entire spiritual movement. In fact, although I have pointed out this problem at the Foundation, it was really less evident there than in several other groups I have known. In the Community, the tendency to be negative about negativity was offset by a generally good community perspective and a high level of humour, as well as a great deal of love and caring. Also, Peter and Eileen, whose personal training was in learning how to overcome the personality and concentrate on higher levels, supported me a hundred percent in my work and began to take a fresh look at their own personality challenges. They have my highest respect for the way in which they proved their openness to growth and to new ideas, qualities that make them good leaders.

* * *

Two [other] factors, experimentation and the high activity level, also contributed to the problems the Foundation and individual members have faced. Growth is a process of deepening, not just activity in the direction of newness and change. Because it can create temporary experiences of instability, it is good if growth can be nourished by a stable environment. Traditionally, this stability is provided by family structures and by those in one's peer group who can provide a sense of caring and of support. A rhythm of growth — a cycle of inbreath and outbreath — is also very important.

When I was at the Foundation, such a rhythm was often spoken about but was not always evident. Instead, there was a constant sense of activity and growth without adequate periods of assimilation and consolidation. The winter period, when visitors were few, was considered the time of consolidation, but it was often as busy in its way as the summer. Over a period of time, however, such a rhythm did begin to emerge, but the overall feeling remained one of constant activity and energy in motion. While this need not be a bad thing, it can work against the deepening process of growth, substituting instead a sense of motion and change that masks as growth.

This was heightened by the frequent turnover of personnel and the amount of work that needed doing. There were always more jobs than people, and sometimes a person would be allowed to stay simply because he had a needed skill, irrespective of whether he understood or supported the deeper objectives of the Community. Such people rarely worked out and often created more challenges than they solved; in fact, it was these people who usually had the most personality problems, since they did not have the spiritual dedication or motive of unselfish service which can give a person a perspective beyond their own feelings. Often, people would be trained for a skill, such as running a printing machine or working a loom, and then would leave the Community. Also, the bulk of the Community's population were foreigners to Britain, mostly Americans, whose stay was limited by their visas. The youth of many of the members, their lack of previous experience or of skills and sometimes their inability to carry through with responsibilities also increased the work pressures.

All of these factors detracted from the overall stability of the Community, and also created a situation that demanded full time commitment from the members in order to deal with the many tasks that arose. This demand of the Community for the greater part of an individual's energy had a dispersing effect on families that came to live at the Foundation, as well, bringing into conflict the allegiance of husband and wife to each other and to their children with their new allegiance to the Community.

Many intentional communities are designed to pull families apart in order that the community itself can emerge as the family. Such programmes develop in reaction to the limitations and separation that family life can produce: the possessiveness of families that can ruin a person's life. However, the family remains an important link in the processes of growth and stability and needs greater understanding not destruction. In fact, a recent report indicates that in the Israeli kibbutzim, where the family was broken up, it is reforming in the third generation, with the support of the original pioneers! They recognise its importance after all and are seeking creative ways of incorporating its advantages into community life.

Families have never had an easy time of it at the Foundation, and some have broken up, as recent criticisms have suggested. However, as a marriage counsellor, I observed that in every case where families broke up in the Community and husband and wife separated, the seeds of that separation were already there before the couple came to the Community. The Foundation simply intensified and speeded up their confrontation with the realities of their relationship (or lack of it). This can be a good thing, but sometimes the process became glamorised, that is, seen as evidence of a spiritual process, and others were encouraged to split as well.

A combination of factors — the new morality, the love flow in the Community, a certain lack of responsibility — all combined to make it easier to seek another partner than to work out the problems with one's mate. Some marriages were borderline; they were in that phase, which all new marriages go through, when the problems of adjusting to another being seemed all-encompassing. Normally, couples work through this period and come out stronger but when there are opportunities to form other, more attractive partnerships where possible personality challenges are obscured by the flush of romance, when the demands of the Community are asking for as much as one can give, and when the seeking of a new mate is interpreted as a spiritual experience (such as the finding of a soul mate), then everything is working towards pushing that marriage over the line.

All of these matters could be subjects for articles in themselves. All I want to show now is that conditions exist at the Foundation to create instability, and while the Community is filled with loving people, love alone without a wise structure to support it is insufficient to restore that stability. The fact that the Foundation has few rules places a premium on self-discipline, but self-discipline is also a matter of training and can be difficult to develop in the vulnerability of an intense growth process. As a consequence, the Foundation can appear as an emotional jungle where people are left exposed to the heat of the sun and unprotected from the ravages of their own contradictions and those of the Community.

* * *

It is important to remember that Peter and Eileen did not set out to build a community; it developed out of the work they were guided to do. The Foundation was built out of faith, not out of ambition. Neither Peter nor Eileen nor Dorothy were trained or prepared to deal with the problems of running a community; they have learned through trial and error, supported by their guidance and their faith.

The Foundation has not been easy for them, either. They, too, have been subject to the same growth forces as everyone else. I have seen them change tremendously over the past six years, until now they are simply not the same people we met in 1970. They have grown in wisdom and in love, but they have paid their own price for their growth. They have gone through periods of profound inner change and instability, and this has been reflected into the Community as well, creating further problems.

The fact remains that the Foundation has been meeting its problems and continuing to grow. I have described what I observed during my three years there; they are challenges which I believe the entire New Age movement or community is facing in one form or another. Perhaps new sets of problems have developed at the Foundation since I left. The point is that the Community does have its jungle aspect, but it is learning to deal with it in creative ways. When I think of the problems we faced while I was there, the wonder to me is not that emotional conflicts arise but that the Foundation has survived at all. That it has is a testimony to the people who have lived there and given much to help the Community develop.

Now the Community and all concerned are facing what will be their greatest challenge: success and glamour that surrounds it. How will this affect the Community? Peter and Eileen, after years of being considered crazy for their beliefs and their work, are now making triumphal world tours and being met with wide acceptance and acclaim. They are human beings and share our human vulnerability to praise and acceptance. How will this affect them? Time will tell. I have witnessed in Peter both an attraction towards publicity and a sensitivity to the dangers of glamour. His one-pointedness on the Foundation and its success may be a liability as he moves in a wider arena of contact and tries to create a planetary community of cooperating individuals, for he can give the impression that the Foundation and the New Age are synonymous. He also concentrates on the positive aspects of the Foundation and may fail to give a balanced presentation. However, this is not wholly his fault, for how many audiences want to hear about another jungle when they came to hear about a garden? Most people feel they already live in a jungle in modern society and long for inspiration and for a piece of heaven on earth. Peter's training is to project positive images, so that positive realities will manifest; he will meet this desire within people if he can. His challenge is to do so in a way that promotes a balanced understanding and perspective along with inspiration and new vision. Because the Foundation is a physical place, its concreteness can obscure its vision. People hear of it and rather than see its reality within their own lives and environments, want to travel to Scotland. Peter and the Community must find ways of dealing with this, but it is as much our problem as it is theirs.

We see and hear what we wish. We create our dream worlds and try to project them into reality. We desire a heaven on earth. We can have such a heaven if we are willing to create it in our own lives and where we are, which means confronting the challenges of growth. This is all they are doing at the Foundation. The problems that arise there are human problems; the triumphs are born out of the spiritual potentials and realities within all human beings. The essence of the Community is everywhere; the challenge of the Community and of Peter as its primary representative is to communicate this and help us all to realise it. I believe they will meet this challenge and succeed, but we will probably observe the process of their lesson-learning as they do. We need a balanced perspective that can tolerate imperfection in those people and places that we select as our guiding images even while demanding and reaching for the perfection we know is there; in short, we need wisdom.

What the Foundation needs is help to meet its vision. It needs people who can accept its promise and make it work in their own lives where they are. It needs people who can go to the Community with the right motives of service and commitment to growth and responsibility, people who understand the growth process, can work creatively with negativity, can strengthen family patterns; people who are balanced and who are not looking for a personal utopia as much as for a place to serve according to the service that is needed, not according to their own glamorous ideas of the kind of service worthy of them. The Community is both garden and jungle, but so are we — so is the world. What we all need is a consciousness that can work with both in order to touch the greater life that is the Source.

THE PRESSURES WITHIN

David Spangler

(A transmission through David Spangler, circa 1972 — amended)

I am a disciple of the Christ. Any other identity is not important for our purposes, for what I have to say will either have merit within the human understanding of your consciousness and it will meet a need or it will fail to do these things, in which case my words should not be given any importance simply because of my identity. I am, however, one who has an abiding interest in this centre and the work it is doing as part of the overall plan of the Creator. It is from this interest and from my experience as a disciple that I would speak with you.

The Source of Pressure
The nature of spirit is dynamic and irresistible motion. The nature of matter is resistance and non-motion. Out of the conflict between these two arises consciousness. Consciousness is a flaming light born of the friction between that which moves and that which is still.

These statements are fundamental expressions of the nature of creation, though limited in their meaning for having been expressed in such concrete terms. God is both spirit and matter, but humanity has polarised its consciousness to identifying God as spirit.

Because human beings, being evolutionary entities, seek freedom from matter, seek more dynamic expression, they will necessarily view God, which is their goal, as being spirit, spirit that is increasingly refined and dynamic, until they reach the point in realisation where they know, not just intellectually but through the direct experience of their being, that God is both spirit and matter and where they can embrace this wholeness in their consciousness.

I begin with these statements because if God is understood as spirit, then he must also be understood as pressure. He is that presence which moves, and moves through and beyond the restriction of matter. This is the God-image that humans are presently working with. Again I say this is only an aspect of God.

Humans themselves, emerging out of matter, are on the whole more polarised to matter, its consciousness, and its qualities, than they are to spirit. Herein lies the source of their conflict. The characteristics which represent the majority of human consciousnesses are characteristics of inertia and resistance. When these characteristics come under the impact of the continually moving stream of energy that is the active presence of God, what consciousness experiences is pressure.

In the long run of evolution, consciousness can simply move along the lines of least resistance, moving no more quickly than the gradually developing and growing rhythm of its matter-nature will permit. On the other hand, any consciousness that takes on to itself the self-initiated responsibility of the initiatory path enters into a state in which it is deliberately accelerating its evolution. This will highlight the various dualities that exist within the consciousness of the disciple until that point is reached where these dualities can be resolved back into wholeness, equilibrium. In this case, the inertial, matter-like qualities within the human become intensified. All that resists becomes intensified as the individual seeks to bring the course of his or her evolution out of the slower rhythm of nature and under the direction of the soul.

At the same time, all that would move and stretch itself and reach toward its goal of liberation also becomes intensified; although in the initial stages of the disciple's experience, because he is emerging out of matter, the qualities of resistance are usually experienced as being the stronger of the two. The meeting of these two polar forces within the experience of the disciple creates pressure and it is from this that the ancient definition of God evolved. God is pressure. God is that which irresistibly seeks to move through inertia to transform resistance into cooperation, awareness and complementary rhythms.

The path of spiritual initiation which all of you are upon,

having entered upon it before this life, is in itself a path of pressure, for you are attempting to accomplish the work of millions of years within thousands of years and even hundreds of years. You are accelerating your evolution. Therefore your soul, as it increasingly is given access to the control factors of your personality life and becomes the control factor itself, initiates and draws to you experiences which will be most useful in accelerating the expansion of your consciousness. In other words, your soul itself is like a pressure, a divine discontent, determined to overcome all resistance of the lower nature and transform that lower nature into oneness with the soul's divine rhythm.

Let us consider the Findhorn Community for a moment. It represents the gathering together of a group of people, each of whom is at some stage of progression upon the path, in order that together they can more fully invoke the energies of evolution and accelerate their progress through accelerating the growth of the capacity to serve. Service is the natural rhythm of the soul.

All who come to this centre must understand what they are entering. For the Foundation will always be a centre of pressure, because it is a centre of spiritual experience. That which creates the pressure, however, is in essence the conflict between spirit and inertia or habit. As this becomes increasingly resolved, pressure disappears. Psychologically, this means that the conflict is born between the intent of the soul, as it reflects the will of the inner God, conflicting with the resistance of the more sluggish and conditioned nature of the personality. As the personality learns to blend itself into its soul, surrendering its will to the will of its higher perceptions, the pressure diminishes.

Within this Community it is apparent that a consciousness of pressure is both generated and experienced. This needs to be dealt with creatively because the pressure that exists here should be evolutionary in nature and not self-propagating. By this I mean that the pressure should lead to creative illumination, change, wisdom and growth. It should not lead to an unending circle of fatigue, of discontent, of non-awareness and of dispersal of energy.

Therefore I now wish to address my comments to the more practical consideration of what you can do to deal with this challenge of pressure, and to place it into its proper perspective and into its proper use as a tool. It is a tool that is also a reflection of the present stage of human evolution. As I have said, the consciousness of pressure diminishes to the extent that the being can resolve within itself the dichotomies of spirit and matter, soul and personality, Divine Will and personal will.

Dealing With the Challenge of Pressure
Awareness
First: Pressure cannot be overcome by the application of more pressure. We are not here dealing with an obstacle which can be shattered through application of energy. Specific obstacles and resistance can be met and swept aside, but in the sweeping aside there may build up a sense of frustration and a backlog of pressure on the emotional, etheric and mental levels. This will mean that there will build up in the creative environment of the Community a reservoir of unfulfilled, discontented and unanchored energy.

Therefore the first area of awareness comes within the responsibility of those individuals who have as their trust and their responsibility the expansion and development of the centre. You may call this the leadership of the centre and in one sense this is so. This would be focused within the person of Peter who embodies in himself the energies of expansion. This also touches upon the subject of guidance, which some may believe to be the source of pressure .

The question that is most important when dealing with this subject of pressure and the right use of pressure is not "Should guidance be received?" For the rhythm of the spiritual unfoldment of humanity now revolves around the individual and collective capacity to attune to higher states of consciousness. The question is "How can the energy which guidance releases best be translated into usable energy within the corporate structure?" An answer to this lies in communication, ensuring that there is an understanding, as much as possible, within all pertinent areas of the Community as to what the guidance is saying and why it is being given, and thus generating an energy of cooperation, rather than that of simple obedience.

This has been said in other ways here at the Foundation: that the time has passed when Peter can carry the full energies of expansion. They must be shared increasingly by the Community, which means that each member of the Community must take unto himself and herself the responsibility that comes of being a part of a whole and of exercising deliberate awareness, conscious awareness, of the need and rhythm of the whole, so that through intelligent understanding and awareness they can contribute their part more effectively to the whole. One source of pressure comes from the fact that if this is not done Peter, feeling his responsibility but not finding aware cooperation, will seek to implement with the power of his will the will of God as given through his partner, Eileen. Pressure results. As he encounters irresponsibility, lack of awareness and resistance to obedience, pressure grows.

Pressure will always result from this time onward if the polarity of power in the Community resolves itself into purely that of leader and followers, orders and obedience. The only way this can be successfully dealt with is to have a Community of people who are themselves aware and dedicated to the path that the Foundation serves, a path of service freely chosen with awareness of consequent possibilities of personal sacrifice.

Many times it has been stated that the Community is not for everyone. I would state this again in the following way: the Community is not a place for people to learn only the lessons of the personality. Certainly these lessons will be learned but the focus should be on learning the lessons of group synthesis, service and meeting the needs of the whole. The consciousness of an individual is as important as his or her skills because out of consciousness will arise the harmonious force which, by helping to resolve unnecessary pressure and resistance, permits the emergence of skills and talent. Those whose consciousnesses, though skilful in meeting communal needs on a physical level, cannot meet the needs of the Community in terms of awareness and responsibility and synthesis with the greater whole, will, in both the short run and the long run, pull energy from the Community and be a source of increased inertia, increasing pressure and causing the energies of more attuned people to be used simply in holding balance rather than in opening to a more creative flow.

This is a challenge and is one which should not be met entirely by Peter or Eileen, or by any one or two people exercising responsibility or leadership in the Community. Each individual should be aware and should be wise enough in love not to criticise, not to condemn, but to work with new people and older people to see that their consciousnesses grasp what this centre is about. Each should learn the wisdom not to encourage people to remain who cannot take the fundamental steps of self-awareness and dedication to self-transcending service which the Community asks, and at the same time not to look with criticism nor with disrepute upon a person who does not remain or cannot remain. The leaders and the workers in this Community must work as one in their consciousnesses and love.

Attunement
The second factor to realise in the positive use of pressure is that people should first be encouraged to become attuned, not simply to receive guidance. This is important because attunement is the foundation on which guidance can rest with safety and discrimination. To see the receiving of guidance as a goal is to encourage people often to put the cart before the horse, or to attempt to grasp the sacred fire before they have yet constructed the proper kiln in which to house it. The first step for individuals is to learn how to use their minds and emotions to create not resistance and inertia, but attunement and flow and communication, and to experience how

to have a balanced personality in relationship with others, in relationship within oneself.

This Community is ideally organised to accomplish this because it is a community in which people have to work and interact together. The primary training ground is this interaction so that people learn how to serve others, to respect others, to listen to others; how to be inwardly silent and peaceful in the face of the pressure of others; how to communicate.

These are fundamentals and you must be master to some extent of your physical, emotional and mental environment before you should attempt to venture into a greater environment. You should learn how to work with the sacredness that is within your human environment. You should learn how to touch the divinity that is in your everyday lives and relationships before you attempt to draw down a divinity of which as yet you have little understanding. To reverse this process is to run the risk not only of contacting the planes of illusion but also, even if valid contact is made, to so unbalance the personality levels that the contact is withdrawn, leaving behind only that which is greatly distorted.

To receive guidance, the process should be first to learn how to use one's wisdom and mind and feelings as skilfully as possible and to be open to communication with others, and to be open to those who have demonstrated that they are successfully and in a balanced way receiving from higher levels. Then you will find that guidance, rather than being something that must be brought through under great tension and stress and through great discipline, begins to bubble and well up within you. As the personality life becomes more balanced, attuned, more regular in its rhythmical expressions, more harmonious with its surroundings and its fellow beings, then the channel is clear.

Remember, God is pressure. He is moving. It is inertia and resistance that stop his presence. As you clear away the qualities of resistance within your being the Pressure of God will move through you and you will find the attunement developing (to the point of your need and not necessarily to the point of what you want). If your motive for seeking attunement is to become a guiding light within the Community, then your motive is one of self. If your motive in seeking attunement is simply to be a better human being, more divinely expressive, no matter how simple, how mundane, how apparently ordinary your task may be in the Community, then you will receive that attunement and God will be your identity and your beloved. To know whether a person is acting with spiritual pride and under the glamour of illusions of the self, or not, the person must learn to know herself in terms of her reactions and relationships with other people.

In time all within this Community, who remain within this Community, will receive guidance and it will come from the same Source. It will express to each according to the need and according to that which promotes the harmony of the whole.

There should be a clear understanding of where guidance should be used and where it should not be used. To seek guidance on all matters is to dilute the power. It is also to discourage the development of wisdom and to encourage the development of dependence and of obedience. Obedience can be a necessary discipline to weaken the power of resistance and inertia. However, at some point obedience must be superseded by illumined understanding and wisdom, as one becomes more at one with the rhythm of the Divine Spirit. Many in this Community have yet to learn how to overcome resistance. They have yet to learn the liberating value of simply obeying in trust and love. To obey because that is necessary in order to remain within the Community while carrying within oneself elements of frustration and non-understanding will ultimately increase the vicious circle of resistance and pressure. As much as possible people must be encouraged to use their consciousness, their wisdom and attunement in taking responsibility and in discharging it well, and as much as possible the *energy* which guidance releases (for truly one of the fundamental purposes for guidance on human levels is to release an energy of accomplishment and empowering spirit into activity and manifestation) must be communicated and synthesised into the Community as skilfully as possible.

Now, in dealing with this, it becomes the responsibility of each person to know her attunement and centre and balance. The wise disciple is not one who does all things. He knows his capacity at the moment and does not exceed it. He gives balance to his life so that when certain periods arise when greater energy must be given forth to meet a greater need or an emergency, it is there and can be given freely and without a sense of strain. The rhythm of meditation, of going into silence and drawing upon that silence, the practice by an individual in finding a centre of peace within and drawing on it consistently, will reduce strain and pressure.

Care should be exercised that a continual sense of emergency is not generated. This is possible with the rapid expansion of the Community. Therefore, this expansion must always be understood and balanced out with an intelligent understanding of the capacities of the Community. By the same token, a great deal of pressure that is being felt is due to inertia within individuals. Help should be given to overcome this and to assist people to find and work more from their centres of silence and peace.

A person should know not only when to say yes but when to say no. A disciple should know that, having been given a vision of what the will of God is, what the plan is, she must answer wisely the question, "How can I best fulfil this vision?" The best way might not be to move into action, it might be to stand steady in non-action and to allow someone else to step forward into the active role. This is wisdom in action and will reduce considerably the feelings of strain and the feelings that any one person is being asked to go beyond her capacities.

Yet this is a challenge which will always be with you until you resolve your own separation from your divine state; for you, yourselves, are the ultimate creators of your pressure. It is your drive, your self-initiated choice to accelerate your evolution and to accomplish in a short time the consciousness of illumination and of the liberation of the soul that you may become a more skilful and wise server of the race. Do not feel guilt if you must say no and say, "I understand the guidance but I cannot fulfil it within my present capacities. I will step aside, continue to function on my present level and allow someone else to step in and fulfil it." But counterbalance this with an awareness that true guidance is not an order, it is an opportunity. Perhaps you can accomplish more than you think you can. Balance the wisdom of your true energy capacity against the illusion of inertia which the consciousness of matter can give into your being. Within that balance and discrimination you will find your true path and relationship.

Dedication

Thirdly, I would say the Community itself must be seen for what it is: not a place where people can live but a place where people come to learn service. The time is not yet for communities to be formed here for the sake of the community. The time is now when people come together to learn how to serve the planet and the whole of consciousness. Service is the dominant theme and quality of energy moving through this centre. All who come here should realise that this is not a place simply to come and live. If that is their expectation then they will find challenge, for the energies here demand that a person continually go beyond himself in learning how to serve, in learning how to understand, in learning how to give, in learning how to reconcile the conflict between spirit and matter and to restore wholeness.

Those who come here must be dedicated and must know that to which they are becoming dedicated. The leadership must exercise wisdom not to draw in people who, though strong in one way, in what they can give to the Community, are weak in dedication and understanding. The Community must exercise love and compassion and strength to help those who are struggling to externalise that dedication to achieve it, and not simply to carry the individuals, overlooking or compensating for weaknesses that truly distract from the vision and growth of the whole. We do not wish to develop a spirit of criticism or of negatively pointing out each other's faults. What we do wish to develop is the consciousness of awareness of where people may not be fulfilling the good either of the whole or of their own development, of where they may be letting down the whole and themselves, and a consciousness of what can lovingly, wisely, creatively be done about it, for the growth and blessing of all. If you restrain from communicating this awareness and help to people, you encourage them in weakness and non-awareness and you may build up in yourself a pressure of resentment or a pressure of added work. Do not attempt to carry another's burden unless there is clear evidence that you should because that other person in that moment is undergoing a particularly trying period. Then you can rally around him in love and support.

Help each other to fulfil the dedication which this centre demands and do not be under any illusion about why you are here or what you think the Foundation can give to you. This is my message to this Community and to the people who are part of it and it should be understood by every new individual who enters. This centre is created to fulfil a certain need for service within the greater plan that has as its object the fulfilment of the will of God for humanity and for all lives upon the planet. I will now open myself to any questions that may be present.

Balance

Question: Many have been feeling a pressure to leave the Community. It seems to be contagious: others feel it and wonder if they should go too. Now certainly we know there are those who are ready at this point to leave. Can you give us anything that might be helpful to those who are not ready and yet feel the pressure? Certainly all you have said to us would indicate a release of this pressure but if there is anything that you would want to add further, we would be very happy to receive it for these individuals.

Certain energies of a more universal nature are being invoked and experienced here by individuals. It will at some point lead to the formation of a group of those people whose interest in this centre is less on the day-to-day workings of the centre itself and more on helping the centre to integrate within the greater pattern that is taking form over the planet. Such people will be part of the rhythm of the centre but yet will occupy a different position within it. This is forming and creates a certain restlessness which can be met by those individuals who have moved beyond present tasks, and who are now being given greater tasks or more broad-reaching tasks relating the Community to the larger society, as well as integrating those who come from the larger society as new members into the Community. Then there are those people who are truly reaching a point where they must move out. Also there is the energy of expansion within the Community itself, as it comes into greater contact with the larger society.

Most of all, pressure comes from a sense of pressure which becomes communicated to others and which causes individuals to turn more in on themselves and what they are feeling and on their fatigue and hence diminishes the quality of communication which depends on opening out to what others are feeling and saying. As communication is diminished, pressure increases.

It is important for each of you within this Community to know how to balance your energies. Some may use my words as an excuse to justify inertia. If so, this will be seen and observed, for it will become readily apparent and it will need to be dealt with. Others will heed what I say and will not attempt to stretch themselves beyond what they can do in the moment and still maintain effective communication with their environment. This is important. You are not machines and you are all at different levels of energy. This is what I also meant when I said that the intent to accomplish the divine will must be wisely balanced and adapted to the capacity of the Community.

I can express this best by using a physical analogy. A disciple may, through the power of her will, force her body to do many things above and beyond its endurance and thus discover resources within herself she may not have known were there. This is a stage which every disciple goes through but it does not represent a balanced condition, for the will should never be developed above and beyond wisdom, love and intelligence. There are lives where people experience the development of love and wisdom, lives where they experience the development of intelligence, lives where they may experience the development of will, lives where certain aspects are especially focused on, but eventually balance must be learned.

The corporate body of the Community will at some point be able to respond, and should be able to respond, immediately, with power, with awareness, with wisdom, with intelligence, to that which is perceived as being the will of the beloved. But for will alone to attempt to drive the Community forward before the corporate body is strong and secure and healthy is to run the risk of disintegration, or, at the very least, of over-fatiguing the corporate body to where it greatly reduces its efficiency. Your corporate structure is still in the process of evolving.

So finding the balance between will, manifestation and timing is a creative challenge. You need now to build into your structure the elements of strength, communication, love and synthesis that will permit a healthy body to develop and will give to Peter or to whomsoever manifests the will, the corporate structure that will respond. The kind of willpower Peter has developed in his own life rhythm others here have not, nor is it necessarily important for them to do so. It is important for each to play his or her responsible and aware part within the corporate body. If this one factor were achieved you would find greater harmony and a significant reduction of pressure.

Now I give this challenge to the Community; you can take my words as justification to resist that which flows through Peter, and such resistance has sprung up from time to time, or you can take my words as a challenge to act cooperatively with Peter to achieve a balance. Justification can be a mask to hide inertia and to resist the divine moving through you. Each person in his own heart must answer this question of motive. Otherwise, where is the responsibility which they claim to have for the whole?

Resistance is not only non-obedience and outright denial or refusal to follow the path of the whole. Resistance can be simply unawareness and lack of intelligent and responsible and loving communication and action. Resistance can be frustration and it can be that which prohibits the person from being aware of the whole and which focuses his attention in upon himself to too great an extent. All of these things increase the inertia with which you are dealing.

I say to those who are truly the dynamic motivators within the Community and are the source for much of the energy which moves through it: you must do what you must do to be true to your highest. Do not allow the inertia of others to discourage you or to make you feel, "Why should I continue when others are not fulfilling their role?" You continue because you have a vision and are dedicated to it. You do not do it because others are following or are not following. You do not do it necessarily because that is what is expected of you in the Community. You do it because in this way you demonstrate your attunement and are true to yourself and to the God within. By the same token, do not attempt to carry the weight of the Community when others should be carrying their full share. In other words, do not promote weakness by stepping in to fill gaps, to fill holes, to fill vacancies that others should be filling, if by doing so you simply prolong the condition of non-awareness, pressure and weakness. Far better for an aspect of the Community to cease to function and to collapse to some extent and for the lessons to be learned than for that aspect to be shored up with makeshift energies and to bring the whole down to that degree. I can say these things because I consider you wise people moving into greater maturity. Only children in spirit will take my words as excuses to justify non-action or unwise action.

Where there is pressure, there is often a desire to escape

it and this is contributing to much of the restlessness as well. Also understand that expansion is not always outward but can be inward and to fulfil expansion may not mean to incorporate an ever-growing number of activities unless this is done in balance. It may mean to purge your centre of activities and individuals if by so doing you result in being a much more cohesive and harmonious group, creating more inner expansion, which can then expand outward again with greater effectiveness. For those of you who feel pressure, do not bow to it as to a god. It is only illusion, but an illusion that must be dealt with, with wisdom and with the clear insight of an illumined heart and mind. Do not magnify it, but do not underestimate its strength. Just deal with it as effectively and creatively as you can, and seek to promote in the consciousness of others a sense of strength and peace and calm.

I extend my blessings to you each: and to each, Love from the heart of God.

Seven

Relationship of the New Age to Formal Religious Doctrines

INTRODUCTION

David Spangler

The New Age represents the emergence of a new world view rather than a new religion. As a world view it can have a spiritual or religious component, but by itself the New Age is a vision of cultural possibilities rather than a set of beliefs about God or a way of relating humanity to the sacred.

Of course there are groups that identify with the New Age, such as the Findhorn Community, which are spiritual or religious in nature and which do have particular beliefs about God and practices of realising the presence of the sacred in everyday life, but such practices or beliefs might not be universally shared or agreed to by all the groups and individuals who otherwise share the New Age vision.

Likewise, there are other groups who see themselves as New Age who have no particular spiritual orientation at all, concentrating instead on technological or social issues, such as renewable forms of energy, environmental protection, new designs for housing, or alternative economic systems.

A person can believe in the New Age and be a Christian, a Muslim, a Jew, a Buddhist, a Pagan, an agnostic, or even an atheist. An individual does not have to believe in God to believe in a better future.

On the other hand, there is a value system which is generally emerging throughout the New Age movement and which to some extent defines the boundaries of that movement. This value system honours the interconnectedness of everything; is holistic in its perspective; values both the individual and the group; sees men and women as equals; is compassionate and cooperative; values nature for its own sake and not for its utilitarian value and therefore has a strong ecological ethic. It also tolerates paradox; is open to ambiguity; values human potential, imagination and creativity; and accepts that there is more to reality and more to human consciousness than a materialist philosophy may admit.

I would not call this value system a religious one. It basically strives to see the world and all within it as a wholeness rather than as separate parts and calls us imaginatively to envision and create a culture that embodies that wholeness.

However, this value system is 'spiritual' in that it claims that the materialist perspective is incomplete and that there is a non-physical or transpersonal side to reality which must be considered as well. Beyond this, though, it does not prescribe a particular way of believing about or interacting with that non-physical or non-ordinary reality. For example, acknowledging and working with nature spirits and angels, as the Findhorn Foundation does, may be part of a new cultural world view — a New Age — but it need not be; one could approach the same end by acknowledging that there is simply a little-understood energy within thought and emotion which has an impact on the environment because we are interconnected with that environment psychically as well as physically. Also, belief in the existence of non-physical or spiritual worlds and their inhabitants — or the mere exploration of such a possibility — is not necessarily a religious enterprise. It could be seen as a scientific or an artistic enterprise. It is seen as religious only because in our culture we have over time relegated any topics of that nature to the religious dimension, considering them to be supernatural and thus (like religion itself, in some ways) not part of the 'real' world.

An additional challenge is that one word — spiritual — is used to describe two different things: the quality of being non-physical or non-material, and the quality of having religious or sacred value or of being connected to spirit. In pushing the boundaries of consciousness and interaction past the limits which current materialist western culture accepts — in other words, by exploring a non-material component to reality — the New Age seems also to be pushing a particular religious world view. By having a 'spiritual' component to its world view, it can appear as if the New Age has a 'religious' component to its world view. In a way this is like saying that when Columbus sailed west to prove the earth was round, he was actually on a religious journey and was espousing paganism because many pagan beliefs described heaven or a blessed state as being an island in the sea to the west. Columbus may well have seen what he was doing in religious or spiritual terms (though not necessarily according to a pagan tradition), but what he was actually *doing* was not a religious venture in itself.

This confusion can appear in other ways. Channelling is a major phenomenon in the New Age movement, and it is often seen as a dominant New Age religious or spiritual practice, by both outsiders and by New Agers. The channel becomes the new priest, dispensing wisdom and insight — for a fee — and allowing the believer to touch the presence of spiritual realms. However, channelling has nothing to do with spirituality, being simply a phenomenon of perception and communication. It may be appropriate for a media-saturated age that an act of communication itself becomes raised to the level of a religious epiphany, but it is a gross distortion of a spiritual practice. When a person is considered spiritually evolved simply because he or she can be a telephone between two levels of consciousness, the understanding of what constitutes spirituality has become twisted.

Equally distorting is the assumption that because a life-form is without a physical body and inhabits a non-material dimension it is consequently 'spiritual' in the sense of being an embodiment of sacredness, compassion, wisdom and truth. This is a profoundly dangerous assumption to make. Channelling may under some circumstances be a useful tool, and it certainly is encouraging people to reconsider the existence of non-physical realms, but to equate it with spirituality or with a spiritual practice only suggests how impoverished our language and ideas about spirituality have become.

Of course, as I said at the beginning, there are religious and spiritual (in the sense of being connected to spirit or the sacred) aspects within the New Age movement. The Findhorn Community is a good example of this, for it does not identify itself as a secular or technological community but as a spiritual one, and part of its work has been to demonstrate the reality and value of each person finding a personal communion with the God within. There are New Age groups that take on all the trappings of a church and behave as if they were the proponents of a new religion. Because such groups are often organised around a charismatic teacher or prophet and have definite codes of behaviour and doctrines of belief, they can take on the trappings of a cult.

However, in my own experience, the dominant religious or spiritual strain within the New Age movement has nothing to do with any leader or dogma; it is simply the desire of individuals to find a spiritual path in which they can relate in a direct, guilt-free, loving and empowering way with the sacred without the need for an intermediating priesthood or clergy. Many, if not most, of the people I have met or known over thirty-five years of involvement with the New Age movement were exploring ways of knowing God directly and intimately. Their route might be circuitous and take them in and (hopefully) out of strange situations, including cults of one kind or another, but ultimately this was their goal: to discover within themselves their own spiritual nature and its union with the sacred as a personal experience and not just as a theory or teaching.

In a way, this is the path of the mystic or the shaman, and it can be highly individualistic, since each person's relationship with the sacred is unique, intimate and private. The phenomenon of increased interest in this path suggests that for many people, formal religious institutions and doctrines, particularly of a Western variety, are not meeting their spiritual needs. It also conveys an implicit — and often explicit — criticism of Western, particularly Christian, churches and religious life (though interestingly the majority of people I have known still see themselves as followers of the Christ but are seeking a new and more intimate way of knowing the Christ within their own hearts and of giving birth to the mystical Christ within). This criticism can itself be a source of friction between the New Age movement and formal religious institutions, though it can also be an inspiration for renewal within churches open to change.

The negative side to this is that, whereas a mystic or shaman pursues his or her individual and unique relationship with spirit and the sacred within a context of belonging to and serving a larger community, a seeker into the New Age may find himself or herself apart from such a context. Rather than *transforming* the personality while retaining its unique qualities, the spiritual path becomes *shaped* by that personality and its needs in idiosyncratic and sometimes ego-inflated ways. If the only reference a person has is whether a particular practice or teaching feels good and each person is his or her own prophet, then the stage is set for the possibility of usurpation of the spiritual process by the selfish and self-referencing aspects of the ego. A community or tradition can provide a context for critical self-reflection and quality control by providing guidelines of wisdom and discernment and also by demanding accountability. Because the average New Age seeker has often abandoned his or her tradition of origin, this context may not be present or available.

A tradition does not have to be a religious one, however, as long as it provides training in discipline and critical discernment and a larger community context that can inform and balance the individualistic aspects of spiritual development. It can be artistic or scientific, and in fact, I personally believe that science — or more appropriately, the methodology of science — is a primary tradition which will assist and inform the development of a New Age spirituality. The methodology of science has been practised within a materialist context, but there is no reason it — and the disciplines of observation and thinking which it promotes — cannot also be practised in a more holistic context that also includes a non-material reality; in the process, both science and spirituality would be redefined and re-imagined.

Inherent in the scientific method is the power of the individual to learn about the truth of creation for himself or herself through using rigorous and disciplined modes of observation, thinking and discernment; in a spiritual context, this discipline and discernment would also extend to and include the training and use of such inner faculties as intuition, imagination and attunement, leading to a spiritualised form of cognition. This development stands in contrast to approaches which ask individuals simply to believe and to follow — usually without question — someone else's revelation, approaches common to many mainstream religious practices.

Unfortunately, New Age spirituality often fails to live up to this ideal of disciplined, spiritual cognition, nor does it live up to the ideals of compassion, surrender or sacrifice found in mainstream religious traditions. Instead, it often seems to outsiders to be very self-referencing, focusing on self-development and one's own well-being to the exclusion of others, and therefore devoid of compassion (the 'it's their karma, let them work it out' syndrome). It seems — and often is — mired in subjectivity, a mask for personal opinion and prejudice. Furthermore, many New Age spiritual groups and beliefs embody a fundamentalism just as intolerant and demanding as that of any mainstream religious denomination, and they can be just as insistent upon obedience and blind faith.

Another major criticism is the undiscerning way in which New Agers tend to eclectically mix and match elements from various religious paths such as Christianity, Buddhism, Hinduism, paganism, shamanism, native traditions, and so forth. The criticism is two-fold. The traditionalist sees elements of his or her religion taken out of context and used in ways that he or she does not approve of (and which actually may distort the original meaning and power of that element), and the resulting mixture can be grotesque and spiritually impotent, as symbols, taken out of context, lose their meaning and power or take on other meanings never intended. Secondly, this eclecticism can lack the organic integrity of a tradition that truly arises from a cultural context; it can lack coherence, like a collage of conflicting images put together because the artist liked each image individually but never considered how they might look or fit together as a whole. I once went into the sanctuary of a New Age centre where every conceivable image of the sacred, including photographs of the stars, the earth from space, and so forth, had been placed on the altar. The intent was probably to be universal and all-embracing, showing the many ways in which the sacred can manifest to human consciousness, but the effect was one of clutter, confusion, and a diffusion of energy and power. Just one symbol — or no symbols at all — would have been far more effective and powerful.

On the other hand, what the New Age offers is an arena for religious and spiritual experimentation and exploration, as well as in social, artistic, political and economic fields, too. Not everything that arises from such a grand mixing together of elements is going to be beautiful, functional, useful or healthy. Some of it will be silly, frivolous or even toxic. But at the same time, there will emerge from this exploration new insights and combinations that will be holy, powerful and transformative. It is these combinations that will give us hope for the future and insights with which to build a new world vision and culture in which spirituality will be a living, creative and healing presence in everyday life, the birthright of each individual born upon this planet.

OVERVIEW OF THE WORLD'S MAIN
RELIGIOUS TRADITIONS

Alex Walker

Members of a community dedicated to living out the truths underpinning all the world's great religions might be expected to have a working knowledge of, or at least access to, information about the fundamental beliefs of these traditions.

There is no place here for anything other than a brief overview of these, and a short extract from their teachings as an introduction to humanity's rich heritage of spiritual teachings and practices. As the majority of new Community members will be most familiar with Christian cosmologies I have tended to use those as a reference point. I hope readers from other faiths and traditions will forgive this technique — it is purely intended as a means of effective communication, and certainly not meant as a device to imply that Christian teachings have a more (or less) special place in our own pantheon.

Hinduism

The Hindu faith is the oldest of our living traditions, and in many ways the hardest to categorise. It is historically inspired by the teachings incorporated in the Vedas, which originated 4,000 years ago. However, although certain key beliefs inform all Hindu thought it has branched out into a bewildering variety of forms which frequently leads to confusion in the minds of Westerners about the true nature of this religion.

For example, it is not pantheistic but essentially monotheistic, although (un)like Christianity[1] it allows the Godhead to divide into a variety of forms such as Vishnu the maintainer or Shiva the destroyer. It is also extremely tolerant of minor gods, and many institutions and households have their own

---

[1] Many Christians would think of the concept of the 'Father, Son and Holy Ghost' as 'One God in three Persons'. Muslim scholars, on the other hand, have argued that this is not monotheism but tritheism.

particular deities to whom they offer devotions. This is further complicated by the doctrine of avatars, by which the Godhead will 'for the protection of the good and the destruction of evil-doers, incarnate from age to age'. God/Vishnu may therefore be bequeathed with different historical titles such as Rama or Krishna.

The sanatana dharma (eternal duty), as Indians call their religion, is largely free from dogma, and has a long tradition of toleration for other religious beliefs. The main tenets are essentially:

● that the universal Brahman is the substratum of all existence
● a belief in both reincarnation or the transmigration of souls and
● karma or the law of cause and effect
● the need to adhere to spiritual duty or dharma
● and by doing so to achieve liberation from the endless wheel of time in which both microcosm and macrocosm are locked.

The means by which this is to be achieved are however extremely varied.

One of the main dramas of Hinduism surrounds the life of Krishna, and the Mahabharata is a great epic poem which tells this story. The key part of this tale, and central to Hindu thought, is the Bhagavad Gita — the 'Song of God' in which the great warrior Arjuna drives out to the centre of the Plain of Kurukshetra between two great armies poised on the brink of civil war. Krishna goes with Arjuna as his charioteer and offers him the following insights.

Arjuna sees that his own army — the Pandavas — is on the side of good, whilst the opposing army of the Kauravas is a force for evil, yet he trembles at the thought of this conflict and suggests to Krishna that although he is a warrior it might be better for him to eschew the conflict and the inevitable slaughter of kith and kin.

Krishna reveals himself as an avatar — an aspect of God come to earth to liberate humankind — and explains to Arjuna that life and death are but part of a great cycle, and the death of the physical body should be treated by him as little different to the changing of a set of clothes. He goes on to say that there are three kinds of person — the slothful, the passionate, and the noble ones who seek enlightenment through detachment and renunciation. Arjuna's task as a warrior is to take this balanced or 'even-minded' approach and release his attachment to his own life and all earthly things and to strive in battle to achieve the victory of good against evil. He must see renunciation as the release of attachment to the fruits of actions which must be offered to God, not the giving up of all action.

Arjuna is convinced and goes back to his lines. The battle commences and with Krishna's help the triumph of the Pandavas is achieved.

The Gita is of course a symbolic means of describing the conflicts of perception between personality and soul.

It is an extraordinary paradox that despite this apparently war-like ideology Christians often view Indians as fatalistic. Perhaps it is easy to forget that hunger and exhaustion can significantly contribute to such attitudes. Hindus, on the other hand, have the greatest difficulty in imagining a God prepared to die meekly on a cross, far less that this icon could be central to the mythology of a people with a reputation for military aggression.

Buddhism

Buddhism is of course based on the teachings of Gautama Buddha who was born some 2,500 years ago in northern India, and rests on his famous Four Noble truths and the Eight Fold Path.

The Truths are:

- The Truth of Suffering
- The Truth of the Arising of Suffering
- The Truth of the Cessation of Suffering
- The Truth of the Path Leading to the Cessation of Suffering

The nature of the Path is often interpreted as having three constituents. These are:

- Moral self-discipline, incorporating a peaceful, truthful, upright and disciplined way of life.
- Meditation, meaning the cultivation of proper states of mind in addition to proper actions, equanimity and control. Meditation is not thought of as a practice undertaken only by sitting in solitude, but something that can be brought into everyday life.
- Wisdom, i.e. a perception of the world based on the Four Noble Truths.

In today's world Buddhism is practised in a variety of forms by the majority or significant minorities all over south east Asia. There are two main schools. The Hinayana, or Small Vehicle, largely found in Burma, Sri Lanka and Indo-China, does not diverge from the original teachings. The Mahayana, or Great Vehicle, attempts to investigate the nature of nirvana about which the Buddha himself remained silent, and is important in Japan and China. Zen is a particularly direct (i.e. non-symbolic) form of Mahayana Buddhism, much influenced by Taoist thought. In this part of Scotland we have most strongly felt the particular influence of Tibetan Buddhism, due to the presence of the centre of Karma Kagyu lineage at Samye Ling in Dumfriesshire. Although stemming from the Mahayana, Tibetan Buddhism has its own characteristics.

Buddhists are the great spiritual psychologists and technologists of formal religion. So much so that many practitioners of this faith find Christian teachings can seem rather naive by comparison. For example, the notion of original sin can be seen as a somewhat over-simplistic interpretation of karma, the idea of heaven, purgatory and hell a trivialisation of the complex bardo states in between incarnate life and so on. On the other hand, Buddhist cosmologies can appear both nihilistic and indeed atheistic to Christian observers.

Readers must judge for themselves, but here follows a fragment of Buddhist thinking that may be of practical value and give those unfamiliar with its techniques a taste of the richness this faith is heir to. It is taken from *The Tibetan Book of the Dead*, and involves a description of different states which occur due to a greater or lesser separation from the 'luminosity', which Christians might call God or the Holy Spirit.

The Realms

The hypothesis is that the mind produces certain projections which seem to exist objectively and inhabit the external world. Depending on the state of the mind there are different 'realms' that a being may appear to him or herself to be in. These realms particularly refer to the 'bardo' or transition state in between one life and another, but they may also be usefully applied to living and waking states. The Book of the Dead concerns itself for the most part with various practices which will aid a being in such a bardo state. We need not concern ourselves with those here, but the realms can be described as follows.

Firstly there is the **Hell** realm. Here the being imagines a state of terror or paranoia, which turns inwards, and a degree of violence is felt towards the self. In this realm it is not so much a question of punishment meted out by some external agency, but of a self-inflicted environment of fear. It could be one of fiery rage, or frigidity and loneliness.

The **Hungry Ghost** realm is one in which the desire for possessions becomes overwhelming. The more you consume, the hungrier you become for more of this nourishment which you desire. It is not a state of enjoyment of things, but of the endless pursuit of more.

The **Animal** realm (which is a slightly misleading name from a Western point of view) is dominated by a lack of a sense of humour. Dour religious observance, dogged but joyless work, or a rigid family life all characterise this realm. It is entirely lacking in spontaneity or unpredictability.

The **Human** realm is one of passion, which involves some of the hungry ghost demands for endless striving, and an element of animal realm predictability, but the prime characteristics are slyness, and a desire to maintain achievements and successes at all costs, despite the inevitable impermanence of life.

The Realm of **Jealous Gods** is one of great intelligence, but also one of fear. It is like a game which involves intrigues, deceits and diplomacy, but one whose rules demand a concentration on survival and winning. This is a realm in which many personal relationships exist.

The final stage is the Realm of the **Gods**, also known as the realm of pride. Here there is a state of peace and bliss, but also a recognition of self as separate from the luminosity.

These terms may not be familiar to everyone, but these six realms have been said to make up the entirety of our psychological world. If it appeals to you, you may find it helpful to observe which of these states you are in at any given time, and to learn techniques for moving into other states you may find more suitable.

Judaism

The religion of the Hebrews is important partly because of its contemporary influence (although it is by far the smallest of the religions under our consideration), but also because it is the root from which the stem of Christianity, and thus Western religion, philosophy and culture, has grown. Its historical beginnings as related in Genesis concern the call of Abraham, who migrated from the Euphrates estuary to Canaan c.1850 BC.

The holy books of Judaism are the Torah and the Talmud. The former is essentially the Written Law, and includes the Pentateuch of the Old Testament in the Christian Bible. The Talmud is largely a later codification of the Oral Law. Although it is a religion with ancient roots, it would be entirely wrong to think of Jewish thought and practice as being in some way more old-fashioned than its children. Like the Vedas it provides deep insight into areas untouched by other religious traditions.

Judaism has for instance a well-developed moral philosophy in the realm of commerce, equalled perhaps only by the Islamic tradition. Alas, there is certainly nothing to compare with this in modern Christianity to temper the activities of amoral business practitioners. Judaic practice is also the font of the Kabbalah, probably its greatest contribution to contemporary esoteric ideas.

A detailed description of the 'Tree of Life' is not possible here, but there follows a brief overview of its treasures.

> *On penetrating into the sanctuary of the kabbalah one is seized with admiration in the presence of a doctrine so logical, so simple, and at the same time so absolute. The essential union of ideas and signs; the consecration of the most fundamental realities by primitive characters; the trinity of words, letters and numbers; a philosophy as simple as the alphabet, profound and infinite as the Word; theorems more complete and luminous than those of Pythagoras; a theology which may be summed up on the fingers; an infinite which can be held in the hollow of an infant's hand; ten figures and twenty two letters, a triangle, a square and a circle. Such are the elements of the kabbalah.*
>
> Eliphas Levi

Islam

The prophet Muhammad, after the mention of whose name it is customary to say 'Peace be upon him', was born in 570 AD at Mecca in what is now Saudi Arabia. His religious work began in earnest when at age 40 he received the call from God through the Angel Gabriel while meditating in a cave.

He is the central figure in Islamic teaching but he is considered to be human rather than divine. Through his revelations came the Koran which contains 114 surahs or chapters and is taken by Muslims to be the Word of God.

The Five Pillars of Islam are:

- There is no God but Allah, and Muhammad is His Prophet.
- The daily performance of prayers.
- Regular payments to charity.
- The making of a Pilgrimage to Mecca.
- Fasting during the time of Ramadan.

Muhammad (Peace be upon him) died in 632 AD, or the 10th year of the Islamic calendar. In 622 AD the prophet and his followers had been forced to escape from Mecca to Medina after growing opposition to his teachings in the former city.

Despite the impression one might gain from Western media reports the Islamic faith is tolerant of other traditions. For instance, it was common in Islamic mediaeval cities for there to be Jewish quarters at a time when the persecution of Jews was rife in western Europe. Jesus is considered to be a great prophet by Muslims, but they believe Christians err in perceiving him as divine. (Jews and Christians are known to Muslims as 'The People of the Book'.)

The great majority of the followers of Islam are 'Sunnis' who accept certain traditions derived from the Prophet's political successors as authoritative. Shia Islam, which rejects this path, and follows the traditions of his family successors, is predominant only in parts of Afghanistan, Iraq and Iran.

Sufism is an esoteric sect of Islam, and although Sufis can trace their heritage back to the roots of their religion, and perhaps even further, the order which operates in the West was founded by Hazrat Inayat Khan who was born in India in 1882. The modern leader of this movement is Pir Vilayat Khan. Sufism has probably had more direct effect on our communal life than orthodox Islamic practice. The Sufi order is very ecumenical aiming at a direct understanding of the nature of God which goes beyond the specific creeds of formal religion.

Sufis love allegorical spiritual anecdotes and stories, of which this is one.

Caravanserai

A visitor appeared in the city and marched straight into the palace and demanded an audience with the king. Such was the strangeness of his appearance that no one dared question him.

On approaching the king he said: "I should like a place for the night in this caravanserai."

The king answered: "This is not a caravanserai — it is my palace!"

"Who lived here before you?" demanded the stranger.

"My father."

"And before that?"

"My grandfather."

"And this place where people come and go, staying and moving on, you call other than a caravanserai?"

Christianity

Christian teaching is based on the life of Jesus Christ of Nazareth who lived in Palestine from approximately 3 BC to 33 AD. His life and work need little elucidation here, but three main points may be made.

The Doctrine of the Trinity envisages God as having three major aspects: God the Father, who is transcendent (outside of our ordinary experience), the Holy Spirit which is immanent (pervading our experience), and God the Son, i.e. Jesus himself.

Christianity replaces the Old Testament notion of a system of moral balance of 'an eye for an eye', with one of 'loving one's neighbour as oneself' and 'turning the other cheek'.

The Crucifixion of Jesus is seen as a central moment in human history when a new pact between God and humankind began. Christianity thus involves a uniquely personal God 'who gave his only son' so that humanity might be saved from its errors. Early Christian philosophy may lack a comprehensive inquiry into the nature of reality[2], but the simplicity of its message and its emphasis on a loving God may be the main reasons for its continued success.

The three main forms of Christianity currently extant are Roman Catholicism, Eastern Orthodoxy and Protestantism (of which there are over 20,000 denominations). To outside observers the differences often appear more administrative and cultural than philosophical, although the current Papal stance on contraception is a significant exception. Often still thought of as 'the white man's religion', today over half of all

---

[2] This is widely acknowledged by Christian theologians, e.g. "There is absolutely no system of theology or doctrine to be found in the Bible; it is simply not there." Emmet Fox; *The Sermon on the Mount*; Grosset & Dunlap; 1934

Christians are non-white.

There is no history of acceptable esoteric Christianity outside of monastic houses, but other themes of interest are:

The Essenes, a spiritual community which existed in Palestine shortly before the ministry of Jesus and whose philosophies arguably bear similarities to both Christian and New Age ideas.

Gnosticism, widely viewed by the orthodox as a heresy, in which contact with, or 'knowing of', God can be made directly rather than through priestly intermediaries. It is not simply a philosophy of mysticism but a set of doctrines which perceives humanity as trapped in an alien world.

The writings of **Pierre Teilhard de Chardin** who attempted to bring together the rigours of scientific inquiry and Christian faith, through his theology of creative evolution.

Creation Spirituality, which is a modern movement largely based on the work of Matthew Fox which seeks to explore the mystical Christian tradition and attempts to reconcile the spiritual side of ecology with Christianity.

Finally, here is a delightful short story about community life which brings out the simplicity and compassion at the heart of Christianity. It may be of Jewish origin, but one hopes this will not offend. Perhaps its place here might even be seen as an acknowledgement of the debt Christianity owes to Judaism. After all, Jesus himself is sometimes referred to in the Bible as 'Rabbi'.

The Rabbi's Gift

A once-renowned monastic order had fallen on hard times. All the daughter houses had closed and the mother house was kept alive only by the efforts of a handful of ageing monks. Although the individual faith of these monks was strong, collectively they had begun to accept the inevitability of the death of their order. There had been no new recruits for many years and as their numbers slowly dwindled the buildings crumbled into greater and greater disrepair.

At last there were only a handful of monks left and the abbot knew the end was close at hand. One of the few real joys left to him was his occasional visits to an old friend, a rabbi who lived in a nearby forest. Yet it was with a heavy heart that he made his journey through the woodlands on this occasion. His old bones complained every step of the way and he wondered how often, if at all, he would be able to visit with his spiritual companion again.

At length he arrived at the rabbi's quiet abode amongst the trees. "How goes life in your order?" asked his friend.

"Not good, not good," replied the abbot. "We are now but five, and none are young enough for the heavy tasks."

The rabbi viewed the monk with empathy and compassion. "Alas," he said, "it is the same for me. The young do not visit the synagogue, and I fear for my faith in this barren and God-less time."

They commiserated with one another and read holy texts together, weeping as they compared the memories of their youth with their worries for the future. At length the abbot had to leave, and in his heart he wondered if he would ever see his old friend again. "I am glad that we met," he said, "but before I leave is there any advice that you can give me that might help to save my dying order?"

"No, I am sorry," the rabbi responded, "I have no advice to give you, but I can tell you this. The Messiah is one of you."

The abbot left the clearing puzzling over this last remark, and when he returned to the monastery he told his fellows about the rabbi's concerns, and his enigmatic statement.

"Whatever can it mean?" they asked themselves. "The Messiah is one of us?" and they retired to their cells pondering the riddle. At first it seemed to them simply a jest, perhaps an off-hand comment that the abbot had misinterpreted. He was getting old after all, and maybe he had mis-heard the rabbi. But in the quiet of the night they mulled their thoughts over and began to consider the possibilities.

"It must be the abbot," thought Brother Jeffrey. "Although he is old and prone to forgetfulness, he is the most venerable and wise of us all. If the Messiah is here it must be him. Mind you, Brother David is so quiet and gentle, so unassuming. If any one of us is close to God, surely it is Brother David. He is always on hand with his compassionate advice and helping hands.

"Although it could be Brother William. He is very rigid, but perhaps that is a measure of his faith. He is so dedicated to prayer and worship. Even when no one else can come through illness or duty he always can be found in the chapel ready to take a service for us or our visitors and guests. Yes, it could definitely be Brother William.

"I don't think it could be Brother Roger, he is so crotchety. On the other hand, he knows the history of our order like no other, and he is very knowledgeable about the scriptures. He goes everywhere with a Bible in his hand. He always has something useful to say, and when he is critical it is usually because he has seen something important.

"At least I know it's not me," thought Brother Jeffrey. "I am not the Messiah type at all. I have too many faults and failings for that role. I am dedicated to being your good servant, Lord, but I am not ready for that — am I? Oh please Lord, do not let it be me!"

And so the monks were left alone with their thoughts, and although they never discussed them with one another a mysterious change came over their house. When they met they remembered the rabbi's words and started to treat one another differently, just on the off chance that one of them might indeed be the Anointed One. They were more caring, more willing to take time for one another, more ready to see each other's virtues rather than faults. They also began to view themselves in a new light. "It might be me," they all thought, "and even if it is not, God must value my work if he has chosen me to serve the Messiah."

Soon, the occasional visitors to the monastery began to notice the change. The atmosphere of the whole place seemed to them to have become sanctified, and imbued with a deeper sense of spirituality. The visitors told their friends of their experiences, and the trickle of guests grew into a regular stream. From time to time one of the guests would become so inspired by what they saw that they asked to stay and become apprentices to the order. In time the company of monks began to grow and as the years passed the order flourished once again and, thanks to the rabbi's gift, brought spiritual solace to all who encountered it.

A version of this story has been publicised by M. Scott Peck in The Different Drum: Community Making and Peace. *See Section 10 for publishing details.*

THE COMMUNITY AND CHRISTIANITY

Alex Walker

Mysticism is not a sect or a creed;
it is a conviction deriving its authority from
the natural instincts of the human heart.

Manly Hall

We live within a Christian culture and most Community members have some experience of the Christian tradition. However, many come here partly because they have struggled to make sense of their Christian upbringing, and are reacting against it. It may then be worthwhile considering our relationship to this religion in a little more detail.

First and foremost it is important to state that we are not in any way anti-Christian. Christian ministers have joined the resident membership of the Community from time to time. Every year we welcome many professed Christians to our courses, and even organised groups of Christian believers. Many of them view our work as embodying the essentials of Christianity. Whilst we do not of course confine our work to Christianity, we agree, for many of our members consider themselves to be Christian too.

Secondly, it would be possible to categorise most if not all of Eileen's guidance as belonging to a Christian tradition. Although we are more than this, we are nonetheless in large measure a Christian mystic community. The fact that such mysticism is less well understood by some Christians than it might be is neither here nor there — the similarities between Eileen's contribution to our lives and the teachings of, for example, Julian of Norwich or Hildegaard of Bingen are evident.

Thirdly, it is worth reiterating that the New Age is not a religion which is attempting to supplant Christianity; rather it is a context within which we can honour and respect our differences without having to give up the specific cultural and religious forms which are important to us. Such respect involves a recognition that the inability of some of Jesus's later followers to put his message of toleration into practice can be no more blamed on the messenger or the message than can the shortcomings of any other religious (or political) group attempting to control orthodoxy.

Perhaps the fundamental point of conflict between ourselves and many Christians is in the interpretation of Jesus's statement , "No one goes to the Father but by me" (John 14:6). Many, perhaps most, Christians interpret this as an injunction to follow the teachings of the Christian church. They may be right, although of course the church was not founded until after Jesus's death. Our interpretation might be that no one can approach the kingdom of heaven until they have learned to emulate Jesus's compassion, wisdom and dedication to God, whatever the specific practice they choose to perform.

You may reject both of these explanations, and that will not be an issue for us. Community life is surprisingly free of theological debate, for what does matter to us is the consciousness with which an individual lives and works, not the specific belief system which inspires them.

THE CHRIST AND THE BUDDHA

David Spangler

In the summer of 1993 David Spangler and Craig Gibsone came together to present a Christ and Buddha Nature workshop after years of thinking it would be a good idea to explore these two roots together. Craig's background includes a long-standing interest in Buddhism and David's background includes an interest in esoteric Christianity. Departing from the established routine of other workshops where a small group gathers together for a week and focuses mainly on themselves and their subject, this workshop gathered each evening in the Universal Hall to open itself to the Findhorn Community as a whole. This paper is the transcript of one of those evenings.

I'd like us to think for a moment of what it is that precedes our images of Buddha and the Christ. And while you're thinking of that, I want to harken back for a moment to the beginning of the Findhorn Community. In many ways this Community has incorporated into its teaching and into its life an image of the Christ — the Christ energy, Christ consciousness, or the Cosmic Christ — and some of that incorporation evolved out of the work I did here some twenty plus years ago. But before the Community was talking about Christ consciousness, its initial impulse was one of attunement to the sacred or to God, going directly to the source without intermediaries. The Community was built on Eileen and her hearing of the 'still, small voice', upon Dorothy and her hearing of the 'still, small voice' and then Peter's willingness to execute the guidance and information that came out of the respective attunements of these two women.

Even though the Community became famous because of its garden and because of the idea of cooperation with nature, which was the image that went out into the world and attracted people to come here to see this marvellous garden and to explore further the dimension of cooperation and interaction with invisible kingdoms, the real message of the Findhorn Community — what Peter and Eileen and Dorothy themselves thought of as the basic message — was attunement to the sacred and obedience to what came out of that attunement. This is a very mystical approach.

All of the great religious traditions, in one way or another, invite us into a relationship with the ultimate, a relationship with the ground of being that is the answer to our most pressing existential questions: "Why am I here?" "Why is there life?" "Where are we going?" Different peoples in different times have experienced a connection with a source that has offered them what they have felt were the answers. Some people looked at the ultimate through one lens and some looked at it through another and out of those respective visions grew traditions, just as here in this Community traditions grow and spring up and thrive.

Going back to my original question about what it is that comes before the Christ or the Buddha, we come to this condition of attunement and relationship to the sacred or what many Native Americans have called the 'Holy Mysterious'. I think this is an important place to start because there is already an immense amount of material — discussions, probings, insights, questions — that has emerged out of the Buddhist/ Christian dialogue. What I want to do is to use the images of Christ and Buddha to enliven within us a sense of what is our most basic relationship to the sacred, because that is the defining, formative impulse for this Community.

In doing this, it is important that we also realise that we are taking a journey into imagination and that Christ and Buddha, to some extent, exist for us as images in our imagination.

Over the past thirty years, for most of the Community's existence, the image of the Christ has played an important role in the spirituality of the Community. It is, however, an image drawn mainly from the mystical side of Christianity and, as well, from that inner tradition that could be called esoteric Christianity. What distinguishes a mystical or esoteric image of the Christ from an exoteric one is that the Christ is seen not simply as a being outside of us and separate from us but as a presence that is at the heart of our soul's existence. It is a state of being that we can share and in which we can participate.

The interesting thing about this image of the Christ is that it has much in common with the Buddhist concept of the Buddha nature. I can bring the spirit and life of Christ to birth in me, just as in Buddhism I can unfold the Buddha nature and become Buddha. In fact, I already am Buddha — we are all Buddha — it's just that we don't realise it, and that's the problem. But the moment we awaken to that fact and realise it, then we just are what we have always been anyway, and the illusion of separation and of self falls away.

In a similar way, in esoteric Christianity we all are the Christ; we are that principle of Logos, that presence of love, and our task is to awaken to that reality. Different schools or traditions have different processes for how that awakening takes place, exactly as in Buddhism there are various schools and traditions that give different techniques and processes for how the awakening into Buddhahood or enlightenment takes place. What I am particularly interested in is the way these figures live in us as powerful spiritual images and help to take us to our own experience of the sacred.

Looking at Christ and Buddha imaginally, the task is to go into those figures and through them and out the other side. There is a well-known statement in Zen Buddhism that if you meet the Buddha on the road you must kill him, because in Zen the object is to go direct to truth and truth is beyond form. So if Buddha appears, it is just another form, just another illusion that you want to cut through. It would, however, be very unusual to find a similar statement in the Christian tradition — "If you meet Jesus on the road, kill him!" — because in Christianity the form of things is often considered important, and Jesus is the most important form of all, being the incarnation of the sacred into a form. But our task is to use the form, the image, to go more deeply into the spirit that may lie behind it.

If we want to encounter the essence of Christ and the

essence of Buddha, which may not be identical and may be two very different qualities, we come to that essence not by looking to those individual figures, but by going through them to that which existed before they did, and then coming back and asking the question: What is it about soul life, about human life, about planetary life, that made it necessary for such figures to be evoked in the collective imagination — both as real, historical individuals, and as images that have grown and been elaborated upon through history?

The figure of Jesus is not set; when I say 'Jesus' not everyone agrees on exactly who I'm talking about. In the two thousand years of Christian history the image of Jesus has changed dramatically, almost once per century, and the image we have of Jesus now is not identical to the one that was held in the first century after his death and resurrection. It is not the same as was held five hundred years ago. There is a process of imaginal development or change as each period of history and each culture reinterprets this individual and the spirit he represents. But why do we reinterpret? What is it about these figures that we can't allow them to be set in concrete? Instead, they have a dynamic life, a transforming life of their own that acts almost mirror-like to the changes and evolutions of our culture. This is because our own soul life is changing in relationship to the sacred. Just as we grow to understand the nature of physical reality more deeply and clearly, so we grow to understand the mystery of the sacred more deeply. And as we do, those images that mediate that mystery to us change as well.

In a sense, the Findhorn Community reflects the current historical collective process in which a new image of the sacred is seeking to emerge. It is for that reason that I want to bring our attention back to the founding impulse of this centre, which was attunement to the sacred: attunement to the 'still, small voice' of God, however one defines and experiences that.

This Community was founded on a process of attunement to the sacred within. This specifically manifested here through the guidance that Eileen Caddy received for Peter and the Community. However, one day Eileen was instructed no longer to get guidance for the Community because increasingly the act of getting guidance was being confused with the principle of attunement to the inner divinity or ground of being. Her specific way of getting guidance and her way of perceiving God was beginning to crystallise as 'the way' to do it in the Community, which was not what the Findhorn Community was about. It was not for all of us to learn to stay up late at night and receive guidance; this was Eileen's way. However, what Eileen was in touch with, the mystery of the sacred within us, was what we were all asked to be in touch with.

For the Findhorn Community to become a Christian centre, or even an esoteric Christian centre, or a Buddhist centre, or an Islamic centre, or a Human Potential centre or anything quite so specific, I think, is to miss the nature of the mirror that this place is called to hold up. In a way we are where St Paul was when he went to the Greek world and said, "I bring you teachings of your unknown God." Of course, for Paul, Jesus Christ was the face of the unknown God. But there is a part of God that is always unknown. That is an esoteric teaching. So every age confronts its own unknown God and then forces arise to bring a new knowing out of that mystery. But it will never be a final knowing. The moment a new aspect of the sacred emerges, a new unknown God emerges too! But it is important in moments such as these, when human culture undergoes such a deep shift as it is attempting to do now, that our ability to name ourselves and to name the sacred makes a commensurate shift.

That shift is that we, each in our own way and collectively in our own way, can hear the 'still, small voice'. That to me is the Findhorn Community's task, and it mirrors the task that Peter and Dorothy and Eileen had when they arrived. But what is this still, small voice? What is the sacred as it seeks to live in our time? Is it the Christ? Is it the Buddha Nature? Let us look further at these images.

Christ

The word Christ comes from the Greek word 'Christos' which is a version of the Hebraic 'Messiah'. It means 'the anointed one'. There is a significant difference between imaging someone who is anointed and imaging someone who is awakened (the Buddha is the awakened one). We all know what awakening is like because we do it every morning, more or less. At some point in our lives we have all had an experience of awakening from something but we may not feel we have ever had an experience of being anointed. Anointing is an act in which something is transferred, bestowed and confirmed upon someone else and it can be thought of as an act of giving. In the New Testament, in the Gospel of John, it says that God so loved the world that he gave his only begotten son. He didn't loan, sell or barter — he gave him as a gift.

In that notion of giving we have a vision of a way of interaction that runs as a theme throughout the New Testament and describes the Kingdom of God. One of the qualities of this state of being is that it is not transactional: it doesn't have a debit sheet, it doesn't keep accounts — I give and I do not give with the expectation of return. So in this idea of the Christ as the anointed one, or the gift, is a sense of liberation and freedom from reckoning and keeping tabs, a freedom from all the kinds of internal accounting. In a sense it is a liberating openness to new possibility.

Giving and being a gift has a transformative and uplifting effect and this is one traditional way to describe what we experience as the Christ. It is the message of Jesus throughout the New Testament: Watch what I'm doing and do likewise; be a giver too.

There is another side to the image of the Messiah that is more problematic because the image of the Christ enters into our history through a particular cultural heritage that is looking for a warrior hero — a priest king that would come and be a saviour to a specific people. The image of the Messiah in that context is that of a leader, someone who stands at the pinnacle of government and at the pinnacle of the people.

Certainly over the past two thousand years the image of the Christ as mediated by various church institutions has often been presented to us as a kind of kingly lord who one day will rule the world and who is the summit of human aspiration. In Revelations, John says, "When he comes again he will come in a cloud garbed in power and majesty," which is an interesting image when contrasted to Jesus's own words when he said, "I come as a thief in the night," secretly and quietly. This image of Christ as a symbol of power makes it more challenging for us to receive the Christ and find our own anointing in the ordinary surrounds of our daily life because most of us do not live wrapped in clouds of majesty and glory.

In those quiet, intimate and ordinary moments of our lives when nothing particularly spectacular is going on we may not recognise that the Christ can be there and this is because we are trained to look for something very much like an earthly king, a kind of esoteric master or a God-realised individual that stands out from the ordinary. I feel we place a tremendous burden on ourselves by thinking we are not worthy or kingly or queenly enough to experience the Christ. While we are watching a sunset or listening to a piece of music or having a good meal or working in the garden, if for some reason we have the immanence of the Christ break in upon our consciousness and we feel a sense of oceanic love and oneness and delight and pleasure and ecstasy, then it is easy to come up with all kinds of excuses about why we shouldn't be feeling it. It is easy to deny it or, on the other hand, to think that since we are feeling this, therefore we must be a great realised master or a king or a queen. Instead, we could be feeling that this is an experience of the most ordinary and natural state for a human being.

There will always be moments when we touch the Christ in an extraordinary way and we are taken beyond ourselves, but most of the time we can find the Christ in the very non-Messianic moments of our lives when we are with other people, eating, drinking, cleaning our houses and doing all the hundred and one things with a good heart, good intelligence and with skill of body.

There is a famous document of Christian mysticism called 'Practising the Presence' in which a monk would experience his union with the Christ in doing very simple things — baking bread, washing dishes, cleaning the floor and so on. In new age circles this sometimes gets misinterpreted in the assumption that it is the act itself that is the practising of the presence — my practice is baking bread, my practice is sweeping the floor, and so forth. These can be good things to do in a skilful way, but what makes something a practice is not just the ordinary doing of it, but the sense that in this moment we are giving ourselves, in love, to the universe through this action. I'm not in any way struggling with it — if I am washing this dish, I wash it with the sense that I am caressing the consciousness of a multitude of beings and asking that my touch may be a gifting touch, bringing love and a sense that I am touching my Beloved.

In this sense, we anoint the moment with our love and with our attunement to the sacred. We make that moment a messiah, a liberator, a revelator in our lives. We redeem that moment from being trivialised and contained and open it out to be a sacrament of communion with our Beloved. This is very much part of the Findhorn Community's spiritual teaching: work is love in action; love whom you're with, where you are, what you do. Then the still, small voice comes alive in that moment, and its message is the love that spreads out from your mindfulness and attunement.

Buddha

Although this Community uses the language of Christianity to talk about itself and its mission, it is in some ways a Buddhist centre and this can be illustrated through the image of community.

When this was a small gathering of people it was very easy for us to experience community here; everyone worked with everybody else, we knew everyone's first name, we were together through the day and we had sanctuary all together.

As the Community grew, jobs became more specialised and people worked further afield, and being together with everyone else became more difficult. Then the quality that makes community had to arise from something more than just physical proximity and daily encounter.

Some years ago, a friend of mine, David White, gave a talk on Celtic history and Christianity. He said that the best way to think of the Celts is that they were a 'community of the imagination'. I have been using a similar image for a number of years and have talked about the 'community of consciousness', a phrase that originated here. Community is not something that is created when people come together and live together; rather it is something that is pre-existent and we can awaken to it. There is never a time when we are not in community, but there are many times when we don't feel ourselves to be in community, and our practice is to awaken to that experience of communion.

When I meet you, though I don't know your name, though we do not work together, though you may have just newly arrived and I have been here for many years or vice versa, I can immediately see and experience you as part of my communion. Community is for me something like the Buddha nature — always present, always infusing what we come out of and what we are immersed in, but I need to awaken to it.

One of my friends was a Tibetan Buddhist monk and is now a professor of Tibetan Buddhist studies at Columbia University, and he gave a talk once in which he discussed a set of practices for enlightenment that had seven steps — six steps of meditation leading to a seventh step of realisation. The first step was to meditate on the realisation that all beings are our mothers — in the countless millennia of time in which we have lived countless millions of lives, every being has probably been our mother. And we honour our mothers and we recognise that our mothers nurture us and give us life and birth. The second step is just to remember the kindnesses that have been paid to us by our mothers. The third step is to meditate on the desire to repay all that kindness — every molecule, every star, every world, every being anywhere in the vast extensions of the cosmos is looked upon with a remembrance of tenderness of the gift of love they have given to us and we want to repay that. The fourth step flows out from that: it is to meditate on that feeling of great love that is invoked by that remembrance. The fifth step is to meditate upon the compassion that that love ignites. And the sixth step flows out of that compassion, love and remembrance and it is pledging ourselves in service.

All those meditations together lead to the seventh step which is the will to achieve enlightenment because the way in which we may give service, express compassion, give love and repay tenderness to all beings is to become enlightened — not for ourselves, but on behalf of all sentient beings. That is the meaning of the Buddhist Bodhisattva vows.

Bodhisattvas exist in a wide continuum from baby Bodhisattvas who have only been Bodhisattvas for a couple of hours to cosmic Bodhisattvas who have been Bodhisattvas for three uncountable aeons of time and are right now trembling on the brink of Buddhahood.

The wonderful thing about this image is that you never know, just by looking, who is a Bodhisattva. But we do know that all of us at some point need to become Bodhisattvas because the deepest task of life is to serve other life in becoming enlightened and liberated — in being at one with all other things. But how do I awaken to that oneness? The world is full of practices, but we can use community as a mirror in which, by encountering each other, the other, we can awaken to that deeper communion. This is the practice of community.

The practice of Buddhism enjoins me to go out into the world and see all other beings wherever I may be as part of my being, as part of Buddha nature, sharing that great community of existence. However feebly I can attempt it, my task is to act for the well-being of all these others in my great community. Maybe in the beginning my actions can only be feeble, tentative or half-hearted; I'm so filled with myself that I can't do more than make a half-hearted gesture towards someone else's well-being. In the Bodhisattva tradition it takes a long haul to become a Buddha and that is a way of saying that we should be prepared to be gentle with ourselves but also make consistent effort.

Here in this Community the intent is to inspire a practice where I would not think of myself as a 'Findhornian', but instead as a member of a community of consciousness, and my community is the world. In community I can learn to be a baby Bodhisattva. If all the structure of the Findhorn Community fell away and all the buildings disappeared, you could still look at each other and say, "I know you — we're in community together." We can hear the still, small voice of communion that links us as one.

In this awakening to the 'enlightenment' of community and the anointing of each moment with our awareness and our love that redeems that moment from triviality and makes it sing with presence, we use the images of Buddha and of Christ to find the deeper strata of living the sacred in the midst of the ordinary. That, to me, is what the Findhorn Community is about: to live the ordinary as if it were sacred, and the sacred as if it were ordinary. In this lies for me an emerging image of the sacred for our time, one that weaves Christ and Buddha in a new dance but that remembers the Holy Mystery that is at the dance's centre.

(David Spangler; Christ and Buddha Nature; One Earth Magazine, Winter 1993, Issue No 12. Reprinted with permission. Further edited by David Spangler for this book.)

READING LIST

Kerry Brown and Martin Palmer (editors); *The Essential Teachings of Islam*; Rider; 1987

Michael Carrithers; *The Buddha*; Oxford University Press; 1983

Richard Causton; *Nichiren Shoshu Buddhism*; Rider; 1988

Pierre Teilhard de Chardin; *The Phenomenon of Man*; Fontana; 1969. *The Divine Milieu*; Harper & Row; 1960

Chogyam Trungpa; *The Myth of Freedom and the Way of Meditation*; Shambhala; 1976

Church of Scotland; *Young People and the Media*; Board of Social Responsibility report to the Church of Scotland General Assembly; 1993; especially Appendix C, Rev Dr John Drane's 'Coming to Terms with the New Age Movement', which whilst detailing a strong critique of the New Age, also identifies key weaknesses in Church thinking, e.g.

> *We also have to grapple with the fact that we have often lived in a reductionist and materialistic way: our exploitation of the environment, our male chauvinism, or just our ordinary church life — in which we frequently major exclusively on believing the right things (rationally), without any real interest in direct experience of God. We could go on. But we need to move from mere analysis to action. Most unchurched people in Scotland today are more likely to construct their world view from aspects of the New Age outlook than from elements of mainstream Christianity.*

Ronald Ferguson; *George MacLeod: Founder of the Iona Community*; Collins; 1990. Required reading for anyone who believes that the Church of Scotland belongs in the Jurassic. Especially interesting are MacLeod's struggles with the establishment of his day which echo many of our own difficulties. He also had his 'miracle' stories. See for example page 183:

> *'In September 1940, when the incendiary bombs were raining on London, it looked as if the re-building [of Iona Abbey] might have to be stopped because of lack of timber. Then the deck cargo of a Swedish ship, carrying wood from Canada, had to be jettisoned. The timber floated all the way to Mull, directly opposite Iona — all the right length. "Whenever I pray", said the beleaguered Dr. MacLeod, "I find that the coincidences multiply." '*

Matthew Fox; *Original Blessing*; Bear and Co; 1983.

Guru Rinpoche; *The Tibetan Book of the Dead: The Great Liberation Through Hearing in the Bardo*; Shambhala, 1975. This incorporates a commentary by Francisca Fremantle and Chogyam Trungpa.

Manly P. Hall; *The Mystical Christ*; Philosophical Research Society Inc.; 1951

Heinrich Harrer; *Seven Years in Tibet*; Harper Collins; 1988

Hermann Hesse; *Siddhartha*; Bantam; 1971

Christmas Humphreys; *Zen: A Way of Life*; English Universities Press; 1962

Anthony Judge; *A Conference Towards Spiritual Concord as a Metaphor of Spiritual Concord*; Union of International Associations; 1992. Tony, who is a Fellow of the Foundation, is an excellent contact for those interested in Inter-Faith Dialogue. Interestingly, he reports the Dalai Lama as having recently stated that attempts to imagine there is a single truth underlying all religions are 'hypocrisy'.

Hazrat Inayat Khan; *The Unity of Religious Ideals*. See Section 1 for details.

Eliphas Levi; *Transcendental Magic*; Rider; 1968. The quotation is from page 19.

Henry Renckens; *The Religion of Israel*; Sheed and Ward; 1967

David Spangler; 'The Christ Series'; Findhorn Foundation Original Series Study Paper; 1972. See especially 'A Letter to Graham', which is a reply to a minister who had raised a question about David's interpretation of the Christ.

Idries Shah; *The Way of the Sufi*; Pelican; 1968. A version of the story 'Caravanserai' appears on page 260.

Gordon Strachan; *The Bible: An Ecological Perspective*; in Vance Martin and Mary Inglis (editors); *Wilderness: The Way Ahead*; Findhorn Press; 1984

Eric Voeglin; *Science, Politics and Gnosticism*; Gateway; 1968

Alan Watts; *The Way of Zen*; Pelican; 1957

R.C. Zaehner; *Hinduism*; Oxford University Press; 1966

Eight

Esoteric Influences

THE WESTERN MYSTERY TRADITION

Nicholas Rose

*(First appeared as 'Findhorn and the Western Mystery Tradition',
One Earth Volume 2 Issue 6, 1982.)*

When I first came to the Findhorn Community some seven years ago, one of the regular events was Peter Caddy giving talks on the 'Foundations of Findhorn'. He would bring a most amazing range of stories and experiences into these talks, including masters and magic rings, power points, travels in Tibet and UFOs. Sometimes I had to keep my mind very open: file the information 'for future reference' as it were. One of the things he would say almost casually, was that the Foundation was of course a mystery school in the Pythagorean tradition — and everyone would nod as he then moved on to another subject and we were all swept on to the vaster vistas of the universal cosmic role of the Community.

It wasn't clear to me at the time how the Foundation fitted in with the ancient wisdom teachings that have come down through the centuries, but I have long been interested in the so-called mystery tradition and during my time here I have given attention to where the Foundation stands within that tradition. And I can now see how much I have come to experience the Foundation as part of the continuous revelation of the spirit in daily life in a form appropriate to our age.

There are various theories about the nature of evolution. Perhaps the simplest is the Darwinian one, in which it appears that through a process of natural selection the pinnacle or crown of evolution is humanity. Teilhard de Chardin adds to this theory the idea that behind the scenes there is a spiritual blueprint seeking to come into full manifestation. As life forms become increasingly complexified, so there is an equivalent growth in spiritual consciousness. According to him, there is an archetypal image of the perfect humanity — Omega Man — which has never yet been fully born but towards which we are evolving. Sri Aurobindo says something very similar. He talks about the pinnacle of the evolutionary wave being the Supra-Mental manifestation — again the spiritual archetype or ideal of humanity which we have never yet been able fully to incarnate, largely because the life-forms or the substance have not been responsive or adaptable enough really to manifest the body of light.

One way of looking at evolving humanity is to see it like a child growing up. Many of the mystery teachings say that at some point in time the evolving life forms on this planet became sufficiently complex for the spark of individuality and spirit to be inseminated into them — rather like a soul coming into a baby. And at that stage there needed to be parents, guardians and wise teachers to guide the growth of infant humanity. The mystery tradition goes back certainly as far as the schools of ancient Egypt. The ancient Egyptian civilisation, which was extremely stable for almost a thousand years, can be seen as an example of the parent-child relationship. It aimed to be a manifestation on earth of the spiritual realms, and the Pharaoh was seen as being the embodiment of the divine on earth. Every facet of society corresponded with spiritual law. The buildings reflected divine proportion and each person knew their place in a very structured hierarchical order.

This rich reservoir of spiritual teachings had a profound influence on the Hebrews, who went on to ground the monotheistic concept of one creator, which seemed to be a necessary preparation for the coming incarnation of the Christ and the birth of Christianity.

In the centuries prior to the birth of Christ there was a great proliferation of mystery schools and spiritual teachings. In the 6th century BC, for example, Pythagoras, Confucius, Lao Tzu and Buddha were all living at the same time. In the mystery schools great emphasis was laid first on the lesser mysteries — the integration of the personality, the balancing of the elemental essence within the body and the preparation of the personality as a chalice — and then on initiation into the greater mysteries. Initiates were taught to open themselves to the higher soul qualities, to align themselves with the power of spirit and to bring that spiritual power into the personality vehicle and out into daily life. However, these mystery schools were very much for the elect and remained the privilege of the few. There were stringent and difficult initiation rites, and the heart of the mystery teaching remained secret and hidden from the multitude.

This changed with the advent of Christianity. In the life of Jesus we have what the mystery tradition calls the exemplar pattern of initiation, someone who through the example of his own life showed us the Way — which was how to purify and align the personality with the soul and then through an act of sacrifice to make that substance holy. The essential message of Jesus seems to be that initiation is for all, that the kingdom of God is within and that we are all potentially gods in the making. There is also a strong emphasis on groups — "Where two or three are gathered together in my name, there I am in the midst of them." It seems that at this time the seed was being sown for the next step humanity needed to take, which was the development of brotherhood, and a sense of the oneness of humanity. The message of Jesus was taken up by the early Christian communities, which despite attack and persecution seemed to embody the essence of the Christian teachings. Certainly the gifts of the spirit were made manifest in a very powerful way.

However, with the growth of the Roman Empire and Constantine's taking on of Christianity as the official religion, much of the original purity of these early groups was lost. Christianity became institutionalised and then with the break-up of the Holy Roman Empire there came the entry into the Dark Ages, and the flame of the spirit seemed to burn very dimly in Europe.

Towards the end of the 11th century there was a rekindling

of the light by groups like the builders of the Gothic cathedrals, who through the use of the flying buttress created huge soaring buildings that seemed to transcend the heaviness of stone and reach up into the heavens. There was also the advent of the Troubadours, many of whom were said to be initiates, who travelled round Europe with songs that were essentially subversive. Some of their songs were of the Reynard the Fox type, little fables about the fox who got the better of the establishment. They were underground revolutionary material attacking the powerful structures of a materialistic society and church. This was part of a general erosion of the feudal and monarchical patterns of the establishment which were essentially keeping the evolution of consciousness in a parent/child position. The Troubadours also had songs dealing with the courtly chivalric tradition, of knights and imprisoned damsels who needed rescuing, and these were symbolic of the longing of the personality to be reunited with the soul — the soul being seen as feminine according to the ancient wisdoms.

Then there were the Knights Templar, who travelled through the East keeping the routes open for the Crusaders, and in their travels coming into contact with groups like the Essenes and the Sufi orders, who had kept the flame of the ancient traditions alive. Many of them became initiated in these traditions and through their own fraternities brought the teachings back to the West.

All this led up to the Renaissance when there was a rebirth and return to many of the Hermetic and mystery teachings which had existed before Christianity. In the early 1600s the Rosicrucian manifestos appeared which put forward a new pattern for initiation in which the individual initiated himself through study, self-observation and experimentation. The Rosicrucians also taught the qualities of liberty, equality and fraternity, which were of course absolutely necessary if there was ever to be a unified field of consciousness. This was very threatening to the crystallised monarchical patterns in Europe and so you had the founding fathers going off to try to ground those qualities in the supposedly virgin territory of America. In Europe itself it took the French revolution to begin to shatter the old patterns.

In the centuries following the Renaissance we can see an increasing division between science and religion, and the very rapid growth of materialism. In one way this allowed us to explore the mysteries of matter very extensively, but it also created an increasing identification with matter, with the subsequent loss of connection with our real source. However, alongside this there were always groups keeping the mystery tradition alive, such as the Rosicrucians, Alchemists and Freemasons.

In the last century or so the mystery teachings have become increasingly popularised, and it seems we are coming out of this period of deep materialism and beginning once again to re-identify ourselves as spiritual beings. The early 19th century saw a revival of the magical tradition through an intense interest in spiritualistic phenomena, and in 1875 there was the founding of the Theosophical Society, which through the work of Madame Blavatsky brought many of the Eastern teachings to the West, particularly the ideas of reincarnation and of the masters of the spiritual hierarchy. At the same time there was the founding of the Order of the Golden Dawn, which drew together many of the threads of the Western mystery tradition, including the Pythagorean, Hermetic, Gnostic and Rosicrucian teachings, numerology, astrology and the Kabbalah.

Both of these groups acted as seed points for the development of other groups and teachings. The Order of the Golden Dawn splintered into a number of occult groups that are still active today. Out of the Theosophical Society came the work of Rudolf Steiner and his anthroposophical teachings. He broke away partly because he felt the Theosophical system didn't state the centrality of the mystery of the Christ and the crucifixion, which he felt were of tremendous importance. Another elaboration from the Theosophical system were the Alice Bailey and Arcane School teachings.

What is the relevance of all these teachings to the Community? It is interesting to see how in the persons of the founding group, many of the themes of the mystery tradition are blended together. Eileen is obviously very much in the mystical tradition, concerned primarily with union with the source. Significantly her first book was called *God Spoke to Me* — not an angel or a guide or anyone else, but God. Peter, on the other hand, is clearly an exponent of the occult method. The mystery teachings associated with this path are those concerned with the creative use of the mind, with learning about the machinery of creation and the workings of the intermediate realms between spirit and matter, with ceremonial magic and ritual, and working with the masters of the spiritual hierarchy.

Roc was also very much in the magical tradition. Part of his role in the Foundation in the early days was to be the guardian of the Community on the inner planes. He was very much the magician. He also had a close contact with the elemental kingdoms, but generally his world was more in the Hermetic tradition, while Dorothy Maclean, through her attunement to the devas and the nature kingdoms, was able to present much of the Orphic tradition, which is associated with the nature mysteries.

Through the coming together of these very diverse personalities and approaches it was as if the role of the Foundation as a place of synthesis was being formed. Part of the difficulty in the past has been that the different religions, different mystery traditions, different paths — all different aspects of the universal truth — have seen themselves as separate and alienated from each other, and have had problems communicating. Part of the challenge in the world today is to help nourish the concept of universality and the qualities of liberty, equality and fraternity for the whole of humanity. With the incoming of the Aquarian energies it seems that the time is now ripe for a greater understanding of group consciousness and the overcoming of the apparent differences that separate us, with a recognition of the underlying unity in diversity that surrounds us. And the Foundation, in attempting to blend the paths of the mystic, the occultist and the nature mysteries, is contributing to this.

One of the main features of the mystery traditions is that they all come out of a consciousness of wholeness and a knowledge of the reality of the spiritual realms. All the maps that were produced — whether these were the Hermetic sciences, the astrological or alchemical symbolism, the Rosicrucian teachings, or even some of the pre-Christian approaches — sprang from the idea of oneness and the interrelatedness of the spiritual reality and the material world. Our culture has lost that awareness, but we are now trying to regain it in ways that are appropriate to our age. And certainly that is the consciousness that underlies the work at the Findhorn Foundation.

So the Community brings together many of the themes of the mystery tradition and also represents a return to the essential core of the mystery teachings; and it is clear to me that this centre is very much part of the ongoing revelation of spirit and of the evolving spiritual consciousness of humanity. But how about the Foundation as a mystery school in its own right? What are the lessons here that in the mystery schools of old would have been associated both with the lesser and the greater mysteries?

The lessons of the lesser mysteries were concerned primarily with initiations of the personality, with the integration of mind, emotions and the subconscious aspects of ourselves and then the grounding of that in the elemental essence of the body. Many of these lessons have now become externalised in the world today, largely through the development of psychology and the different psychotherapeutic approaches. At the Foundation, much of the work of the lesser mysteries goes on just through the process of living in the Community — the rubbing off of rough edges, the gradual shaping and pruning as people increasingly take responsibility for their own realities, for what they draw to themselves and for what they express, and as they stop blaming others or their environment and do the necessary work in character training and personality integration. But that is only the first stage of the work.

The second stage is one of re-identifying ourselves as spiritual beings, of shifting from a personality-level orientation to a soul-level orientation, and of opening ourselves up as a chalice to the life of the spirit. It is the shift that David Spangler describes of moving from the old laws of manifestation, which are personality based, to the new laws, which are soul based. Very often, as people make that shift, whether on an individual or a collective level, we enter into a difficult transitional period, a period of dryness, doubt and despondency, when the old patterns no longer seem to work. In some ways the Foundation as a collective entity has been working with this over the last five to ten years. The old patterns of splendid manifestation which worked so well in the early days of the Community no longer seem to be effective, and it is as if a different level of consciousness is being asked of us.

The switch is rather like the experience one has in changing from two-finger typing to touch-typing. As a two-finger typist you are able to produce a reasonable result, but you are very conscious of the machinery and the process is rather slow. Nevertheless, it works. Then when you begin to learn to touch-type you are told "Cover the keys," and suddenly you enter a period of helplessness: you fumble around and seem to produce nothing. But if you persevere you begin to get a new creativity till you find you are far surpassing your previous capabilities. You are still using exactly the same machinery but you are no longer so conscious of it and you have much greater freedom.

In the Community I have seen this process at work again and again. There is a lot of what can be called 'heart energy' here, and as people join the Community they begin to soften and open and reveal much of who they are. An opening of the heart centre takes place — which in the mystery teachings is associated with the birth of the Christ within, a movement of consciousness in which we dis-identify from the personality centre and re-identify with the soul centre. At the same time part of the process often involves this period of doubt and disorientation. People catch the vision and respond to it, and then somehow it seems to get lost and they find themselves in the middle of a wilderness experience. Luckily we don't all go through this period simultaneously, and so we are able to support one another moving through it, encouraging people to stay with it till they come through with new insights and a knowledge of the spiritual truths that is rooted in their actual beings rather than just in their minds.

And that is really what I see as the main function of the Foundation as a mystery school — the work to re-align ourselves with the soul centre. The personality work is important, but we have to watch that we don't get bogged down in it. We need to do our character work and integrate our personalities, supporting one another in this process, but we also need to open ourselves up, constantly and consistently, to the inflowing of inspiration As we take responsibility for our personal universes in this way, we then move on to take responsibility for the universe of the group, then the universe of the Community — and so on out to the universe and the planet. Because as the connection with the soul is made and strengthened, we move to a state of consciousness that is naturally group conscious. It is naturally inclusive, it naturally sees the connectedness and relationship between apparently separate groupings, and it naturally perceives a much clearer image of the divine pattern. From that level we are automatically able to help bring through the archetypal blueprint for humanity and this planet. And as more and more people do that, both in the Community and elsewhere, the combined power that is generated will transform the planet.

THE THEOSOPHICAL LEGACY

Alex Walker

In the early days of the Findhorn Community much of the literature was couched in theosophically influenced esoteric terminology. This has become less commonplace, but an understanding of these influences is nonetheless important. The Community's founding took place on 17th November, as did the purchases of Cluny Hill and the Caravan Park. This date is also the anniversary of the creation of the Theosophical Society in 1875.

Helena Petrovna Blavatsky (1831-91)

HPB, as she was known to most of her associates, was the child of Russo-German nobility. Married young to a man much her senior — Nikofor Blavatsky — she escaped from an escort a few weeks after this unfortunate liaison and did not re-surface in a verifiable way until her arrival in the USA some 25 years later. By all accounts she travelled widely during this time in Europe, Asia, Russia and perhaps Tibet, where she claimed to have lived for seven years.

Here she met some of the spiritual Masters who were to guide and direct her later life, which was to be dedicated to bringing a form of Eastern esoteric knowledge to a disbelieving West. Not long after her arrival in the US she met up with Henry Olcott, a colonel with a distinguished career behind him, who became her partner in this ambitious scheme.

Much of Blavatsky's work now seems obscure at best, and during her own life there was certainly no shortage of sceptics who scoffed at the idea of letters from the Masters precipitated out of thin air, and hidden sources of oriental wisdom. Nonetheless she amassed many powerful friends, and for over half a century there was genuine public interest, in both India and the West, in the Theosophical Society and the humanitarian and internationalist principles it espouses.

The legacy of her work was primarily the popularisation of a genuinely world-embracing esoteric system. This remains of considerable significance, even if the Society she founded to promote it has failed to achieve the mass audience it once promised to reach.

The linchpin of Theosophical teachings is the brotherhood of adepts and Masters who work behind the scenes controlling world affairs and guiding humanity towards its spiritual destiny. These Masters include Koot Hoomi, Maitreya, St Germain and the Buddha. The head of the hierarchy is known as the Lord of the World, and his HQ is located at Shamballa in the Gobi desert. Much of Blavatsky's writings are quasi-scientific attempts to describe a spiritual history of the world, and the workings of the principles, dynamics and artefacts the Masters use.

During its heyday the Theosophical Society had over 45,000 members world-wide, and it retains an International HQ in India and centres in almost every Western country. Her main successors were Charles Leadbeater, and Annie Besant. The former's life was dogged by sexual scandal, while under Besant's benign but somewhat costume-and-ceremony-oriented control the Society reached its peak membership in the late 1920s.

Krishnamurthi (1895-1986)

The career of Jiddu Krishnamurthi began on a beach near Adyar in India when Charles Leadbeater stopped to watch some young boys at play in the sand one evening in 1909. Observing the aura of one of the children he was convinced that he had happened upon a great teacher. One of his assistants already knew the lad and had pronounced him a dunce, but Leadbeater was insistent.

Taking Krishnamurthi in hand he informed Annie Besant of his find and set about instructing this semi-educated Brahmin youth in the wisdoms of Theosophy. At the age of sixteen Krishnamurthi produced a short book called *At the Feet of the Master*, and although clearly ghost-written in part if not in whole by Leadbeater, it sold well. In 1911 Besant received his father's permission to take Jiddu and his brother Nitya to England. He was eventually to spend some time there, completing his education in a rarefied upper-class environment.

Soon after his discovery Krishnamurthi had been proclaimed by the Society as the World Teacher — the Theosophical messiah. At first he seemed happy enough with his task. His ability to inspire individuals by the steady intensity of his discourse on spiritual matters convinced many who met him that his destiny in this role was assured. He never used notes and the constantly recurring themes of his talks — compassion, honesty, personal responsibility and so on were in accord with Theosophy's own teachings. There is little doubt that his personal charisma was a major reason for the growing membership of the Society at this time.

However, after a long apprenticeship, Krishnamurthi broke with Theosophy in 1929, setting up his own base at Ojai, California two years later. His rejection of Theosophy in favour of an individually based spirituality without recourse to the trappings of esoteric terminology, religion or gurus would be his consistent message for the rest of his life.

Despite the inherent paradox of a spiritual teacher telling the faithful to reject leaders he remained a compelling figure for a wide audience until his death in 1986. Although his teachings remain influential, as might be supposed from his insistence on individual spiritual inquiry, there has never been a recognisable group of Krishnamurthi disciples in our Community.

Rudolf Steiner (1861-1925)

Although Rudolf Steiner's parents were Austrian he was born in Kraljevec on the border of Hungary and Croatia, his father having been stationed there for a period whilst in the employ of the Southern Austrian Railway.

A somewhat solitary and serious-minded individual, Steiner discovered a psychic gift whilst very young, and as maturity dawned and he realised not everyone was blessed with his capacities, he decided to devote his life to enabling others to discover and use similar faculties. These, he imagined, were latent in most humans.

He entered the Technical University of Vienna in 1879, where he was much influenced by Goethe's ideas of humankind's spiritual role and the place of science within the sphere of human achievement. During the 1880s he came across the theosophical writings of Blavatsky which gave him a partial explanation of his own psychic abilities.

He left university in 1884 and became a tutor to a family with four young sons. One of the boys suffered from water on the brain, and in the course of the next six years Steiner's relationship with the child became the bedrock of his later theories for curative education.

In 1890 he moved to Weimar in Germany to work on the Goethe archive there, and in 1891 he received a PhD from the University of Rostock. Whilst at Weimar he published several books, including *The Philosophy of Spiritual Activity* and began lecturing on spiritual matters. In 1897 he moved on to Berlin, where two years later he married Anna Eunicke. In 1902 he attended a Theosophical congress in London and shortly thereafter he took over the leadership of the Society's German Section. He remained associated with mainstream Theosophy for the next ten years.

During his time as a Theosophist he became increasingly uncomfortable with the allegations of sexual misconduct levelled at Leadbeater, Annie Besant's fascination with the orient, and above all Leadbeater's claims that Krishnamurthi was the reincarnation of the Lord Maitreya/Jesus Christ. Steiner had little time for hierarchies of which the Christ was but a part, and less for the notion of Krishnamurthi's messianic identity. For Steiner the life and work of Jesus was always a matter of vital and unique significance. He was also increasingly unhappy with both the lack of rigour in the teaching of Theosophy and its rejection of most of European mainstream thought.

In February 1913 he broke with the Theosophical Society (an action which coincided with separation from his wife) and formed his own Anthroposophical Society based in Dornach, near Basle, in Switzerland. The headquarters of the new organisation was a specially constructed wooden structure of heroic proportions called the Goetheanum. This splendid building was completely destroyed by fire only nine years later but it was quickly replaced by a concrete one of similar design which exists to this day. Although the anthroposophical movement continued to prosper, the fire seems to have had a serious effect on Steiner himself. By the time of the inauguration of the new building on Christmas Day 1923 he was already ill with the sickness that took his life fifteen months later, age 64.

Steiner's legacy is a tour de force. His written work covers an amazing array of subjects including the relationship of religion to ecology, agriculture, children's education, alternative medicine, economics, the nature of humankind and the cosmos. The continuing success of Anthroposophy is in large measure due to his ability to link his theoretical ideas with eminently practical activities, the Moray Steiner School being the most visible example of this influence in the Community today. Because he was trained in the German academic tradition, Steiner's written style is not particularly accessible to everyone, but of all the elements of the Theosophical movement, his work has been the most enduring.

Alice Bailey (1880-1949)

Unlike Steiner, Alice Bailey made no attempt to credit her own spiritual perceptions for the equally voluminous material she published during her lifetime. Rather she believed herself to be simply a channel for the teachings of a Master who intended to bring spiritual teaching to the West and used her as a vehicle.

She was born in Manchester, England in June 1880 and her early life was one of a typical upper class Victorian child — a mixture of luxury and discipline. Although outwardly fortunate by birth she suffered the tragedy of both of her parents dying before she was nine years old. Brought up by a series of relatives and governesses, as a youth she claimed to be 'morbid, full of self pity through loneliness, exceedingly introspective and convinced that no one liked me', having twice attempted suicide by the time she was 15.

By this time she had become an active orthodox Christian with a firm belief in the power of Christ. When the opportunity arose she would go to lonely moors and try to feel the presence of God and listen for his 'Voice'. It was therefore perhaps less surprising to her than it would have been to many of her contemporaries when, whilst she was staying in Kirkcudbrightshire in southern Scotland, a tall man dressed in European clothes with a turban on his head, came to visit her. He explained she had an important spiritual mission and that he would be in touch with her again. Quite naturally she assumed she had met her Master, Jesus.

As an adult she commenced a career as an evangelist amongst British troops in Ireland, a task which suited her profoundly fundamentalist approach to religion. Aged 22 she was posted to India where she served in a number of Soldier's Homes. A life of excitement perhaps, but also one of considerable privation and loneliness.

One night in Lucknow she again heard the voice of her Master who simply encouraged her, and said that the ideas he had earlier outlined were still planned, but in a way which she might not recognise. However the burden of her work began to tell and she was eventually invalided back to England. There she married Walter Evans, a soldier she had met in India who was studying to be a preacher in Ohio. She followed him to America, and although he found employment in California, and they had three daughters in quick succession, they were not well matched. He developed a violent temper and left her in poverty when he found work in Montana. She never saw him again.

The next period was one of desperate poverty. She worked in a sardine canning factory and struggled to bring up her young family as best she could. It was at this time that she first contacted Theosophy, having met two elderly ladies who had been personal pupils of HPB. Convinced of the authenticity of the Divine Plan, the Masters, and the laws of karma and reincarnation, she joined the local Lodge and started to teach and hold classes.

For her this new philosophy was a kind of sophisticated version of Christianity, with Christ as the head of the Masters. She moved near to the American Theosophical HQ at Krotona in Hollywood, and when she joined the Esoteric Section in 1918 she was admitted to a certain lodge. There she saw a picture of the man who had visited her over twenty years before and was astounded to discover that this was apparently Koot Hoomi and not Jesus!

In 1919 she was divorced and came into contact with the two individuals who would dominate the rest of her life. Foster Bailey, her second husband and partner-to-be, was an ex-lawyer and the National Secretary of the Theosophical Society who was living in a tent at Krotona when they first met. Secondly, in November of that year she first clairaudiently heard from 'the Tibetan', whose channelled ideas were soon to bring her to international prominence.

At first she rejected the entire notion of working in this way, but convinced by Koot Hoomi she began writing down what she heard. The first few chapters were printed in 'The Theosophist'. However, this was a time of trouble for the Society. First of all Bailey discovered that she could not be a disciple of the Masters unless officially informed of her position by Annie Besant — something of a problem as she had felt herself to be just that for more than two decades. Secondly, the Esoteric Section was at loggerheads with the main movement, and the Baileys were firmly on the side of the latter, more democratic body. After various internal wrangles, during which they found themselves on the losing side, she and Foster left for New York in 1920, and ultimately founded the Arcane School based on her channelled writings.

At first the identity of this Master remained hidden, but the authority and scope of the teachings gave rise to considerable speculation and at length it was revealed that the *deus ex machina* was Djwhal Kul, otherwise known as DK.

Although her/his works are in some ways at odds with the teachings of the Theosophical Society, the Tibetan's cosmology has a striking resemblance to Mme Blavatsky's. The congruencies include the identification of Shamballa as the seat of the Lord of the World; the existence of a secret brotherhood of wise Masters, adepts and chelas; a history of humanity based on the development of root races, and the existence of Lemuria and Atlantis; the existence of divine Rays etc.

The scope of this work is too great to be covered here, but its influence on the Community should not be underestimated. Possession of at least one book by Bailey — published by the Lucis Trust — was de rigeur in the Community of the 70s and early 80s, and a working knowledge of the Rays, Masters and techniques described therein a prerequisite for any serious candidate for high office.

These works still command considerable respect, but such views are however less prominent than they once were. The reasons for this are not wholly clear but it should be remembered that at the time of their writing and for many years thereafter the Lucis Trust publications formed a significant part of a relatively small corpus of teachings about the New Age. Today they are just another set of books on the groaning shelves of New Age bookshops, with an archaic written style and a claim to authority based on an alleged channelling rather than a documented history and living presence. A generation with access to the visible masters and teachers of the East perhaps has less time for a discorporate and (possibly) long since silent Master, however erudite his message. On the other hand, popularity is not the same as authenticity, and for many people the work of Alice Bailey remains the apogee of Western esoteric thought.

EASTERN INFLUENCES

Alex Walker

G.I. Gurdjieff

Of all the gurus who have influenced Western thinking in this century, the life of George Ivanovitch Gurdjieff is perhaps the most enigmatic. Little is known for sure about the first four decades of his life, and his own descriptions of them are both fantastic and contradictory.

It is likely that he was born in what is now the state of Armenia (which was until recently part of Soviet Central Asia) sometime between 1866 and 1886. His formal education was sketchy at best, but he was street-wise and crafty to an extraordinary degree. He may or may not have been a Russian secret agent under the Czars, visited Tibet and married a Tibetan, and been a member of a mysterious esoteric sect (the Sarmoung Brotherhood) in the Himalayas. He was certainly a dance teacher, a hypnotist, a carpet dealer and a story-teller.

The influences he claims on his life, in for instance his 'autobiographical' work *Meetings with Remarkable Men*, defy the ordinary, even as some kind of obscure metaphor, but he was clearly influenced by Sufi thought, especially the Naqshbandi dervishes, and also by Theosophical teachings. His approach was however unique.

A charismatic figure with bristling moustaches, he delighted in playing tricks on his devotees to test their mettle. His 'system', to which he often referred, defied comprehension even to his closest disciples. It usually involved chanting and breathing exercises, dance, fasting, encouraging internecine strife, lectures on esoterica, admonishments, etc, all of which were designed to get his pupils to awaken from the machine-like state he perceived most ordinary humans to exist in. He claimed to have invented a *Fourth Way*, distinct from the development of the physical, the emotional or the intellectual, which involved a harmony created by the opposition of powerful forces rather than the absence of activity.

History records his first formal teaching as having begun in Moscow in 1912 and continuing there (and for a while in Finland) until 1917. After a variety of travels and hardships, he and what remained of his group had escaped from the upheavals of the Russian Revolution to Constantinople by 1920.

Despite these vicissitudes, earning a living seemed to come with almost magical ease for Gurdjieff, and although often short of funds for the institute it was his desire to create, he never seemed to lack commercial schemes to stay afloat whilst he built up a new supply of pupils. Tiring of Turkish intrigue, he quickly moved on to Germany, then England, before finally arriving in Paris in 1922. This remained his main base for the rest of his life.

With financial help from English supporters he quickly established the 'Institute for the Harmonious Development of Man' at the Chateau du Prieuré des Basses Loges near Fontainebleau. Here he conducted an ongoing experiment in spiritual development which attracted individuals from across both Europe and the social spectrum, and achieved considerable notoriety.

Pupils could only expect the unexpected at the Prieuré. Days of harsh living with little or no food available would be followed by lavish banquets. Unlike Theosophy, physical work was extolled as a virtue, and English aristocrats would find themselves chopping wood or cooking soup along with everyone else. It would sometimes be well past midnight when work for the day would finish.

In 1924, after a mysterious (and possibly staged) road accident, Gurdjieff closed down most of the Prieuré's activities and kept on only a skeleton staff. He turned to writing, and increasingly to tours of America. His negligence eventually forced the sale of the Prieuré in 1933 over an outstanding but trivial debt to a coal merchant.

From 1933 to 1935 Gurdjieff was mostly in the USA but he returned to Paris where he lived in a flat and taught only a small group of pupils until the outbreak of World War II. His activities for the next six years, when he remained in Paris throughout the entire German occupation, are typically obscure. Despite the obvious threat from the Nazis he seemed to live well and joked that he received supplies from a distant planet.

The post-war period ushered in a short revival, but this Indian summer of his fortunes ended with his death at Neuilly in 1949.

Gurdjieff's teachings were also much publicised by his disciple P.D. Ouspensky and by J.G. Bennett. The groups they founded influenced a number of prominent Community members in the 70s, but it would seem that his teachings were too much an extension of his own fabulous personality to maintain their influence indefinitely.

Sri Aurobindo and the Mother

Aurobindo Ghose was born in India of Indian parents on August 15th 1872, but he received an essentially Western education. Age seven he was sent to Manchester and he remained in England until shortly after graduating from King's College, Cambridge in 1892.

On his return to his native land in 1893 he began an academic career as an English professor, but from 1900 to 1910 his desire for India to win her freedom from imperial rule drew him into political activity. Inevitably this led to conflict with the British authorities and he was arrested for sedition in 1907. Later he spent a year in prison awaiting trial for conspiracy, only to be acquitted of all charges.

His time in jail was to prove of great significance however. As early as 1893 he had experienced a profound mystical state, and shortly before his imprisonment a meeting with the teacher Vishnu Bhasker Lele led to his instruction in meditation. Thus the months he spent in solitary confinement in Alipore jail he was able to put to good use, meditating on the Gita and practising yoga.

He continued to be politically active for a short period after his release, but in 1910 he left northern India for Pondicherry, having resolved to dedicate his life to a renewal of Indian spirituality, and karma yoga or selfless action. During the next seven years he published most of his major written works.

In 1914 he met Mira Richard, a spiritual seeker, a psychic, and the wife of a French diplomat. They immediately recognised a spiritual kinship with one another. Aurobindo soon acknowledged her as 'the Mother' of his ashram, and in time as his appointed successor.

In 1926 Aurobindo completed his great written masterpiece, *The Life Divine*, and on November 24th of that year he withdrew into seclusion after a mystical experience he interpreted as a 'descent of Krishna into the physical'. It was only in 1938, after fracturing a hipbone, that he began to make himself available again to a few close disciples.

In a move that went against the grain of Indian popular opinion, in 1940 he and the Mother announced support for the Allies in the war effort, and later in this conflict, their approval of a British proposal to allow a greater degree of Indian self-government in return for Indian cooperation. It was clearly a matter of great satisfaction to him that India achieved formal independence on his 75th birthday.

Sri Aurobindo died in 1950, aged 78.

Aurobindo himself stated that the main achievements of his life were not to be discerned from his outer activities, and today he is acclaimed as one of India's greatest yogis of modern times, and by some an avatar. His philosophy is wide-ranging and, unlike that of many traditional Indian schools, is aimed at the bringing of divine consciousness into matter, not the transcendence of the material. He was opposed to his teachings becoming any kind of religion as he stressed the need for individual self-development.

The Mother saw her primary function as bringing aspirants to Aurobindo rather than as a person of great significance in her own right. Nonetheless, she announced that she had experienced 'the descent of the Supermind' in 1956 in accordance with Aurobindo's predictions.

Shortly after Aurobindo's death, the Mother created the Sri Aurobindo International Centre of Education in Pondicherry.

She also predicted that 'the supramental consciousness will enter into a phase of realising power in 1967'[3].

Arguably her greatest work was the founding of the Auroville International township community as a means to ground this consciousness. This task began in 1968 and Auroville has grown to become an international spiritual community of over five hundred members, with the extraordinary Matrimandir temple at its centre. Spread out on a site of over 11,000 acres it comprises over forty different settlements. Activities include reafforestation work, crafts and the construction of small-scale renewable energy systems. Overseen by the Auroville Cooperative, the structures are highly decentralised and there is a strong emphasis on self-reliance.

The Mother left the physical on November 17th 1973 at age 95.

There have been regular trips and exchanges between Auroville and the Foundation over the years, including, for a time, a computerised link-up.

Sai Baba

Sri Sathya Sai Baba's direct influence on our collective life is a more recent phenomenon than any of the others mentioned in this section. Prior to 1987 few members had any interest in his teachings, but since that time there have been annual organised trips of groups of members and guests to his ashram in India (usually including a stay at Auroville as well) and many individuals have undertaken private visits. When considering such a visit, Eileen received the following guidance:

> *Go and do what he is doing — turning people within to find the divinity within them, and to live and move and have their being from that divine centre.*

Some Community members now believe that the 'God' whose words Eileen Caddy channelled is synonymous with Sai Baba.

---

[3] See also Section 2, 'Building the Community' for parallels with our own Community history.

His story is certainly an extraordinary one. Born of poor parents on 23rd November 1926[4] at Puttaparti in the state of Andhra Pradesh, his early life was attended by many strange stories about his knowledge and powers. At age 13 after an apparently serious affliction which lasted two months, young Sathya announced himself to be 'Sai Baba'. Immediately he began giving teachings on the Vedas and quoting passages of scriptures he had apparently never read. He did not begin his first public ministries in Indian cities for another 17 years, but as disciples sought him out in his remote home, an ashram began to develop there.

He states quite unequivocally that he is the Avatar of our age, and that his present life is one of three Sai incarnations destined to lead humankind back to the path of spirit from which we have strayed. The first of these lives was that of Shirdi Sai Baba, a saint or fakir who taught devotees from his base in a deserted mosque in Bombay state, and who died in 1918. He predicted he would return as a boy eight years later. Sathya Sai Baba predicts he will die at age 96, but return within a year as Prema Sai who will be born in the state of Mysore. These are grand pronouncements, and although the claim to be an Avatar is one for which there are unfortunate precedents, his followers now number at least 50 million worldwide[5], and include many influential leaders and politicians, especially in India.

His teachings are not easy to encapsulate. He often talks in parables which have a biblical simplicity, but he is equally capable of producing erudite discourses on the nature of inner reality. Nonetheless, he himself has said: "It is enough to

---

[4] By coincidence or otherwise, this is the day before Sri Aurobindo's period of withdrawal commenced.

[5] This is an incredible figure, making his followers the fifth largest spiritual movement in the world. There is little reason to doubt the veracity of the statement, but it makes the almost total absence of media coverage of his work in the West hard to understand. He has apparently indicated that he is deliberately withholding the growth of recognition of his role for the present.

cultivate the love that knows no distinction between oneself and another — because all are limbs of the one body of Almighty God."

His four main watchwords are Satya, Dharma, Shanti and Prema (Truth, Duty, Peace and Love). According to one devotee:

The three main tenets of the teachings of Sathya Sai Baba are first, the universality of all religions; secondly, that the atma, or divine spark is indwelling in all human beings, which is the basis of the Brotherhood of Man and the Fatherhood of God; and last, that God is Love, and that the quickest and most direct way to Him is through love in action, or selfless service.

Ron Laing, in *The Embodiment of Love*

There are therefore many similarities between these teachings and the work of our own Community, as has been expounded on at length by Carol Riddell in her book *The Findhorn Community.* The Hindu basis of ashram life is hard for some Westerners to feel comfortable with, but his teachings are very ecumenical and he has frequently advised those searching for spiritual truth to work within the religious format they are already familiar with. His claim to be the reincarnation of Krishna is not one to be taken lightly, but when asked outright if he was God, his reply apparently was:

The only difference between us is that I know that I am God.

Those interested in learning more will find no shortage of companions in the Community.

The Maharishi

The Maharishi Mahesh Yogi is probably the world's most well-known living spiritual teacher, and for many people the archetypal guru figure.

Surprisingly little has been published about his early life, although it is clear that he was a disciple of Guru Dev, a great teacher of the Vedic tradition. The Maharishi spent 13 years with Guru Dev, a period about which he later said, "Right from the beginning the whole purpose was just to breathe in his breath. That was my ideal."

In 1953 the Maharishi retired to live a life of retreat in the 'Valley of the Saints' high in the Himalayas. Two years later he left to visit the holy city of Rameshvaram near the southern tip of India, and here he began his first public teachings. These were and are based around the premise that the apparent gap between the Vedic teachings that *ananda* or bliss is the true nature of life, and the wretched suffering of ordinary people can be bridged quite simply, namely through the practice of what has come to be known as Transcendental Meditation, or TM.

Towards the end of 1957 at a 'Seminar of Spiritual Luminaries' he announced his plan to regenerate the world spiritually. His first few centres were located in India but soon he began his first world tour, travelling to south east Asia, and reaching America and Europe by 1959. His fame spread quickly — by 1961 the open session of the first World Assembly in London was attended by 5,000 people.

The extraordinary growth of his organisation, which today spans the globe, has however been largely overlooked. This is primarily because he is indelibly linked in the popular imagination with his most famous followers, the Beatles, who dallied with his techniques and ideas in the mid-1960s at the height of their popularity.

The quiet but steady growth of his work has continued all the same. By 1974 over one million people had been taught TM, and today his ambitions remain nothing if not bold. In 1988 he announced his world-wide programme to 'Create Heaven on Earth', the central focus for which is his Vedic Science and Technology which attempts to fuse the scientific with the spiritual. For example, it is claimed that 30 scientific research studies have shown that when a tiny fraction of a population practise the Advanced TM-Siddhi technique, or 1% practise regular TM, crime, accidents and sickness are all reduced.

In Britain his largest centre is in Lancashire at Skelmersdale, but the most well known recent contribution of TM to modern British culture has been the unfortunate antics of the

Natural Law Party, a wholly unsuccessful attempt by TM's political wing to field candidates adept at 'yogic flying' at a recent general election.

The Maharishi's genius has been to create a simple and accessible introduction to meditative techniques, which has allure for many beginners, and then to back this up with a mastery of Vedic philosophy which becomes available to those who wish to probe more deeply into the mysteries. There is much in common between the Maharishi's philosophy and Community thinking, particularly in stressing the importance of meditation and that humanity's role is not to escape matter, but to infuse it with spirituality.

Unsurprisingly many Community members (including Eileen) have been initiated into the TM technique, and there are some who have taken a more formal role in the TM movement at one time or another. Regrettably, however, in the UK at least the TM movement tends to take a fairly exclusive approach, and formal links between our respective communities are virtually non-existent.

Other Teachers

A complete list of the many other teachers and teachings who have influenced members of the Community would be as impossible to create as it is unnecessary. Such influences include A Course in Miracles, Ken Carey, Bhagwan Shree Rajneesh (Osho), Mother Meera, Pak Subuh, Babaji, Yogananda, Dion Fortune et cetera, et cetera.

Various works of fiction have also been influential in the Community from time to time. Interestingly it is often works of science fiction or fantasy which strike the deepest chord. Tolkien, Doris Lessing and Ursula Le Guin are probably the most prominent of such authors to date. Carlos Castaneda has also been widely read — although whether his writings are held to be fact or fiction is a moot point.

THE AVATAR OF SYNTHESIS

An Esoteric Myth about the Foundation
of the Community

William Bloom

There is an esoteric myth about the founding of the Community that I particularly like. There is no exact source for it that I can name, but it seeped into my brain in the early 70s. (At that time the Community was full of folk who studied and practised Western esoterics, particularly Theosophy, Rosicrucianism, Alice Bailey and Steiner.)

According to this myth, in the 20th century Planet Earth and one of her major centres, humanity, was trying to take herself through a very difficult transformatory shift. Seen from our perspective, this entailed moving from an isolated atomic perspective and experience, into one of holistic synergy. The process of change was so difficult that Earth and humanity were sounding out into the cosmos a tense note of pain and effort. (This is not surprising, considering the tensions of the World Wars, the Cold War and the divide between South and North.)

Somewhere on the other side of the universe there was a system — planetary or stellar — which recognised this particular sound of distress. It recognised this note of distress because it too, in its history, had been through a similar difficult transformation. In consultation with the Great Heavenly Consciousness this system asked if it could help Earth and humanity. The GHC said "Okay" and the system sent an aspect of its consciousness to incarnate into Earth and humanity.

This aspect of its consciousness is sometimes known as the Avatar of Synthesis. The Avatar of Synthesis brings into Earth and humanity the principle of Synergy. It could not, however, just descend as a cloud to permeate everything in general. A plot, therefore, was hatched by the Great White Lodge of saints, adepts and rishis (humans who have liberated themselves from the cycle of incarnation, are 'perfect' and remain usually invisible on Earth to help us). They planned to build some centres made of human beings through whom the Avatar of Synthesis could incarnate. They were also, at the same time, planning the re-creation of certain mystery schools. Perhaps it was possible that one centre could serve both purposes. "Whom shall we use to set this up?" they asked. Aha! They spotted three disciplined and willing disciples who would make a perfect seed-group and who would see the founding of the project through to completion.

Thus it was that Eileen heard the voice of God, Peter obeyed and Dorothy worked creatively with the angelic aspect. (I believe that Auroville is another place where this happened.) So Eileen, Dorothy and Peter were indeed following very clear guidance as they set down roots and foundations for the Findhorn Centre. It is thought that the particular Adept or Rishi who oversaw the founding was that Western teacher known variously as St Germain, Ragoczi and Christian Rosencreutz. The Universal Sanctuary in the Park Building was always dedicated to him and until recently there was a picture of him in the entrance to the Park Building.

This whole story is interesting because it suggests that people come to the Community essentially to be permeated by this new attitude-quality of synergy — to let the Avatar of Synthesis incarnate more fully. Synergy means an emerging creative and cooperative connection between everything — at all levels and dimensions, between all levels and dimensions: emotional, physical, etheric, spiritual, mental, cellular, solar, cosmic, earthly and so on. Visitors and students at the Community may think they are doing a workshop, visiting a community, having a new age romance — and focalisers may believe they are facilitating that — but behind everything what is really happening is that people are being impregnated by the Avatar of Synthesis. So even when workshops appear not to work, something esoteric and powerful is taking place. Visitors are always changed.

It is widely recognised that the Foundation has had and still has a planetary importance though, often, people do not in fact understand why. Perhaps the Avatar of Synthesis and its response to Earth's and humanity's need is part of the answer.

READING LIST

Sri Aurobindo; *The Life Divine*; Sri Aurobindo Ashram Trust; 1973. *Essays on the Gita*; Sri Aurobindo Ashram Trust; 1976. *Sri Aurobindo On Himself*; Sri Aurobindo Ashram Trust; 1985

Alice Bailey; Various; Lucis Trust. There are many volumes of channelled material of which the most accessible are *Initiation Human and Solar* and *Letters on Occult Meditation*. In the latter, Letter IX on 'Future Schools of Meditation' is particularly tantalising. Also of interest, *The Unfinished Autobiography*; Lucis Trust; 1951

Michael Baigent & Richard Leigh; *The Temple and the Lodge*; Jonathan Cape; 1989. A somewhat disappointing follow up to the outrageous but compelling *The Holy Blood and the Holy Grail*, but certainly of interest to those wishing to know more about the Western mystery tradition in general, and Scotland's role in it in particular.

Anne Bancroft; *Modern Mystics and Sages*; Paladin; 1978. Brief summaries of the lives and work of several prominent influences on the New Age including Steiner, Gurdjieff, Alan Watts, Pak Subuh and Krishnamurthi.

H.P. Blavatsky; *Isis Unveiled*: 2 volumes; *The Secret Doctrine*: 3 volumes; Theosophical University Press; 1888. The latter is somewhat opaque, although highly regarded by Steiner. The former is rather more speculative.

A Course in Miracles; Foundation for Inner Peace; 1976

Ram Dass; *The Only Dance There Is*; Doubleday; 1970. *Journey and Awakening*; Bantam; 1990

Dion Fortune; *The Mystical Qabalah*; Aquarian Press; 1987

L. Francis Edmunds; *Rudolf Steiner Education*; Steiner Press; 1977

Findhorn Foundation; 'The Story of the Tibetan Ring'; an audio tape archive in which Peter tells the story of an initiation on Ben Macdui.

G.I. Gurdjieff; *Meetings With Remarkable Men*; Pan; 1978. Originally published by Routledge and Kegan Paul; 1963. *Beelzebub's Tales to His Grandson*; Arkana 1985

Stuart Holroyd; *Krishnamurthi: The Man, the Mystery and the Message*; Element; 1991

Satish Kumar; *No Destination: An Autobiography*; Green Books; 1992. This includes a brief but delightful account of a visit to Erraid and Iona.

Mary Lutyens (editor); *The Krishnamurthi Reader*; Penguin; 1970

Robert McDermott (editor); *The Essential Aurobindo*; Lindisfarne

Press; 1987. The quotation regarding supramental consciousness cited above is from this source. The editor acknowledges 'Mitra; *The Liberator*, p279' as the original source of the information.

Maharishi Mahesh Yogi; *Thirty Years Around the World: Volume 1 1957-64*. The quotation regarding Guru Dev is from page 37. *Maharishi's Programs to Create Heaven on Earth*; Global Video Productions; 1992. *On the Bhagavad-Gita: A New Translation, Chapters 1-6*; Penguin; 1986. Many believe this to be the Maharishi's masterpiece.

Caitlin and John Matthews; *The Western Way*; Arkana; 1985

Peggy Mason and Ron Laing; *Sathya Sai Baba: The Embodiment of Love*; Sawbridge Enterprises; 1982. The quotation is from page 215.

James Moore; *Gurdjieff: The Anatomy of a Myth*; Element; 1991

The Mother; *Collected Works of the Mother*; Sri Aurobindo Ashram Trust; 1979-91.

Mother Meera; *Answers*; Rider; 1991

Jacob Needleman; *The New Religions*; Doubleday; 1970. Includes material on the Maharishi, Subud, Tibetan influence on the West etc.

P.D. Ouspensky; *The Fourth Way*; Routledge and Kegan Paul; 1957

Wilf Parfitt; *The Qabalah*; Element; 1991

Robert M. Pirsig; *Zen and the Art of Motorcycle Maintenance*; Bodley Head; 1974.

Bhagwan Shree Rajneesh; *The Mustard Seed: Discourses on the Sayings of Jesus from the Gospel According to Thomas*; Rajneesh Foundation; 1975

Jane Roberts; *Seth Speaks*; Bantam; 1974

Charles J. Ryan; *H.P. Blavatsky and the Theosophical Movement*; Theosophical University Press; 1975

Bhagavan Sri Sathya Sai Baba; *Discourses on the Bhagavad Gita*; Sri Sathya Sai Books and Publications Trust; 1988

Satprem; *Sri Aurobindo or the Adventure of Consciousness*; Sri Aurobindo Society; 1970

A.P. Shepherd; *Rudolf Steiner: Scientist of the Invisible*; Floris Books; 1983

Rudolf Steiner; Various; There are many volumes of his work covering a huge range of subjects, including for example *The Restoration of Man*; Anthroposophic Press; 1971. *An Autobiography*; Steiner Publications; 1977. This work was unfinished at the time of his death.

Peter Washington; *Madame Blavatsky's Baboon*; Secker 1993. A harsh but highly readable critique of the Theosophical influence.

The ground covered includes Gurdjieff, Steiner and Krishnamurthi, but for unexplained reasons the Lucis Trust is not even mentioned.
The Story of the White Eagle Lodge; White Eagle Publishing Trust; 1986
Colin Wilson; *Rudolf Steiner: The Man and His Vision*; Aquarian Press; 1984
Paramahansa Yogananda; *Autobiography of a Yogi*; Rider; 1969

FICTION

Richard Bach; *Illusions: The Adventures of a Reluctant Messiah*; Pan; 1977
Carlos Castaneda; *The Teachings of Don Juan*; Penguin; 1970
Alan Garner; *Elidor*, Macmillan; 1982. A children's book in which the leading characters have to teach a unicorn called 'Findhorn' to sing in order to save the world. First published in 1965.
Hermann Hesse; *The Glass Bead Game*, Picador; 1987
Nic Inman; *Canoeing Through Life*, Findhorn Press; 1985
Jack Kerouac; *The Dharma Bums*; Granada; 1972
Doris Lessing; *Canopus in Argos: Archives,* a series of five books comprising *Shikasta*, *The Marriages Between Zones Three, Four and Five*, *The Sirian Experiments*, *The Making of the Representative for Planet 8*; and *The Sentimental Agents in the Volyen Empire*; all originally published by Jonathan Cape; 1979-83
Ursula Le Guin; *A Wizard of Earthsea*; Penguin; 1992
J.R.R. Tolkien; *The Lord of the Rings*; Harper Collins; 1993

Nine

The Wider Community of Moray

West Moray is the area of Scotland in which Forres and Findhorn are situated. In this section we consider the natural environment of Moray, the history of Scotland and Moray's place within it, and the modern economy and political geography of the county. Lastly, there are some suggestions aimed at improving communications between members of the Foundation and its associated Community, and the resident local population.

Introduction

Scotland is a remarkable country, famous the world over for its mountains and glens, whisky, romantic history, golf courses and tartans. These attractions are certainly one of the reasons many individuals decide to take the long journey to Findhorn. Indeed, in many people's minds there is already an association between Scotland and the paranormal, even before they have heard of the Foundation. Ancient castles imply ghosts, the Celtic mythos hints at mysterious bards, druids and pagan gods, and few are unaware of the enigma of Loch Ness and its fabulous denizen.

There is of course a different side to Scotland, and one that is more real to its people than the country depicted in tourist brochures. For all its beauty it is a country with a short growing season, and the farmers of the uplands and the crofters of the west and north do not find it easy to make a living. Although Glasgow has seen something of a revival in recent years it still faces many economic and social difficulties, not least in housing. Despite the economic buoyancy of the financial sector in Edinburgh and the oil industry based around Aberdeen, Scotland is still a country with a genuine emigration problem.

304 The Kingdom Within

Indeed, one of the reasons for Scotland's international fame and its reputation for innovation and engineering wizardry is that so many of its talented young people have left to seek work abroad. Today the country's population stands at 5 million. Roughly a half of that number have emigrated from their homeland during the course of the last century.

Furthermore, just as there has been an exodus of Scots, so there has been an influx of outsiders, particularly to rural areas — the so called 'white settlers'. Most Scots are generous in their welcome, just as Scots are themselves welcomed abroad, but many also suspect their indigenous culture is under threat. Yet there is more than one Scotland. The working classes of Glasgow, the middle classes of Edinburgh, and Highlanders of any background live in quite different worlds, often united only by a passion for their nation and, less laudably, a suspicion of all things English.

It is easy to over-simplify. Despite her problems Scotland is not by any means a poor country by the standards of the world, and life is for the most part conducted within a system that offers both opportunity and a measure of justice. Let us now examine in a little more detail her nature, history and culture, with specific reference to Morayshire.

Natural Environment

Scotland has a climate dominated by the Atlantic Ocean. The prevailing westerly winds bring damp air warmed by the currents of the Gulf Stream, which flows from the Caribbean across to western Europe and Scandinavia. Forres is as far north as Juneau, Alaska and further north than Moscow, but these maritime influences bring winters which are cool rather than cold, and summers which are warm rather than hot. The northern latitudes mean long winter nights, but almost endless summer days with no true darkness.

In the west of the country, the rugged mountain scenery, formed in the ancient Caledonian upheavals around 500 million years ago, attracts clouds like a magnet. The island of Skye and the mountain massifs on the mainland experience

over 300 cm of rain per annum. Our outpost on the isle of
Erraid is relatively low lying and receives 'only' about 100 cm
annually. This regular downpour — there is no month where
rain is unlikely — and the cool temperatures produce a water-
logged soil almost everywhere except some sandy coastal
margins called machair. The accumulation of moisture in the
ground prevents bacterial breakdown and over the centuries
huge deposits of peat have built up. The region is largely lacking in woodland, but this is due to the action of humans, both
ancient and modern. Once almost the whole of the country
was thickly forested.

The east coast is in a relative rain shadow and much drier
than the west. Forres has about 70 cm of rain each year, Findhorn less than 62 cm (only 24 inches). The prevailing westerly winds bring warm air, but winter temperatures are
generally lower than in the west as the effects of the Gulf
Stream are largely absent, and the North Sea generates cool
easterly breezes. Such conditions are however beneficial to
agriculture, the sandy soils and dune systems around Findhorn being quite atypical[1]. The fertile acres of lowland around
Forres — know as the Laigh of Moray — have been an important granary throughout Scotland's history. The hills of the
interior are however significantly less productive. Climatic
conditions deteriorate sharply with an increase in height and
the soils above 100 metres are more similar to those of the
west coast than they are to the farmland of the Laigh.

Higher still are the granite Cairngorm mountains. Any hill
in Scotland with an elevation of 3,000 feet (914 metres) or
more is known as a 'Munro' and walkers intent on scaling
them are well advised to take sensible precautions. These
modest heights belie the possibility of blizzards at any time
of the year on the summits and plateaux.

Surprisingly perhaps, Scotland is a net exporter of food.
The abundant seas and modern farming methods provide a

---

[1] Nonetheless, there are many other parts of the east cost with grassy
links. It was such places that inspired the game of golf.

healthy harvest of fish, grains, vegetables and fruits. Yet the agricultural scene is not lacking in challenges. The problems of over-fishing are a hotly debated issue, reduced government subsidies threaten many marginal hill farms, which are heavily dependent on a double crop of wool and mutton, and unseasonal weather is a constant worry for horticulturists. Nor should we take the 20th century's success for granted. Despite the inherent bounty of nature, during the 17th century there was famine in eastern Scotland in 20 separate years.

Gardening for its own sake is a popular Scottish pastime, and many local stately homes have annual open days to show off their floral exhibits. The team of council gardeners in Forres are Scotland's finest. 'Flower of Scotland' (co-penned by Roy Williamson who had strong Moray connections) is the country's unofficial national anthem.

The fauna of Scotland, while containing much of interest, is much reduced from its former glory. *Ursus caledonius,* the Scottish brown bear, is long extinct, and the last wolf in the country was shot in the 18th century. The Victorian fascination with hunting denuded the glens of many of their wild creatures, and the lonely hills are now the domain of the red deer, whose feeding habits keep the re-growth of forest to a minimum.

Nonetheless, golden eagles still soar over the mountains from their eyries, and recently several other important birds of prey have been successfully reintroduced, including the osprey, red kite, white-tailed sea eagle and the fearless capercaillie. There has also been a revival in the fortunes of the elusive and untameable Scottish wildcat, a herd of reindeer have bred successfully in the Cairngorm area, and each county of the country can boast a wildlife secret or two.

Morayshire's most famous is probably the 'Kellas cat'. It is not yet clear if this extraordinary animal, which is long-legged and jet black, is the result of a modern wild cat/domestic cat cross, or a discovery of a hitherto unknown species. There have been regular sightings in the hinterland of Forres, and the mystery has been the subject of several television programmes and a recent book.

Our Community's contribution to the understanding of Scotland's natural environment includes the hosting of the 3rd World Wilderness Congress in 1983 (which was dedicated to the memory of Sir Frank Fraser Darling who was both a resident of Forres and the foremost Scottish naturalist of his generation), and the ongoing work of 'Trees for Life' (see Section 2 for details).

History

Ancient Times

No reliable evidence has been found of Palaeolithic peoples in Scotland. The first recorded human presence is that of Mesolithic hunter gatherers who arrived about 7,000 years ago, and who left signs of their passing in the Culbin area. A major site of local interest from the Neolithic period is the **Clava Cairns** in Strath Nairn, a collection of large burial mounds near, but quite unconnected with, Culloden battlefield (of which more below). Further afield on the Outer Hebrides are the **Callanish** standing stones which rival Stonehenge in their scope and provide a dramatic setting on the rugged shores of the Atlantic. Although lacking the balanced horizontal sarsens of the latter, this site evokes far clearer images of the past than does the combination of tourist trap and military playground that is Salisbury Plain.

The stone builders were followed by the first metal users. They were the Beaker people, so called because of their habit of leaving a drinking vessel in the graves of their dead. They built a small henge in **Quarry Wood** above the Oakwood restaurant to the west of Elgin. These workers of copper, bronze and lead were superseded by the first iron-using Celtic tribes about 700 BC.

The Celts

The Celtic culture exerts a curious fascination for many modern Westerners. Somehow the very word[2] seems to evoke the

---

[2] It is pronounced with a hard 'C' as in *Keltic*. Pronunciations with a soft 'C' (*Seltic*) refer to a Glasgow-based football team.

notion of a pre-industrial Golden Age, when humanity lived in harmony with nature, and discussions of the public sector borrowing requirement were considered tedious by all. Perhaps, goes the myth, the Celtic peoples were a kind of white-skinned American Indian.

Certainly, until relatively recently the lifestyle of those parts of Scotland still retaining a close affinity with the Celtic culture was far removed from that of the urban centres of Europe. Cattle stealing or reiving was a common practice, particularly amongst young men trying to prove their worth. On the other hand, Highland hospitality was renowned. As late as the 19th century 'explorers' from other parts of Scotland could walk the mountain tracks until dusk, and then simply rap on the door of the first cottage they came to and be assured of a meal and a bed for the night.

Many other paradoxes existed. We know of the mysterious druids, whose influence was presumably considerable, but it is not clear why Christianity found it so easy to supplant their role. In some societies royal descent was traced through the female line, and poets and musicians were everywhere held in high regard. On the other hand these apparently enlightened attitudes were balanced by the Celtic fighting men's bare-breasted charges at the enemy which seem to have involved a spectacular lack of finesse, which the Romans attributed to their belief in reincarnation.

These elements of gentility and brutality all exist in the poignant story of Dierdre, who was exiled from Scotland and laments her loss thus.

> *Sweet are the cries of the brown-backed dappled deer under the oakwood above the bare hill-tops, gentle hinds that are timid lying hidden in the great-treed glen.*
>
> *Glen of the rowans with scarlet berries, with fruit fit for every flock of birds; a slumbrous paradise for the badgers in their quiet burrows with their young.*
>
> *Glen of the blue-eyed vigorous hawks, glen abounding in every harvest, glen of the ridged and pointed peaks, glen of blackberries and sloes and apples.[3]*

SCOTLAND

Shetland Islands

Orkney Islands

CAITHNESS

▲▲▲

SUTHERLAND

Callanish ●

▲▲▲▲▲

Skye

Findhorn ●
Forres ●

Inverness ☆

Aberdeen ☆

▲▲▲

CAIRNGORM MTS.

Loch Ness ▲▲▲▲▲

GRAMPIAN MOUNTAINS

Mull

Iona

Erraid

▲▲▲

ARGYLL

Birnam ●
● Fortingall
Perth ☆

☆ Dundee

Loch Lomond

Firth of
Forth

☆ Stirling

Bannockburn ●

☆ Glasgow

● Largs

☆ Edinburgh

☆ Ayr

Firth of
Clyde

Dumfries

● Whithorn

Some aspects of the myth live on. Irish rock musicians eagerly discuss the influence of the traditional craft on their work, and early descriptions of the Celtic fighting prowess might equally be applied to the modern Scottish football team, who usually contrive to provide their supporters with a diet of glorious failures. Notwithstanding the importance of this influence, we should be wary of romanticising the Celtic past of Scotland. Cultural inheritances are sometimes not all they seem; for example, the kilt with its distinctive hues and clan associations is an 18th century invention, the original Highland plaids being made of a much longer cloth and coloured in subdued reds and browns.

A further point of note is that the early history of Moray is largely dominated by the Celts, but by Picts rather than Scots. Regrettably little is known of this former group for they left no trace of their language except a few place names, and less still is understood of their customs, philosophies or religion. Even the origin of their name is obscure, although it may have come either from the Roman *picti,* meaning 'painted ones', or the Irish *cicht,* for 'engraver'.

Sueno's Stone on the edge of Forres is one of Scotland's most impressive monoliths, although its original purpose is not at all clear. It depicts a battle, but whether erected by the Picts to commemorate victory over Viking invaders, or Scots celebrating their defeat of the Picts has never been satisfactorily established.

The Romans
The legions left less of a mark on Scottish culture than is the case for most of western Europe. The Romans held the line at Hadrian's wall on the border of what is now England for a century, forayed northwards to build the less robust Antonine wall between the Firths of Clyde and Forth for a few decades, and half-heartedly attempted to subdue the north.

---

[3] The original story may be 9th century. This extract is from 'Dierdre Remembers a Scottish Glen' by an unknown Irish author of the 14th century, translated by T.F. O'Rahilly in *Measgra Danta,* Cork; 1927, and quoted in *A Celtic Miscellany,* K.H. Jackson; Penguin; 1971.

They built a line of forts up into Tayside and fought and won a battle at a site of unknown location called 'Mons Graupius' — later mistranslated as Grampius, hence the modern Grampian mountains. A Roman fleet sailed along the Moray coast in AD 84 and the SPQR banner was raised at a small encampment by the Moray Firth just outside Forres. The occupants bequeathed the name 'Varis' to this place, and the modern name of the town may be a corruption of that Roman moniker.

Their stay was however short-lived, and Scotland can boast few substantial relics or artefacts of that period. The most evocative Roman site in the north of Scotland is at Fortingall in Perthshire where the site of a fort is overlooked by a spreading yew, estimated to be 4,000 years old and reputedly the oldest tree in Europe. It is hard to remain untouched by the thought of a still-living being in Scotland's most beautiful glen witnessing the coming and goings of the emissaries of that ancient empire.

The Coming of Christianity
Although St Columba's landing on Iona in 563 is the most well known arrival of a Christian missionary in Scotland, he was something of a latecomer. St Ninian was based at Whithorn in the south west of the country 150 years before that, and St Brendan of Clonfert was active in Moray early in the 6th century. Celtic Christianity brought from Ireland was thus the dominant early form. Although this loosely organised denomination continued to play a role in Scottish affairs until the 14th century, the Pictish king Nechtan adopted Roman Catholicism in 710 AD, and by the 11th century there were Roman bishops in the country. The first bishop of Moray had his seat at Birnie, but the greatest ecclesiastical architectural legacies of this period include the later bishops' palace at **Spynie**, and the abbeys at **Kinloss, Pluscarden** and **Greyfriars** in Elgin. The story goes that Kinloss Abbey was founded in the year 1150 by a grateful King David I who became lost in the Moray forests and was led out by a white dove. There is also a rock-hewn well at **Burghead**, thought to be of early Christian origin.

The Scots

The Scots, true as ever to the Celtic logic, are from Ireland. They arrived in Argyll early in the 6th century and quickly organised a kingdom called Dalriada. From here they spread out, and the Picts were effectively absorbed into a greater Scottish state by Kenneth MacAlpin, King of Scots, in the 9th century. The Scots spoke a Celtic language called Gaelic, and this superseded the old Pictish tongue. However Kenneth's kingdom did not include most of the southern half of the modern nation.

The first king to unite the whole of what is now Scotland was Malcolm Canmore (meaning 'Great Head') who reigned from 1057 to 1093. His dynasty lasted for over two centuries, but the most famous name from this period of history is that of the man Malcolm defeated for the Scots crown. MacBeth is probably the most maligned figure in Scottish history. He had a legitimate claim to the throne, and his defeat of Duncan in battle near Elgin was a victory over a man he considered a usurper rather than a legitimate king. MacBeth reigned for 17 years and by all historical accounts he was a strong and self-confident ruler, rather than the troubled murderer encountered by witches on a heath near Forres in Shakespeare's fictitious drama. Malcolm's avenging victory in battle over the old king occurred near Aberdeen, and Dunsinane and Birnam Wood (which are not far from Perth) had no connection with it at all.

During the Canmore dynasty a long process of feudalisation began. In the fifty years after the succession of King David I in 1124 many great Norman and Flemish nobles were invited into the country to this end, and the old Celtic clan system became confined to the wild Highlands and Islands. During much of this period Moray, then larger than today, was virtually an independent kingdom.

The Scots brought with them from Ireland strong elements of the ancient religious practices of that island, although already overlain with Christian interpretations. The basis of these traditions appears to have been a 'cult of nature spirits, or of the life manifested in nature'[4], a feature which re-emerges strongly in modern New Age thinking. A knowledge of the hero/gods Fionn and Cuchualain and of the four quarterly festivals of Beltane, Lugnasadh, Samhain and Imbolc has lingered in the folk memory to this day, yet even in the Gaeltacht they are for the most part echoes of a distant past rather than a genuinely living set of observances.

The Vikings

From the 8th century onwards the whole of western Europe was subjected to incursions from Scandinavia. The Norsemen created strongholds for themselves in Shetland, Orkney, Caithness and Sutherland, and exerted continual pressure all along the west coast. Under Sigurd the Mighty, Moray fell to their influence for a while. Today they are largely remembered for their piratical behaviour; their early forays into the sparsely populated north met little resistance, but the growing pressure of numbers led to increasingly violent struggles. The Norsemen were not Christians, which added a religious element to the fray, and Iona was sacked several times. In the 10th century a number of fleeing monks were killed on the Traigh Bhan shore, and on one occasion the entire monastic community was put to the sword at 'Martyr's Bay'.

Vestiges of their culture remain with us, again principally in place names, although the Northern Isles still had a few native speakers of a Norse tongue in the 18th century, and Shetlanders at least retain a strong affinity to Scandinavia. Their threat to the integrity of the Scots kingdom was only

---

[4] J.A. MacCulloch, op. cit. page 3.

[5] Edward Plantaganet was of course of Norman origin, and a descendant of William 'the Conqueror' who seized the English crown in 1066. What is not commonly understood is that the Norman dukedom was strongly influenced by Danes who had previously annexed part of northern France. This invasion of England was thus to a degree an extension of the Viking raids on the whole of Britain. Fortunately for the Scots they too had absorbed some of this Norman mettle, although through conscious policy rather than conquest. Robert the Bruce, for example, was also a direct descendant of a Norman nobleman who came over with William.

finally repelled at the decisive battle of Largs in 1263.

Wars of Independence

The next great event in Scottish history was this struggle for power in northern Britain. It was a tempestuous time, and Edward I of England's cruelties and attempts to subdue the Scots have lived long in the race memory.[5] Prior to the 14th century Scotland and England had co-existed relatively peaceably and many nobles held lands on both sides of the border. However the depredations of the next twenty years left an indelible mark on Anglo-Scottish relations. Exploiting dynastic weaknesses, Edward's armies quickly overwhelmed the divided Scots nobles. First William Wallace and then Robert the Bruce led guerrilla campaigns against the might of the English occupation. These efforts eventually culminated in the Battle of Bannockburn near Stirling, won so decisively by Bruce and his Scottish army in 1314.

Morayshire played its part in these events. Edward of England came as far north as **Lochindorb** on one of his military expeditions. Daunted by his view of the mountains to the north, he turned to the lowlands ahead of him and burnt Forres, Kinloss, Elgin and Aberdeen before returning south.

Andrew de Moray was Wallace's right-hand man although his role was cut short. He died of wounds received at another important Scottish military victory of this period at Stirling Brig.

Although a great national hero, Bruce was not a saint. He assassinated his great rival John Comyn in a confused incident at Greyfriars Church, Dumfries in 1306. During the same incident Gordon Comyn of **Altyre**, an ancestor of the modern Gordon-Cumming family who still own the Altyre estate outside Forres, was killed by Roger de Kirkpatrick, Bruce's accomplice.

The events at the mis-named **Randolph's Leap** on the River Findhorn also fall into this time. Thomas Randolph was created Earl of Moray with lands previously controlled by the Cummings, who set out to raid Darnaway Castle to avenge themselves. Randolph was forewarned, and laid an ambush in a deep ravine at Whitemire. Defeated in the ensuing battle Alistair Cumming's men fled, and he escaped by leaping the narrow gorge.

An interesting result of these struggles was that English influence led to Robert Bruce, and by extension the Scottish people as a whole, being excommunicated by the Pope for a short period. One consequence of this was the arrival of significant numbers of Templar knights on Scottish shores, seeking refuge from Papal persecution in Europe. A number of Templar graves have been found in Argyllshire.

After the wars were over the Scots nobles met to sign the Declaration of Arbroath. Its main purpose was to assert: "So long as a hundred of us are left alive, we will never in any degree be subjected to the English. It is not for glory, riches or honour that we fight, but for liberty alone which no good man loses but with his life."

A knowledge of these facts is no mere exercise in academia, for the events of this long-distant epoch still play their part in the Scottish psyche. The notion of a small freedom-loving nation struggling and winning over the odds against a powerful and barbaric aggressor may be as much romance as truth, and have little to do with the modern political world, but the myths and legends have long since become at least as powerful as the history itself. Astonishing though it may seem to those coming from countries with shorter memories, it is still common to see banners on the streets and sporting terraces of Scotland which prominently display simply the date '1314'.

The House of Stewart

Thus, despite the widespread changes in the organisation of society, unlike much of the rest of western Europe the emerging Scots culture was still rooted in its Celtic past, and only influenced, rather than dominated, by Roman, Norse and Germanic invasions. Indeed it is likely that her national character was already forged largely in defensive opposition to these external threats. Maintaining Scotland's independent place in Europe was to be the task of Bruce's descendants for the next 300 years.

Robert Bruce's daughter Marjory married Walter, the sixth hereditary High Steward of his country. Their son became in time King Robert II, and so began the rule of the House of Stewart. For the most part, however, Morayshire sensibly kept itself apart from what has been rather uncharitably described as the 'long brawl' of Scottish history. Nonetheless, times were not always as peaceful as the majority of the inhabitants would no doubt have liked.

In 1390 the infamous 'Wolf of Badenoch', slighted by attacks on his private life by the Bishop of Moray, charged down to the plains from his fastness at Lochindorb and burned Forres, and then later Elgin. His nickname implies an outlaw but he was in fact an Earl of the royal line. Such religious conflicts were to bedevil the Stewart dynasty.

In the mid-16th century, when the young Queen Mary returned to her native Scotland from France, where she had been married to the ill-fated Dauphin, she found the country in turmoil. John Knox was preaching the Calvinist doctrine, and the ordinary people, tired of corrupt bishops and prelates, lent him a sympathetic ear. Mary's dramatic reign was brought to an early close largely because of her inept handling of this explosive situation.

The old saying that the Stewart dynasty 'came with a lass and went with a lass' is well known but technically inaccurate. Mary's eventual exile and her death at the hands of her cousin Elizabeth I of England only heralded the end of the Stewarts as a specifically Scottish royal line.

Union

When Elizabeth died in 1603, the succession brought James VI of Scotland, the son of Queen Mary, to the throne of England as well — the 'Union of the Crowns'. James promptly moved his court to London and so symbolised the growing Anglicisation of Scots culture which was beginning to make its mark across the country. James allegedly claimed that Nairn was the greatest city in Europe, on the grounds that the people at one end of the High Street (the Anglicised fishing folk) spoke a different language from those at the other end (the

MORAY AND NAIRN

NOT TO SCALE

farming Gaelic speakers). The Gaelic could still be heard in rural Moray and Nairn until the 19th century, but now it is entirely confined to the west coast.

Over the years this union eventually brought a lasting peace between the two nations, but this was not the case at first. Soon Scotland was embroiled in the English Civil war and its aftermath. This is a complex period to understand, with several of the main characters changing sides, and confused loyalties to church, country and King splitting the nation. Moray's main part in it all was to witness a battle at the village of **Auldearn**, won by the great general Montrose, and in 1650 to host the return from the continent of the exiled Charles II at **Kingston** near Garmouth. This was also an era of religious intolerance, and many an innocent Scotswoman was burned as a witch.

Nearly sixty years later in 1707 amidst some considerable controversy, which continues to this day, the Parliaments of England and Scotland were also merged. By statute, however, Scotland continues to retain a separate legal, educational and church system.

Jacobites, Wordsmiths and Philosophers

The 18th century was hardly less warlike. In 1688 James VII was deposed for his Catholic sympathies in a bloodless coup which gave the throne to James's daughter Mary and her husband the Dutch nobleman William of Orange. James's son and grandson fought back. The Jacobite rebellions of 1715 and 1745 are often portrayed as a national uprising of the Scots, but support for 'Bonnie' Prince Charlie was largely confined to the minority of Catholics and Highlanders. The people of Elgin and Forres cheered their eventual defeat. Although proceeding triumphantly as far south as the midlands of England, his upland army soon melted away to tend the harvests. The prince spent a month in Elgin in the spring of 1746 before leading his remaining forces to the massacre at Culloden. It was the end of Stuart[6] claims to the Scottish throne, and the

---

[6] This spelling of Stewart was assumed by the royal family in the time of Mary.

beginning of the end for the traditional clan system of the Highlands. The atmosphere of this doleful battleground remains strangely charged, as if some black cloud continues to hang over the place where so many men were slaughtered.

More happily, Findhorn Bay was the stage for a dramatic incident just prior to this massacre. Richard Warren, the Prince's aide-de-camp, somehow contrived to be picked up by a friendly French sailing vessel called *Le Bien Trouvé,* and although it was trapped in the Bay by patrolling British men-of-war, the larger ships could not enter the shallow waters to conclude his capture. One misty night the French brigantine escaped from their grasp and subsequently made it safely back to Dunkirk.

This century also saw the births of Robert Burns, Scotland's great national poet (whose health is toasted everywhere that Scots gather on the 25th of January), and that of Walter Scott. Scott's star is now past its zenith, but he was the greatest European novelist of his day. It was also the time of the 'Scottish Enlightenment' that brought a galaxy of thinkers to the fore. The works of the economist Adam Smith and the philosopher David Hume and their colleagues introduced this flowering of Scottish cultural and intellectual society to the attention of the whole of Europe, and set the tone for the political and educational reforms of the following century.

The Recent Past

Four great 19th century events deserve mention. First of all, the Highland Clearances, which drove many of the remaining Gaels from their homes to make way for sheep farming. It was the final nail in the coffin of the ancient Celtic culture on the Scottish mainland. Secondly, religion — the 'Great Schism' of the Church of Scotland took place, dividing many highland parishes between the orthodox Kirk and the 'Free Church', which dared to oppose the landowners and demand election of ministers by the people, a right belatedly obtained by the Kirk only in 1874.

Thirdly, the Industrial Revolution brought the railways and the new commercial era. Scotland and the Scots developed a reputation for invention that few nations can match, having brought for example steam power, the telephone, television and penicillin to the attention of the world. The effects of industrialisation were more dramatic in the great cities of the south, and Moray is the happier for having absorbed its methods whilst avoiding its excesses. Further afield the Scots explorers Mungo Park and David Livingstone carved their names into the history of the growing British Empire. Forresborn Donald Smith, later ennobled as Lord Strathcona, played his part as Governor of the Hudson Bay Company, and as a driving force behind the construction of the Canadian-Pacific railway.

Closer to home a branch line of the main north railway was constructed from Kinloss to Findhorn. Although it was a short-lived experiment, the railway engineers have left a lasting mark on the peninsula, and their efforts are a testimony to the thriving commercial traffic the little port once witnessed. In Moray at this time whisky[7] distilling became an organised industry, and the first modern roads were constructed with crossings of the Spey and Findhorn. The 'Sobieski Stuarts', claiming to be Poles descended from the royal line[8], stayed briefly at **Logie** near Forres in 1829. This was also the year of the 'muckle spate' of the River Findhorn, which after a day of torrential rain rose over 12 metres at Dulsie Bridge, and flooded more than 20 square miles of the plain of Forres.

This is not the place for a lengthy discussion of 20th century history, but a number of events are worthy of attention. The most important event of the early years of the century was of course the First World War. It is well worth standing by the war memorial in Findhorn and pondering the long list of names, and the effects of such slaughter on a small and close-knit community. In the years thereafter Forres experienced a modest growth in prosperity, signified by a successful summer

---

[7] From the Gaelic *uisge beatha* — 'water of life'.

[8] These outrageous charlatans were in fact two English brothers, surnamed Allen. Before their exposure they held a kind of Jacobite court for a while at Eilean Aigas near Beauly.

'Gala Week' which regularly attracted 6,000 visitors, and in 1926 the Australian cricket team played the inaugural match on the new pitch at Grant Park. In 1934 **Gordonstoun School** near Elgin, later to educate members of the British royal family, was founded. The Second World War brought more loss, and the airfields at Kinloss and Lossiemouth in its wake. The great concrete blocks on the beach between Findhorn and Burghead are another legacy of this period, their construction designed to forestall a sea-borne invasion.

Let us now turn to the place of Morayshire within the modern nation of Scotland.

Modern Moray

Political Situation

Briefly, there is a hierarchy of political power leading down from the British parliament in Westminster, to the Scottish Office in Edinburgh, which is an arm of the government of the day. Moray sends a single Member of Parliament to Westminster. There is no elected Scottish government of any kind, although there have been persistent attempts to reinstate one since the original Union. This debate can be seen played out in the parliamentary elections in Moray. In recent years, support has swung between the Conservative and Unionist party and the Scottish National Party (SNP), which is of course anti-Unionist.

The highest level of local government is that of the Region. Forres is in Grampian Region, which is based in Aberdeen. On a second separate tier of local administration is Moray District, whose headquarters are in Elgin. The present British government intends to abolish the Regional Council and create a unitary Moray authority for the provision of all local services.

Last in the chain are the Community Councils which provide valuable input into the District and Regional Council deliberations, but which have little decision-making power of their own. There is one for Forres, and another for Findhorn and Kinloss.

At the other end of the spectrum there is the European Community or EC, which is becoming increasingly important as a supra-national form of government. Unlike many of their continental neighbours, the British as a whole remain somewhat suspicious of giving up elements of their political independence to this body. However, the current MEP for the Highlands and Islands constituency is the SNP's Mrs Winnie Ewing — 'Madame Ecosse' — and the Nationalist view is that it would be better for Scotland to seek its place as an independent partner in Europe and by-pass Westminster altogether.

Religious Life

The Church of Scotland, or Kirk, has an annual General Assembly in Edinburgh where the issues of the day are discussed under the gaze of the elected Moderator. The prominent 'Church and Nation' committee is also a regular contributor to public debate, and the well-known Iona Community participates in diverse activities including the Kirk's international missionary work. The smaller 'Free Church' remains important in many Highland parishes and everywhere there is a smattering of non-conformist belief. The Episcopal Church is the Anglican presence in Scotland. Roman Catholicism is widespread, but only in the Central Belt are the adherents numerous. Many Catholics there are the descendants of Irish immigrants, but there are a few Hebridean islands where Knox's Calvinist reformation never took hold. Other faiths are present in Scotland, but none are prominent in Moray.

Scotland's patron saint is St Andrew, whose protection is recalled on November 30th. The blue and white national flag or Saltire is flown in many places on that day, the white 'X' representing the shape of the cross on which the saint was martyred.

The Local Economy

In simple terms the traditional economy of Moray is dominated by the 'Four Fs', namely fishing, farming, fermentation and forestry, to which may be added tourism and the Ministry of Defence.

Several of the coastal towns are still dependent on the fishing industry, although this activity has been in decline in recent years. Farming continues to be the mainstay of the rural economy and, with 60% of the land under forest, Moray is the UK's most wooded county. 'Fermentation' refers of course to the whisky industry. Although both Forres establishments are currently closed, distilling remains of great importance in many areas, particularly on Speyside.

Scottish tourism has ridden out the recent economic recession relatively well, but it has proven to be a fickle friend to Moray. When Forres Hydro[9] a.k.a. Cluny Hill College was the jewel in the crown of West Moray hotels, the area could be referred to as the 'Scottish Riviera' with only modest irony. The advent of cheap holidays abroad has changed all that. Other than the 'whisky trail' there are few large tourist attractions in the county, and much of the trade is passing. Although this is not good news for hoteliers, the relative quietude suits many residents.

In fact, it is the military presence which dominates the local economy. The air bases at Kinloss and Lossiemouth provide employment for just under 5,000 men and women in a county whose total population is only 83,000. The 'peace dividend' is unlikely to bring immediate or direct benefits to the area, and announcements of impending military closures send shudders through the locale. It is over-easy for those of a liberal persuasion to accept the benefits of this military presence whilst disparaging it. RAF Kinloss provides fishery support and air/sea and mountain rescue services in addition to its traditional role, and many service personnel perform tasks which are genuinely dangerous. The role of the warrior may not suit everyone, but it is a legitimate spiritual path in many traditions. You may recall that Peter Caddy's long service training greatly contributed to his leadership and organisational skills.

Economic benefits brought by the oil industry, whilst real, are nothing like so dramatic as in the areas to the east and

---

[9] Short for hydropathic. There are a number of such hotels in Scotland some still offering healing waters. The holding tank at Cluny is on the hill behind what is now the sauna, but the source of the supply was the mains, not a natural spring.

west of Moray. Unemployment in Forres, particularly amongst the young, is currently at very high levels.

Our own Community's role in the economy is thus small, but certainly measurable. It has been estimated that the Foundation and NFD together contribute over £800,000 annually in direct inputs to the Moray Firth area, and the indirect and total Community impact is probably three to four times this figure in all.

Local Relations

The Foundation's relationship with its neighbours may appear to some readers to be a rather specialised subject, having relevance only to those directly involved. So far as many of the specific details are concerned this is of course true, but the difficulties involved in creating a meaningful dialogue and harmonious relationships between very different communities is a subject of wider import. It may be possible to discern from these particulars some ideas which are useful in other contexts.

The subject may be conveniently divided up into four parts, namely:

  i) Findhorn and Kinloss
  ii) Forres
  iii) the Moray Firth area
  iv) the rest of Scotland.

Let us treat them in reverse order. As we shall see, this will allow for an understanding of the issues as they appear at increasing levels of intensity. Note however that the suggestions offered here apply in all circumstances, not just in the context where they are placed in this text.

Scotland

The above narrative on Scottish history and culture, together with a little common sense, should be enough for anyone living in the Community to avoid too many *faux pas*. We are fortunate to be living in such a friendly and peaceable part of the world. There are alternative communities elsewhere in the Western world that require wire fences and guarded gates to allow them to conduct their affairs safely. A few simple reminders are however in order.

1) Try to avoid using 'England' when you mean Britain, and especially if you mean Scotland.

2) Most Scots, and particularly those in rural areas, don't like a fuss. If you come from a nation with a reputation for loudness or pomposity (German, English and American readers take note) try to be sensitive to this.

3) Begin conversations with a reference to the weather. It is considered polite.

4) If you need help, ask for it. Local accents in west Moray are soft and easily understood. If you meet someone from the West[10] or rural Aberdeenshire, don't pretend you understand. Nearly everyone in Scotland is perfectly capable of making themselves understood to someone with a poor grasp of English. If you don't understand a word, the speaker is probably unconscious of your nationality. Better to request they speak more slowly than leave feigning a knowledge of what you have been asked to do.

The Moray Firth Area

Few people within 50 miles of Forres have not heard of the Foundation — which they will possibly refer to as 'Findhorn'. For most this amounts to a cursory knowledge — something to do with a sacking from Forres Hydro over some missing spoons[11], faeries and elves at the bottom of the garden, and a surprisingly tenacious bunch of 'hippies'.

1) However, many locals recall stories from 30 years ago or more that contain a grain of truth. If someone refers to 'yon chap who cut the trees down so the flying saucers could land', don't flatly contradict them. Such comments are usually a covert way of attempting to discover if you

---

[10] The West' refers to the Glasgow conurbation. The Atlantic seaboard is known as the 'west coast'.

[11] Peter, Eileen and Dorothy were of course dismissed from the Trossachs Hotel, not Cluny Hill, and no reasons were ever given — see Section 2.

are as gullible as the speaker imagines. If you present an appearance of sanity and intelligence the conversation will quickly turn to latter-day events (which are more accessible for the ordinary person anyway), and your encyclopaedic knowledge of building houses made out of whisky barrels may be profitably brought to play.

2) Don't pretend that relations with the immediate locality of west Moray are a state-of-the-art object lesson in clear communication. Most people in this area have friends, colleagues or relatives who read the 'Forres Gazette'.

3) Don't assume the person is a Highlander, or even Scots. There is a good chance they are not, and unless you are very good at placing accents, knowing someone lives in Inverness is a very poor guide to their cultural background.

4) Read a local newspaper from time to time. Don't believe everything you read.

West Moray

Everyone in West Moray knows about the Foundation, although few have or desire anything other than a casual knowledge. Most people are quite content to let us get on with our lives if we let them get on with theirs. A small number actively support our work, but the fact is that if the Community is to be relevant to an international audience it must be observably different from mainstream culture. Inevitably this leads to a degree of suspicion.

1) A common gripe concerns the charitable status of the Foundation. Offering justifications based on the nature of the Foundation's spiritual work will not endear you to the average local. Nor will pointing out that Gordonstoun School also has this status, but receives little or no criticism for it. Admit this is a generous tax break, express thanks to the UK government for providing it, and point out that there are many businesses in the Community which pay their taxes like everyone else. This will surprise most people, and indeed few will believe it, but it's worth a try.

You might also usefully examine your own attitudes to 'charity'. The Foundation and Community are still largely dominated by those with a middle class background and the benefits of a tertiary education. The fact that the Foundation does excellent work which deserves support does not mean that it should seek to avoid its social responsibilities towards those who are less well off. To this end the Foundation has a policy of tithing, and is able to direct a small amount of money to local charitable causes. You might consider making an occasional personal contribution of time or money to such projects as well.

2) Many local people have a genuinely hard time understanding what the Foundation and Community do. The Foundation appears to produce nothing, not even a degree certificate. You might usefully discuss the Foundation's work in bringing people with different cultural and religious backgrounds together in harmony. Recent events in the former Yugoslavia make the purpose of such work more obvious. Refer if you like to our outreach efforts in Eastern Europe and South Africa. Don't bother trying to emphasise the value of 'community'. Most genuine locals have lived in a community all their lives and have little empathy with individuals from alienated urban cultures. If you do get involved in a heated discussion (which is highly unlikely — see point two under 'Scotland' above), ask for help. "What would you do to improve local relations?" is a perfectly legitimate question.

3) Be yourself. There is no point in putting on a spiritual act, or alternatively pretending to be an 'ordinary' person. The very fact that you have most likely travelled hundreds if not thousands of miles to be here without reason of a military career makes you different.

4) Above all, don't be smug. Newer Community members sometimes imagine that they have recently embarked on an immensely important transformational process and world work. It is so, but remember this process is one which demands changes in you, not in everyone else, and it is certainly not designed to help you promote or advertise the Community. It is infuriating to be lectured on the

glamorous achievements of the Foundation by someone whose communication skills suggest they would struggle to arrange a children's party in a toy shop. A little humility goes a long way.

5) The Community is world famous for its work with the nature kingdoms. This does not make you as an individual an authority. Local people who have lived with the changing seasons all their lives do not need to be told that every sunset glorifies God, and that the spring flowers are a miracle of beauty and design. Also, whatever your personal views, note that unlike the Irish, few Scots believe in the 'little people'. And by the way, the geese come to Scotland for the winter, and fly north again in the summer, not the other way around.

6) Take an interest. Local people are proud of their culture and roots. Don't bore everyone by discussing the Community at length unless you are asked to do so. Ask about your interlocutors' own work and life, fears and ambitions, successes and regrets. You may learn something worthwhile.

Findhorn Peninsula

It is a mistake to imagine that the Community is an isolated island in a sea of local uniformity. In the village of Findhorn there are four main resident groups.

a) RAF personnel both active and retired.
b) 'White Settlers', i.e. people who are not originally from the north east of Scotland but who have come there to live. Many are of retirement age.
c) Genuine locals who were born and brought up in the area.
d) Members of the Foundation and its associated Community.

In addition there are:

e) Holidaymakers. Many houses in Findhorn village are now second homes or let to visitors.

No-one has ever done a census but the groups are presented roughly in order of descending numbers. You will thus discern that a significant number of 'locals' are themselves incomers. The close proximity of such diverse communities has led to complex tensions, and in some cases outright hostility. This is not solely confined to the Community's relationship with the other groups, but the Foundation is an easy target.

This situation may be exacerbated by the fact that the present village is probably the third to bear the name, the first two having been swept away by time and tide. Fishing, once the mainstay of the village's economy is now a leisure pursuit rather than a serious economic activity, the last commercial salmon nets having been closed in recent years. Subconsciously perhaps, a knowledge of the relative impermanence of certain traditions on the peninsula may add to local fears of a 'Foundation take-over'.

Furthermore, the relatively high turnover of Foundation staff — the average length of stay is about four years — makes it hard for local people, of whatever stripe, to relate to a large organisation with a constantly changing set of faces at the helm. In such a complex milieu, 'being nice' is often an insufficient qualification for social acceptance.

1) Never use 'Findhorn' when you mean the Foundation or Community.

2) If you are part of the Community but not the Foundation you may find your activities described as part of the latter. If appropriate point this out, but don't press the matter. For most people the distinction is irrelevant.

3) Avoid hugging and kissing in public. It embarrasses. Never bathe nude in public places.

4) Successive Community Councils in Findhorn have sought (rightly in my view) to preserve the architectural character of the village. Should you purchase or rent a dwelling in the village, take heed of local planning regulations.

5) Don't remove stones from the beach, or 'back shore' as it is often called. The Foundation used beach stones to decorate the roof of the Universal Hall in the 70s. Although done with the permission of the local estate owners this was met with a singularly poor reception locally. During

the 80s large sums of public money were spent on protecting the village from the effects of coastal erosion. Even if you imagine the consequences of a few handfuls of missing stones will be negligible, it is an insensitive and unnecessary activity.

5) Take an interest, but don't interfere. Some locals complain that the Foundation does not contribute enough to local activities. Others complain when Community members do.

Some of the difficulties local people have with the Community seem to stem back to the very early days, and in particular to the persona of Peter Caddy. On being asked "What is the relation of the Community to its greater environment?" he replied:

"First of all, I would like to point out the importance of obeying the laws of the land and the customs of the land which you are in. So in the area around here . . . don't go swimming naked on the beach or upset people in other ways. Flow with them. As Eileen's guidance used to say, adapt, adjust, accommodate.

Some people seem to feel that it's good to blow other people's minds, as it were. Well, that doesn't help at all. So don't upset people by wearing clothing or behaving in a manner that's going to make you stand out and draw adverse comments, etc."[12]

As an ex-manager of a large local hotel he was certainly well aware of local sensitivities. Nonetheless, many of Peter's comments, particularly on the subject of the 'vast city of light' that Eileen's guidance predicted they were building, still rankle in the local memory.

From today's perspectives, the challenges of creating an

---

[12] These words were spoken nearly 20 years ago. Although the principle remains, certainly things have changed since then, and there is no reason to suppose the youth of Forres today is any more or any less in the cultural fast lane than their metropolitan peers. As early as 1960 the Beatles (or Silver Beetles as they were then called) toured Scotland including a gig at Forres Town Hall. According to 'The Scotsman' of 12.3.94 'They were paid a pittance and their finances were so precarious they did a runner from the Royal Hotel.'

ecological showpiece on a 22-acre caravan park are so daunting that the vision of a 'vast city' perhaps appears an unnecessarily large ambition. Certainly, modest and continuing growth of the Community membership notwithstanding, the Foundation has no plans to purchase significant amounts of land on the Findhorn peninsula or anywhere else. Can the God who spoke through Eileen really be planning an influx of tens or hundreds of thousands of spiritual seekers to this small corner of Scotland? It seems highly unlikely.

Maybe the idea was intended to refer to large groups of invisible attendants. It is also true that the current Community occupies a relatively large geographical area, but with a very diffuse population. Furthermore, modern communication methods offer some astounding options, and it may be that the Foundation's connection to the Internet computer communication super-highway with its possibilities of distance learning, will in time lead to thousands of people participating in the work of the Community without causing undue stress to West Moray's physical infrastructure. Perhaps we should anticipate a 'virtual' metropolis.

Whatever the future holds, the entire episode highlights the difficulties of distinguishing between metaphor and literal truth when considering channelled material of this nature.

The Foundation has also been accused of unfairly purloining the name 'Findhorn' which, it is alleged, should more properly refer only to the village. It is true that up until the end of the 1970s the Community fairly freely referred to itself as 'Findhorn', but policy has been to avoid that whenever possible for over a decade. Mistakes are occasionally made, and no doubt a few exist within these pages, but the issue is not as simple as that.

Just as RAF personnel refer to 'Kinloss' when they mean the air base, and academics refer to 'Cambridge' when they mean the University, no one has a monopoly on a name. In fact the derivation of the word 'Findhorn' is not absolutely clear. It may come from Invererne and mean 'at the mouth of the river Erne' or Fionn-Dearn, 'the white river Dearn'. Either way, although 'Findhorn' may not belong to the Foundation, the facts are that its headquarters are located by the Findhorn Bay, in the Community Council electoral ward of Findhorn, immediately adjacent to the historic village of Findhorn. Further confusion of this nature is frankly unavoidable.

It is no doubt extremely aggravating to be a resident of West Moray who happens to live in Findhorn to be mistaken for someone whose lifestyle you do not care for, but there is really very little the Foundation or Community can do about that except to be sensitive to such feelings and hope that perhaps one day Scotland and the Scots will be proud to have been the birthplace of an extraordinary and lasting experiment in positive human values. In the meantime all that can be suggested is that we continue to try to find ways of reaching a mutual understanding.

Finally, this is perhaps the place to settle a minor wrong the New Age has perpetrated on Scotland. It has become commonplace to see the following inspirational quote attributed to a German gentleman called Goethe.

Until one is committed there is hesitancy, the chance to draw back, always ineffectiveness. Concerning all acts of initiative and creation there is one elementary truth the ignorance of which kills countless ideas and splendid plans. That the moment one definitely commits oneself, then Providence moves too. All sorts of thing occur to help one that would otherwise never have occurred. A whole stream of events issues from the decision raising in one's favour all manner of unforeseen incidents and meetings and material assistance, which no man could have dreamt would have come his way.

In fact these words were penned by W.H. Murray, a leading Scottish writer and mountaineer. Continued misappropriation of these thoughts can only fuel Scotland's habitual sense of injustice, which surely her magnificent contribution to human endeavour does not merit.

A Meditation on the City of Light

Imagine yourself in the Sanctuary at the Park on a winters evening. Drawing on the meditational practice of more than three decades it is easy to envision oneself bathed in a mystical glow of divine inspiration which surrounds this spot, and indeed overlights all the Community buildings on the caravan site. Picture the light as it shines from the Community Centre, Guest Lodge, Universal Hall, and all the individual dwellings where Community members meditate and ask for spiritual guidance.

Widening our field of vision we can see this light reaching out to touch the radiance surrounding nearby properties such as Cullerne, Minton, Station House and a handful of other properties in the nearby village. Rising into the night sky it is easy to see this formation stretching out to greet the great Angel of Cluny and its partners which overlight Newbold House, Drumduan and other places in the town of Forres.

This hub of luminosity is in itself connected, both metaphorically upward towards the heavens and the inspiration of yet greater divine beings, and also horizontally, out into the forests surrounding the town where Community activities add their own unique contribution to the dance of light.

This constellation has tendrils stretching further afield away in the darkness of the night is Glen Affric where the dreams of the tree planters add a sparkle , and out on the Atlantic shore there are Erraid and Iona.

We are now beyond any concept of a human city, but travelling a national and international highway, for the gleam of small centres in the cities to the south is just over the horizon. Beyond that are Glastonbury, London, Europe, the Americas, Asia and Australia the Planetary Network of the New Age.

These images will be familiar to most of you, but let us now return our awareness to the smaller scale of Morayshire. With a little change in our focus we can surely see that the Community's contribution to the glow of angelic inspiration is but a single hue in a multi-coloured and multi-dimensional inner landscape. In every town and village there are churches, quiet good deeds, and the simple prayers of children. Everywhere there is the compassion of those working in the medical profession, the hope of teachers, the strength of those involved in law enforcement, the building of solid family virtues, and the religious practices of a hundred different denominations and faiths. From this perspective the City of Light is not a few strands of hope in an ocean of darkness, but a great and complex web of inspiration which lends comfort and offers vision to those struggling to find a way out of the remaining pockets of gloom and twilight.

Not everyone may use the same metaphors as ourselves, but all these activities are surely part of the City of Light too. If our task is one which sometimes claims a little more attention in the global media, that should not be thought of as a measure of its quality. As we return our awareness to the humble timber-framed building at the centre of the Foundations work let us keep in our awareness that we are neither as individuals nor as a Community alone in our hope for a better world, and that there are many people in the local area who are willing to hear what we have to say, if we are similarly willing to listen to them.

READING LIST

George Bain; *The River Findhorn From Source to Sea*; Nairnshire Telegraph; 1911

Robert Burns; *Poems*: Selected and edited by Beattie and Meikle; Penguin; 1977. There are other collections of equal quality.

Nora Chadwick; *The Celts*; Pelican; 1970

Martin Cook; *The Birds of Moray and Nairn*; Mercat Press; 1992. A comprehensive guide to all avian species to be found in these counties. In the early 80s I observed a chough perched on the fence between Pineridge and the Bichans' farm. There are no authenticated records of this colourful member of the crow family in Moray, so you may guess how I feel.

Frank Fraser Darling & J. Morton Boyd; *The Highlands and Islands*; Fontana; 1969

Ian K. Dawson; *The Findhorn Railway*; Oakwood Press; Undated.

Findhorn: A Scottish Village; Findhorn Press; 1981. A short history and guide to the traditional settlement.

Di Francis; *My Highland Kellas Cats*; Jonathan Cape; 1993

Alasdair Gray; *Lanark: A Life in Four Books*; Picador; 1991. If you find Scott's style too inaccessible, try this surreal masterpiece instead.

Neil Gunn; *The Silver Darlings*; Faber; 1969. A tale of the herring fishers who lived on the northern coasts visible from the beach at Findhorn.

Christopher Harvie; *No Gods and Precious Few Heroes: Scotland 1914-80*; Edward Arnold; 1981

Michael Havers, Edward Grayson and Peter Shankland; *The Royal Baccarat Scandal*; Souvenir; 1988. Alas for the Gordon-Cumming family whose ill-luck reappeared in 1890 when Sir William was accused of cheating at cards in the presence of the Prince of Wales. A *cause célèbre* in Victorian society.

T.D. Lauder; *An Account of the Great Floods of August 1829*; J. McGillivary; 1873

Fionn MacColla; *And the Cock Crew*; Souvenir; 1977. Although appalled by the treatment of his countrymen and women in the Clearances, Neil Gunn was essentially an optimist. MacColla's dark tale has a very different slant.

Hugh MacDiarmid; *Selected Poems*: Selected and edited by Craig and Manson; Penguin; 1970. Arguably Scotland's finest 20th century poet. Like Burns he chose a deliberately archaic style which makes his work hard going for the non-native.

Charles McKean; *The District of Moray: An Illustrated Architectural Guide*; Scottish Academic Press; 1987. A fascinating compendium of architectural heritage, themes and oddities. Brodie Castle, the Crown and Anchor, Drumduan, the Universal Hall and Forres Academy all have their place. Cluny Hill College is described as 'suitably exotic'.

Caitlin Matthews; *The Elements of the Celtic Tradition*; Element; 1991

J.A. MacCulloch; *The Religion of the Ancient Celts* ; Constable 1991. First published in 1911.

W.H. Murray; *The Islands of Western Scotland*; Eyre Methuen; 1973; *The Scottish Himalayan Expedition*; J.M. Dent; 1951. The quotation is from pages 6-7.

Donald Omand; *The Moray Book*; Paul Harris; 1976

Stuart Piggott; *The Druids*; Pelican; 1974

John Prebble; *The Lion in the North*; Penguin; 1973. Probably the most readable Scottish history in print. Prebble has produced a fine selection of more specific histories including: *Glen Coe*; Penguin; 1966; *Culloden*; Penguin; 1967; *The Highland Clearances*; Penguin; 1963

Sinclair Ross; *The Culbin Sands: Fact and Fiction*; University of Aberdeen; 1992

Sir Walter Scott; *Ivanhoe*; Everyman; 1983

W.D.H. Sellar (editor); *Moray: Province and People*; Scottish Society for Northern Studies; 1993

Andrew Sinclair; *The Sword and the Grail*; Century; 1993. Although somewhat elliptical in style this book is well worth persevering with. It concerns two fascinating Scottish historical mysteries — the founding of a Scottish colony in Nova Scotia 90 years before Columbus voyaged to the Americas, and the role of the Knights Templar in providing a crucial link between more ancient Gnostic traditions and the emergence of Scottish Freemasonry. Watch out for the brief appearance of ex-Community member Marianna Lines who played a part in the detective work.

Robert Louis Stevenson; *Treasure Island*; Canongate; 1988; *Kidnapped*; Canongate; 1988. David Balfour, the hero of this latter tale, was marooned for a while on the Isle of Erraid. Stevenson's father was involved in the construction of the nearby lighthouses, and the young Robert Louis knew the island well. He was eventually to become Scotland's greatest 19th century novelist.

Elizabeth Sutherland; *Ravens and Black Rain: The Story of Second Sight*; Constable; 1985

Kenny Taylor; *Local Heroes*; BBC Wildlife Magazine; May 1992. An article about the dolphins of the Moray Firth.

Nigel Tranter; *Robert the Bruce* (three volumes); Coronet; 1972; *Montrose*; Coronet; 1972. This prolific author has produced novels covering most important aspects of Scottish history. His romanticised style does not appeal to everyone, but his research into the known facts is apparently meticulous.

Ten

Decision-Making Structures

*In genuine community there are no sides. It is not always
easy, but by the time they reach community the members
have learned how to give up cliques and factions. They
have learned how to listen to each other and how not to
reject each other. Sometimes consensus in the community
is reached with miraculous rapidity. But at other times it
is arrived at only after lengthy struggle. Just because it is
a safe place does not mean community is a place without
conflict. It is, however, a place where conflict can be
resolved without physical or emotional bloodshed and with
wisdom as well as grace. A community is a group that can
fight gracefully.*

M. Scott Peck, *The Different Drum*

This section is different from all the others in the collection
for it is intended to be a solution to a problem, not just a
description or statement of existing philosophy, history or
practice. Before going on to describe what this problem is,
and how it came to be, we begin with a brief overview of the
subject of decision-making as experienced in the Community.

There is then an extract from David Spangler's paper on
'Growth, Authority and Power' (the GAP) which provided
much of the philosophical framework for dealing with these
issues during the 1970s and 80s. For two years this formed
the basis of regular seminars where most of the membership
worked out their authority issues. The lessons learned in those
heated discussions were to carry the Community long after
they ceased being held.

The next section is a history of decision-making procedures
in the Foundation prior to 1994 by Gordon Cutler. Gordon
has been a member of the Community for nearly twenty years
and has given frequent talks on the history of the Community.
This paper covers part of the period discussed in Section 2

but with a specific emphasis on 'Community politics'.

There then follows a short paper on personal decision making authored by the 'Center for the Living Force'. This is another study paper from the 70s but one which strikes a quite different tone from the GAP paper. Some may find its tone verges on the patronising, but its simple wisdom provided considerable inspiration during the work which was required to complete the final paper in this Section.

The subsequent piece on 'The Problem of Individual Empowerment versus Collective Responsibility' identifies reasons why even those with a comprehensive understanding of the above ideas were experiencing confusion when it came to the details of carrying out important decisions in the Community of the 1990s. During the spring of 1994 the Foundation carried out a fairly lengthy exercise designed to clarify all major decision-making systems. This paper also outlines the attempts that were made to find answers to these challenges during this period, and contains a commentary on the agreed procedures.

There is then a listing of the details of these Agreed Decision-Making Procedures for reference purposes.

At the time of writing it is far too early to tell whether these agreements will resolve the difficulties they address. No doubt many amendments will be made in the future. Certainly those familiar with the constitutions of less experimental organisations will shake their heads in disbelief at some of the provisions. It does however seem to me that their existence is a testimony to the high levels of goodwill and dedication to the creation of a workable collective lifestyle which exist in the Foundation.

OVERVIEW OF THE COMMUNITY EXPERIENCE

Alex Walker

"How do you make decisions here?" is one of the most commonly asked questions by guests on our introductory programmes. This frequency is perhaps because Community life often appears relatively harmonious and orderly to such an observer. This contrast with the hurry and aggression of commercial life, the deadness of bureaucratic existence, and the difficulties encountered in both ordinary social interaction and modern political squabblings seems at first to be considerable. Indeed the truth is that the Community has found remarkable success in creating harmony within a wide range of cultural backgrounds.

Beneath all of this apparent tranquillity there are of course complex and thorny problems that have to be addressed, many of them concerned with issues of power and control. However, before we examine the difficulties that exist let us first take a look at some of the positive qualities and practices that have come to be.

An answer to the above question might include some of the following ideas:

1) Service — First and foremost all of the members of the Community are (ideally) people who joined because they wanted to put service to God before their personal preferences and desires. All discussions therefore start from the premise that everyone involved has the interest of the whole at heart. In such a context there is little to be gained in the long term by someone attempting to put personal, departmental or a factional interest before this utilitarian ideal.

2) Attunement — as explained in Section 5, all activities are carried out in an atmosphere which encourages more than a philosophical attachment to the ideal of service. A wide range of specific practices are constantly carried out which aim to actualise this ideal.

3) Management Structures — An attitude of collective endeavour is encouraged because the hierarchy of authority structures is relatively flat. There are only three identifiable levels:
that of member[1], that of departmental focaliser or manager,
and that of the Management Committee — see 'Administrative Structure' diagram. Furthermore, because Community
activities are much wider in scope than those of a business,
an individual frequently finds that this morning's departmental focaliser will be this afternoon's foot soldier on the clean-
up crew. Such changes tend to discourage managerial airs
and graces.

4) Focalisation itself is not intended to be a line management
function in the ordinary sense of the word. There are elements of authority that a focaliser carries but ideally this should
be more because of the qualities the individual embodies than
because the bureaucracy offers them a position of power
(again, see also Section 5).

5) Flexibility — A very large number of decisions need to be
taken in everyday life in the Community. The first principle
is to ensure that everyone who ought to be involved is
involved. There is a high degree of cross-departmental collaboration. Furthermore, many decisions which might simply
be forced through in other organisations are referred to some
wider group, or given a further period of consideration if consensus cannot be reached.

6) Commitment — It takes time and effort to create an authentic sense of community. Neither the Foundation nor its asso-

---

[1]The concept of a 'member of the Foundation' is a very basic one, and
it adequately and clearly described a certain cadre of people. However,
as the Foundation is a charitable trust this 'membership' was purely a
useful descriptive technique, not a legal term to describe a relationship
to a cooperative or similar institution. Confusion between the two ideas
is a classic case of an inability to distinguish the legal and administrative realms — see below. At the time of writing the concept of 'Foundation member' is under review, this category perhaps being replaced
by those of staff and student. If, as seems likely, the term ceases to have
a formal use, minor amendments will be required to the procedures
described later in this Section.

ciated endeavours are created to maximise profits, and while it may be that some of the practices widely used in the Community might be helpful to industry at large, there is an inevitable tension between effective participation and efficient business. Community activities tend to stress the former rather than the latter.

Perhaps this tension may recede in the world as it is clear that 'efficient business practice' is all too often a euphemism for producing short-term gains at the expense of longer-term economic and social sustainability. Note also however that Community life is not free from ordinary economic constraints, and that all organisations strive to find an appropriate balance between these two needs.

GROWTH, AUTHORITY AND POWER

David Spangler

(The following is an abridgement, with interpolations, of the transcript of a talk given by David Spangler to the Community in late November or early December 1973. This version has been edited by Gordon Cutler. In its original form it is part of 'The Seventh Ray' in the Original Series of Study Papers.)

One of the lessons the Community offers is how to come to creative terms with the energies of 'authority' and 'power' and how they relate to the growth of both the individual and the Community.

A question before us is: "How can we best serve our own indwelling God-source and the God-source of the whole within which we might be functioning at any given time?" In looking for an answer or answers we need to consider the following points.

Freedom and disciplined action taken in harmony with the whole are interrelated terms. For example, I have more freedom when my being is enhanced through the energy that is invoked by synergistic cooperative work with others than I can attain by myself. Movement (or action) is never carried out in isolation. Even if alone in a room or a forest, one moves in relation to the walls or the trees that surround one. Much of the joy of movement comes through the awareness of this relationship.

Dance illustrates this very well. I am sure many of you have experienced the pleasure and joy of dancing with another, blending not only your movements, but your partner's into an interweaving wholeness which you could not achieve singly. Life is a dance and its enhancement, glory and greater freedom come through both our relationships within ourselves and with our 'greater' selves as represented by the people and other kingdoms of life that make up our environment.

In order to achieve this freedom, I need to have awareness; I need to know how to blend and how to move in harmony.

If someone enters the dance who is stronger and more grace-ful I must find how I can blend what I am in the loving respect that is due to what I now become in relationship to this stronger force that has entered my environment. Perhaps I will feel threatened, will seek to alter the dance, minimise the steps this stronger dancer can take or even leave the dance itself. But none of these options solves the essential challenge of how to relate to a stronger force on the one hand or a lesser force on the other. How do I relate so that I do not become a satellite orbiting the stronger force? How do I relate so that no satellites orbit me?

The idea of personal liberty is a divine idea; but if it is glamorised, it can become an illusion blocking the way to true freedom. However, as an ideal it is still very potent, so we struggle for liberty and freedom. We struggle against what appears to represent authority and appears to be telling us what to do. Sometimes we get so engrossed in the struggle that that is all we live for; and if we lose it we lose our rea-son for being. Thus before a person can clearly perceive the new cycle and the possibilities it represents, she or he must be clear about these concepts of strength, identity, power and authority.

My response to a strong dancer should be to move in strength to that person and try to grow from that strength and to recognise greater capacities of dancing I may grow into. But I may feel threatened, and so I may shrink from the dancer; or I may feel submissive, so I simply submit and provide no creative direction for that dancer to work against.

When we deny authority in another we are really denying it in our own being. We cannot have authority and deny it at the same time. My authority comes only when I can recog-nise a strength in others which calls out my own strength. Otherwise what I have is not authority but illusion, the glam-our of separation, of being different than, other than, better than and stronger than other beings. Thus authority cannot be dealt with or resolved on the level of reaction to form.

Since power, like money, tends to have bad connotations

in various quarters, it is time that we deeply examine what is meant by it. Humanity has a right to power and at some point in our evolution we have to learn to embody it with wisdom. There may be some question as to the form of expression used in the Aureolis soul-scripts[2], but what they say, in essence, is very true. I am power; and the sooner I recognise it, the sooner I'll be able to move in harmony with the power that resides in others. We think of power as a force that dominates, but it is also a force that serves, and without it we have no capacity to serve. There must be power within me before I can grow, some kind of vitality and surge of life before I can accomplish anything. If I shy away from power then I may not be able to fulfil my part within the dance. If I glamorise power and assume it is most important and enjoy its exercise over other people, then I am not expressing true power. I am expressing my ignorance and have caught myself in a trap. Many people refuse to invoke this particular energy of their divinity except in ways which might be comfortable for them or their environment . . . but God never said that we were here to be comfortable; only to express the sacredness within us.

God is infinitely small and infinitely large; but wherever he is, he is power. It is for this reason that the Community is founded not on guidance from St Germain or an angel, but on guidance from God. This brings us face to face with a concept which must be resolved because every new cycle revolves around a change in humanity's identification of God. Peter and Eileen have a responsibility to help this identification change and the Community does as well. I have noticed quite a number of times that this change is viewed as one aspect versus another, i.e. How can we be free of the domination or presence of guidance or someone's attunement? But the challenge is not to be free of Eileen's or Peter's or anyone's attunement, but to be strong and aware and centred and clear; to be balanced and powerful, loving and wise in one's own attunement, to discover one's own authority. With authority comes responsibility, which is nothing more than the ability to respond with power, with sensitivity, with awareness, and with an appreciation of the whole which is the dance in which one is participating.

The concept of freedom is not freedom from something, but freedom to be. If you think something in your environment is keeping you from being, then you are operating under illusion, the illusion of your essential powerlessness and your lack of divinity. The spiritual life imposes an incredible discipline, but one that leads to freedom, the freedom that God expresses. That is a freedom which most people have yet to comprehend because they are thinking in terms of personal, separated self-freedom, a freedom from that which would limit them, when they are that which limits themselves.

The right that I have is the right to invoke and be Divine. That does not mean we all have to think the same thoughts, feel the same feelings, be the same being, because we are not all the same. We are individual manifestations of divinity and we have a uniqueness to respect and to manifest. Where does this freedom lead us? There is no freedom without awareness. If I am part of a group, if I am being nourished by a communal ritual, then I owe it my awareness. I owe it a sensitivity and the responsibility to fulfil it and myself. By fulfilling it I am also fulfilled. This means walking a fine line of balance and subtle awareness. I am sure that in seeking this line, in seeking to embody this principle, the Community will have its challenges.

People are asked here to embody something which they thought they could not embody or that they did not wish to embody. When serving as focalisers they have to learn how to express authority and responsibility. When not serving as focalisers they have to grow into their responsibility and authority; so that we become partners in a dance and not marchers in a military formation or workers in a factory. There is no simple solution to this except awareness and love and understanding.

Quite often people who end up in focalisers' positions are people who have little desire to be there, but it's a point of growth, so that is where they got stuck. They may feel uncomfortable learning to express authority because they don't want to be a boss. They may not have discovered what true focalisation means; how to reflect the energies in a way that they become clearer and more easily worked with, so the tune is more easily heard and we can dance in greater harmony with it. So in this process extremes may be expressed; there may be uncomfortable moments, but these are a part of growth and this is a growing organism.

As a growing organism the Community often incorporates patterns it later may have to reject because they cannot be integrated. Yesterday I talked about how we have to learn not to judge, but we also have to learn to discriminate. To judge means to put a label on a situation or a person which is absolute, which is somehow indicating that this is part of an individual's nature. But to discriminate is simply to say that this person, this event, this thing is not in the right place in the dance; therefore this person is stepping on everybody's toes and having their own stepped on. This is uncomfortable and unfulfilling so let's find where the right dance for this person is. In any community that is organic there must be this process of attunement, rapport, resonance and discrimination so that the whole ritual is fulfilled; not just the community's well-being, but the well-being of the entire operation. This may require an ability to perceive that the true and proper place for an individual is somewhere else. If this process is understood it can be worked with creatively.

Obviously discrimination can slip easily into judgement, or appear to do so, unless awareness and understanding are exercised and they who have responsibility for the dance of the Community can perceive beyond the level of the personality into the level of awareness that seeks fulfilment for every person.

It is easy to look at specific forms of expression and to say that someone who does not fulfil them is not New Age or part of the Community; it's easy for vegetarians to say meat-eaters are not with it; it is easy for meat-eaters to look at vegetarians and say they are protein-starved. All these dualities are possible; all of these conflicts are possible if we make them possible. But that is not the level on which we will find our power or our authority or our growth. They can be found only on the level where you can recognise that if you are fulfilling the dance, then you are part of it. If you are not, then you are not, so then find out where you can fulfil it. If a vegetarian has to dance with a meat-eater and they are dancing in step it does not matter what their diet is.

It is the essence that we have to look at and not get hung up on the levels where traditionally people have battled for freedom, power and authority. If you deny or resist authority in another, then you deny and resist it in yourself, for it is not through conflict that you discover who you are; it is by affirming what you are, rather than affirming another's power over you, that you begin this great epic of discovery. It means you have a responsibility to the organism that you are participating in to be whole; without wholeness there cannot be the kind of growth required.

If you encounter what could be negativity or a lack of wholeness, you may find plenty within you to respond in kind. Don't. Be true to what you can perceive as your responsibility to the whole, rather than just your emotions. That simply means that if I want to find what is negative about the Community, I can do so very easily because there are a lot of things about it that are not perfect. Because it is an organism in a process of growth, struggling against the imperfections we have been creating for the past centuries, it is not going to change overnight. I have to find how I can blend with it before I can find how I can change it and give it a living, growing vitality. I cannot do this if I have separated myself. Does this mean we never utter a negative word? No; let's not idealise being positive; let's not idealise anything, let us act with awareness. Be prepared to listen as well as to talk; it is in communication that you will grow together.

Help the organism to grow, for thus your own abilities will grow. You will experience the taking on of responsibility which brings authority, the awareness which brings true power, and the love which makes all these things possible, and without which there is no authority and there is no power. This is not just a community. It never has been. It is something beyond that. It is not a place where people can come and live and hope that it's better than the suburbs they left elsewhere. It is a working organism seeking to accomplish what no group has yet accomplished in the history of humankind. Perceive deeply the splendour and magnificence of what you are involved in. Embrace it with awareness, wisdom, and the kind of love that is not sympathetic, but rhythmic, harmonious and attuned to the dance, that wishes for each person that freedom and joy that comes from being in the right dance, in the right movement, and the ability to grow as the dance grows.

THE DEVELOPMENT OF
DECISION-MAKING STRUCTURES

Gordon Cutler

Theocracy

From the very first day of Peter, Eileen and Dorothy's arrival in 'the Hollow'[3], the Community functioned as a theocracy. Guidance, in the form of Eileen's prophetic visions and practical daily directions, Dorothy's devic advice, and Peter's intuition, was inseparably interwoven with the flow of daily life. Dorothy and Eileen wrote down what they received and Peter carried it out. Peter also shared their role in his creation of the garden. The guidance did not always detail directions, yet Peter, once he "had stuck the spade in the soil . . . would know what to do next". Many ideas actually originated with him, and he then received confirmation from Eileen. No major activities or decisions were undertaken or made unless her guidance gave approval. This pattern continued essentially unchanged for the next twelve years and is still visible, albeit with greatly varying degrees of skill and attunement, in every level of decision making in the Community today. Essentially, Peter functioned as patriarch of a family.

A Learning Theocracy

The arrival of David Spangler in June 1970 marked the beginning of an extended period of development and population growth that was to last for the next nine years. The first six months of his stay saw a 300% increase in membership followed by a further 100% increase in 1971. He quickly began to share Peter's role as director and initiator, and Eileen's role as provider of guidance.

His intuitive and humorous grasp of theory meshed well with Peter's pragmatic spirituality. This collaboration resulted

---

[3] The north-west corner of the Findhorn Bay Caravan Park where the 'original caravan' came to rest.

not only in a theocracy where learning awareness, be it via attunement, running a printing press or studying spiritual principles and concepts (such as synergy and group consciousness) was the prime focus, but also in a community where spontaneity, creativity and humour were highly prized. This environment would support the Community for the next several years, and despite the growth in membership its success largely eliminated the need to change the structures of governance and decision making.

Thus, the patriarchal structure established at the beginning continued until the spring of 1973 when David and a large group of members left for North America. Despite the increasing complexity of the Community (the emergence of regular work departments which performed more complex tasks, etc.), Peter still retained a close awareness of day to day activities (though he would gladly let those who knew their business get on with it) and their co-ordination within a strategic framework. No organisational charts existed as there was virtually no organisation. Peter drew on advisors as needed: aside from the Trustees who met yearly there was only a Finance Committee — everything else was done ad hoc. The major change during this period was of course the cessation in 1971 of Eileen's daily guidance for the Community. She had received that many members were becoming too dependent on her guidance and that it was time that they start turning within to get their own. She continued, however, to provide guidance on major issues and decisions.

The Focalisers' Group was created in the late winter of 1973. Peter met with them twice-weekly, mostly to explain policy and co-ordinate activities, but also sometimes to decide where a new member should work. Eileen's abandonment of her previous task meant that Peter was more than ever out front as the role model for many members. Thus focalisers, even on 'kitchen clean-up', more often than not functioned essentially as little Peters. Their meetings were secret and as a rule neither notes nor minutes were shared in the departments.

A Widening Oligarchy — Core Group

In December 1973, Eileen received guidance to create the Core Group, which also specified who should belong to it. This anticipated the travelling or 'planetary work' that Peter and Eileen would be undertaking. It met on average five days a week, though in the beginning it was more of a class for Peter to teach than a decision-making group. In the following year when Peter and Eileen's opportunities to travel and lecture arose, the Core Group started to come into its own. It held strategic and spiritual awareness and functioned as a management committee. It was also self-perpetuating since its remaining members always chose the replacements for departing ones.

By the beginning of 1975, Peter no longer met regularly with the Focalisers' Group as the Core Group took up most of his attention. The start of the Universal Hall's construction required more sophisticated planning and administration which led to several people moving into roles that had previously been occupied only by Peter and a couple of others. A.D. 'Dick' Barton had joined in June 1974 as General Secretary with the brief to help the Community deal with its current growth as well as prepare for future expansion. Information which just two years earlier had been tightly restricted was now flowing more easily. Core Group deliberations were still secret, but Focalisers' notes and discussions no longer were, and were being circulated in work departments and in a Community newsletter, the forerunner of the present-day 'Rainbow Bridge'.

From mid-1974 to mid-1975 various committees, including the General Office and Education Branch, were created and the Personnel Department was firmly established. The Finance Committee continued its weekly meetings as before. To help smooth the transition to a more complex organisation, Dick began producing the Community's first ever organisational charts. They served the dual function of illustrating both the layout of the organisation and its cosmological context using some of the symbolism of the Arcane School and that from his own transpersonal experiences[4]. Thus one knew not only one's location within the Community, but also the Community's place within the scheme of creation.

Despite the increasing complexity and the spreading of responsibility among a larger number of people, the Community retained its sense of cohesiveness and wholeness. The existence of a strong internal education programme and the fact that leadership flowed from the ability to teach (both by example and by articulating the application of spiritual principles to daily experiences) helped to create an organisational climate which was essentially educational rather than administrative. If decisions turned out to be mistakes, the attitude was "Let's learn from them"; little energy was wasted on assigning blame.

The structure of the Community was now very visible. It would not change radically, despite the ups and downs of membership and guest totals, for the next 14 years. Only in the late summer of 1975 were the first community meetings held on the subject of expansion, brought on as they were by the negotiations to purchase Cluny Hill Hotel. They were only discussion forums since it was understood and accepted that the Core Group would make the final decision. Although community meetings would become an occasional feature of life in the Community, occurring at approximately two- or three-month intervals, they were generally used to discuss and ratify processes. (Important exceptions were decisions such as hosting the 3rd World Wilderness Congress and buying the Caravan Park.) In general terms this pattern continued on into 1987.

---

[4] In line with the Community's education culture, Dick created an Admin study group, known as the Red Group. Though it met only for six months, it conducted the first essential theoretical and planning discussions on how we might run Cluny Hill Hotel in the event we purchased it. Its members shared their deliberations with friends and in work departments, thereby supporting the discussions about the possible Cluny purchase going on in the Community.

Expansion

The subsequent purchase of Cluny, the arrival of, on average, over 7,000 guests during each of the next four years and the simultaneous doubling of the membership to over 300 resulted in a bloating of the management and administrative structure. Problems were compounded by the high turnover of administrators — a feature which exists to this day. Peter was often away on tour and thus inexorably began to lose touch with the detailed workings of the Community's organisation. Although his intention was to hand over day to day running to the Core Group, he in fact found it difficult to do so. Too often on returning from trips he would find himself confronted with people in positions whom he did not know or decisions of which he did not approve. The temptation to step in or to deal only with those people he did know was often too much to resist. One example was his raiding of several departments for people to start the renovation of Drumduan when the Core Group had previously decided that the Cluny renovations and the Hall construction should be completed first. Through his actions he undermined both the authority and the morale of the people he wanted to take responsibility for the Community.

The antiquated accounting system could not keep up with the expansion, resulting in regular twelve- to twenty-week delays in providing monthly reports, which made it difficult to impose spending controls and meant that important decisions were often taken without accurate financial information. The establishment of a Management Committee in place of the old Finance Committee in late 1976 was intended to help stem the flow of red ink as was the creation in 1978 of a Management/Finance Department. The best that could be said was that it managed the flow of red ink, essentially prolonging the day of reckoning. It was difficult to deal with this last problem because Peter considered the debt a temporary blip to be solved by purchasing yet another property to be opened up as a workshop centre. In other words consolidation through expansion. (He could not accept that in 1979 for the first time there was a small but noticeable decline in the number of guests.) Some, such as the Personnel focaliser, wanted to reduce the membership to 240 from the then current 320 and revitalise internal education. Others thought all that was needed to resolve both issues was to reorganise the structure, so much of the spring and summer of that year was engaged in a series of discussions about a number of competing reorganisation proposals. None of them was ever adopted.

In late spring 1979 when Peter called all the members of Personnel, Management, Core Group, Education Branch, Internal Trustees and Focalisers to a meeting in Drumduan to introduce François Duquesne as his successor, there were nearly 60 people, or more than 20% of the Community's adult population, present in the room. The over-staffing of administration could not have been more apparent.

At the end of the fiscal year 1979, the reality of the financial crisis hit home. Membership as well as guest numbers fell drastically following Peter's departure and for two years the Foundation tottered on the edge of bankruptcy. An advantage of this was the lightening of the administrative load. Committees such as Core Group and Management with up to 40% fewer members began functioning more swiftly and efficiently. Despite the difficult financial circumstances, and greatly aided by the 'Village Council'[5], the sense of Community identity remained strong; decision-making remained apolitical and unencumbered by long consensus-building processes. Thus, as the financial problems were gradually sorted out, the Community was by 1983 able to complete the Universal Hall, host the 3rd World Wilderness Congress, and make the big commitment to purchase the Caravan Park. These decisions were quickly arrived at with great unanimity of purpose.

---

[5] Most of whose members were not part of the administrative structure. Created in part as a response to the management failures of the late 70s, it served as a discussion forum that provided useful feedback for François and Core Group. It met through most of 1980 and had dissolved itself by mid-1981.

Grass Roots Involvement

In 1983 Jay Jerman took over Foundation focalisation from François. During his three years in the job little changed in terms of decision making and management. Two groups were added: the Land Commissioners to oversee the right and non-exploitive use of the Foundation's properties, and the Village Environment Group (now called Park Planning Group) to act as the Community equivalent to the Planning Committees that are found in local governments throughout the Western world. Whereas François had had to devote the majority of his time to sorting out the Foundation's finances and arranging the caravan park purchase, Jay was able to focus much more on the membership which, following the successful fundraising campaign, resulted in a strengthening of our sense of collective identity and purpose. Community meetings did not occur very often and still tended to be relaxed affairs; Park Family Meetings functioned nearly as much as tea and scone 'socials' as formal meetings.

Developments which had commenced in the mid-1980s, such as the Design Studio becoming a privately run business, and the shifting of profit-oriented departments such as the Phoenix into the separate New Findhorn Directions Ltd, continued[6]. These developments as they multiplied resulted in a manifold increase in social and organisational complexity. No longer was it possible for many members to talk knowledgeably about every area of the Community. Additionally those former members taking businesses into the private sector also wanted to maintain some form of connection with the Foundation which was often symbolised by the wish to continue eating in the Community Centre. There were also an increasing number of individuals moving into the area who wanted to associate themselves with the Foundation yet were not willing to become full-time members. These two groups

---

[6] The reasons for this are complex. They ranged from the zeitgeist (it was the high noon of 'privatisation' in the UK), through the strictures of Scottish charitable law, and Home Office requirements that only EC nationals be allowed to undertake commercial employment.

formed the core of what was to become the Associates of the Foundation.

In 1986 Jay released the Foundation focalisation which was taken on by Craig Gibsone. Craig did not initially acquire the unanimity of support that François and Jay had received, and partly as an experiment he encouraged others to move into this role as well. Craig, Roger Benson and Joan Jerman created a joint three-way focalisation for a while. Though this idea worked well, for the first time Community decision making had become more overtly political. There were two contributing social factors that tended to encourage this:

1) a number of long-term members who had been here since the early 70s and provided stability and continuity returned to North America; and

2) the Foundation's own internal education programme had focused progressively less on its own history (particularly its organisation and its ideas) allowing several generations of new members entry with little even rudimentary understanding of how it had been working with the issues of authority and power for the previous 15 years.

Decisions were no longer educational opportunities, but matters that took on almost life and death importance. From this point through to 1993 a relaxed community meeting became a rare event.

In this difficult period Craig's long association with the Community helped give him the confidence to experiment. He encouraged the dissolving of part of the Foundation's boundaries, allowing the Community to expand beyond them. In 1989 the Core Group was selected by the membership for the first time and its executive powers and responsibilities were transferred to the Management Committee. It was to become a meditation group, responsible for 'holding' the spiritual vision of the Community. Out of this process came the concept of the 'mandate'; meaning that all candidates for important positions — such as Foundation Focalisers and those in Education, Administration and Personnel — had to have community-wide approval before they could take up their jobs. The vacuum of experience and education had resulted in a form of participatory democracy that did not often give authority. Increasingly those members sitting in leadership positions complained of being given lots of responsibilities but no authority to carry them out. Consequently, the number of community meetings exploded such that by 1990-91 schedules of community meetings were drawn up a year in advance.

Foundation and Community

By 1990 the identity of the 'Community' had outgrown that of the Foundation: it was simply too small to contain it any longer. This 'open' Community comprised many different aspects such as NFD, private businesses, individuals working closely with the Foundation, and the Foundation itself. As businesses shifted into NFD, members became employees and the Foundation membership slowly declined towards 120 (it sometimes became necessary to hire employees to fill positions that could not be filled from the membership), the tensions of a mixed employment system simmered. In late 1990 and throughout 1991 they broke into a full boil where in numerous meetings many members complained of their loss of privileges (the average new member paid up to £4,000 for the first two years of membership) to employees and associates who were either paid for their work or themselves paid little for their 'membership' in the Community.

The creation of the Development Wing and Building Department with its special rates and agreements further fuelled the debate. The beginnings of a resolution appeared during the Planetary Game held in the Hall in December 1991. By playing the Game together, the associates, members and employees of the Foundation and NFD got, for the first time, a sense of their essential, collective identity. In the two years since then this particular debate has virtually ceased and long-term associates, employees and long-term subscribers to the Open Community 'programme' have been welcomed into the 'Selectorate'[7] of Community members who choose the Foundation focaliser and ratify important decisions.

In early 1991, based on the success of the Development Wing[8] and on the need to get the lumbering, politicised and increasingly diffuse organisation moving again, it was decided to reorganise the Foundation structure into three 'wings': Education, Development and NFD. The focaliser of each, together with the Foundation focaliser and the General Secretary, were to meet fortnightly as the Admin. Group. An added factor was that Craig Gibsone had released Foundation focalisation at the beginning of the year. Judith Bone took it on in a caretaking capacity as the focaliser of Core Group. For the first time in its history the Community had a group leadership with no one strong individual guiding it. The next Foundation focaliser would be Judy Buhler-McAllister who took it on in late spring 1992 after returning from sabbatical.

Admin. met for two years and its members, for the most part, established a good working relationship with each other. But this tended to mean that the communication between the different parts of the organisation took place only at the top. Thus, if there was a problem between the Building Department and the Education Branch Committee, the focalisers did not talk directly to each other, but rather handed it on to their Wing focalisers who took it to Admin. This round-about communication was frustrating as it sometimes meant that a focaliser would first hear of a problem only after someone else had taken it to Admin.

In early 1993, there was a general feeling that the 'Wing System' had fulfilled its function but that a more thorough reorganisation was necessary in order to encourage continued

---

[7] The list of those on the Selectorate is being kept up-to-date for future Core Group selection procedures and as a guide to those eligible to attend certain community meetings. It is essentially made up of members of the Foundation plus a number of long-term Community members living in the locality.

[8] Its focaliser Patrick Nash had turned it into a minimally structured, smoothly functioning department, so it was hoped that the same thing could be done with the Education apparatus including all the Foundation work departments.

development of the educational programmes. In the resulting shake-up Administration (Personnel, Finance & Accounts, Asset Management, Building, Public Relations, etc.) was separated from Education so that the staff of the latter could concentrate on its own administration (brochures, programme co-ordination, logistics, etc.), income making programmes (Guest Department, workshops, trainings, Outreach, etc.), and its 'campuses' (Cluny, Park, Hall, Erraid, etc.). Admin. was replaced by a new Management Committee which consisted of the Foundation, Administration, Education focalisers, the NFD managing director and the focalisers of Cluny and the Park.

As the year progressed Patrick Nash, its first focaliser, was able to pull Administration together and start to give it a sense of coherence and focus. Education proved more intractable[9] as it became apparent that though the old structure had been disposed of nothing much had really changed. The people who still worked in it merely continued with the 'organisation in the mind' much in the same way as the citizens of the re-united Germany have to deal with what they call the 'wall in the mind'. The clearest example of this was the new Faculty Group which quickly became a clone of the old Education Branch Committee assiduously ploughing through its agenda and just as assiduously ignoring its brief to revitalise the Foundation's internal and external educational programmes.

Further impetus was provided by David Spangler in a lecture given to the Community in late July where he warned, among other things, of institutionalisation and passivity, and of becoming a retirement home for the New Age. His comments lent support to those critical of the current status quo within the Foundation; particularly within Education. Within five weeks Loren Stewart, the Education focaliser, called

---

[9] Most of its structures and working culture dated back to the mid-1970s. In nearly twenty years there had been close to ten almost complete changes of personnel. This regular change of generations had resulted in a highly structured, institutionalised mechanism which lacked the flexibility to perceive and respond to the needs of the membership, focusing primarily on visitors' education instead.

together a group of members from mostly outside the Education edifice (although including some from within it) to address this. This group met from September through the winter, revamping the organisation and giving it more flexibility and much more focus on internal education, both formal (lectures, classes) and 'living' (regular work departments). At the time of this writing the question of who will fill which roles is still being worked out, but the changes are already being implemented. What long-term effects these changes will have remains to be seen.

As the writer concludes this document in late March 1994 change is in the air, the future direction of the Foundation finely balanced. Peter Caddy's death in an automobile accident near his home in Germany a month ago marked the end of an era. The Internal Conference in February was one of the most harmonious in several years: a de-politicisation of decision making appears to be under way. The membership is changing yet again with something of a mini-exodus, as has happened so often in the past, taking place. The vital growth of the wider Community; the strengthening of NFD, the evolution of former Foundation departments such as Trees For Life and the Holistic Health Centre into separate organisations; the continued challenges of providing excellence in education, and the difficult relations with many of the residents of Findhorn village illustrate that many of the Foundation's old structures and customs are out of date. The era of the Founders is drawing to a close. The membership of today faces the task of redefining, re-articulating and, most importantly, learning to embody the Foundation's vision and purpose.

PERSONAL DECISIONS

Center for the Living Force

(This material was originally entitled 'Decision Making; Lecture No. 32; Center for the Living Force'. We believe this archive material was channelled by Eva Petriarchos in the mid-1970s as part of a series of talks she and her husband John gave to the Foundation membership, but we have been unable to trace the authors.)

The subject of DECISION is a very, very important one in a person's life, for everything is a decision. This is true not only of your deeds, your obvious and material choices, but it also involves every *emotional attitude* a decision holds. The majority of human beings are incapable of making clear cut and mature decisions. That is why their souls become sick and suffering. That is why a great disorder is created in the soul, which of course leads to confusion and conflicts. For you who are on this path, it might be very beneficial to start to view your life, particularly your conflicts, from that point of view. Have you made a real decision? Have you decided here and there superficially, not weighing, not facing what is involved and then, as a result of it, when things naturally do not turn out to your satisfaction, do you then feel thwarted? Do you then revolt against yourself, your surroundings, and against life in general?

As long as you are living in this sphere of matter, every decision offers two and sometimes more alternatives. With some decisions and in some cases, there are several wrong ways and one right way. Only mature and responsible searching will eventually show you what the right way is. However, in many instances, it actually does not matter on what way you decide, provided the decision has been made whole-heartedly, with awareness, responsibly, not shirking any issues or possible results. Even in the cases where one way would be right or better for you than the other alternatives, it is infinitely healthier for your soul, strange as it may appear at first, if you choose the wrong way but in the right attitude.

Now what is the right and mature attitude with which to decide? The answer is simply to know what you want; to know what is the price involved; to realise that you cannot fully have what you want on this earth sphere because there is always a price or a disadvantage with every alternative; and to be wholly willing to pay the price even before it becomes a certainty that the possible disadvantage may turn out to be true. On the other hand, let us assume you chose by accident the right alternative. (When I say 'by accident', I mean that you have chosen immaturely, with half-closed eyes, not accepting beforehand the disadvantageous side.) In this way, you harm your soul a great deal more than by shouldering a needlessly more difficult alternative because for the moment it just seems better to you for some reason.

By doing it with the right attitude, you responsibly accept the price to be paid. So beware of making your decisions half-heartedly like a child, going into it with closed eyes, wishfully thinking that the price can be evaded. With each alternative lies on one side an advantage and on the other side a disadvantage, as long as you live in the world of matter.

In high spiritual spheres and realms, this negative side does not exist any more. On the other hand, in the lower spheres of darkness, no alternative carries with it an advantage, so to say. In your sphere there is always an advantage and a disadvantage, as long as you have not raised your spiritual development to the point where, even whilst still living in a body in the world of matter, you have worked yourself up to these higher spheres where no disadvantage can befall you. But to reach such a point, you have to go through the laws governing this lower sphere that is rightfully yours for the moment; you have to fully accept these laws and keep them willingly, not being forced by life to do so. Then, and only then, will you reach that point and not by trying to avoid the laws of your own world, no matter what 'spiritual acrobatics' you may try. By the same token, a human being, bound to the world of darkness, will have the very same conditions governing this latter world, in this earth sphere; in the subject just under discussion, as well as in many others.

To love God means naturally, among many other things, to abide by these various laws — and not only to abide by them, but also to accept them willingly. So one of these laws is that the disadvantageous side of each alternative or decision has to be faced and accepted. To make a mature decision means therefore to deliberate each alternative thoroughly; to face not only the advantageous sides of all alternatives in making your choice, but also equally the disadvantageous. When you have done that, knowing that whatever you choose, there is a price to be paid, you can ask yourself which price you prefer to pay. You can think it over if perhaps you do not prefer to risk a higher price on one side because the possible advantage does not seem worthwhile in comparison with the price. You will then have accepted another one of this earth life's rules: the uncertainty that also has to be accepted. This includes the risk, the lackings of life, and that which offers you no risk-proof plan. This too is an emotional health, my friends. In that way you act as a mature being and your soul must benefit from it.

No one who makes a decision in this way will ever come to grief because of it! Nor will he ever have the conflicts that result from the lack of making a decision in that way. The conflicts are not created because of the possible wrong decision or the less advantageous one, but they are created because you go into it blindly, not weighing and not being ready to shoulder the price. This, my friends, happens with each one of you, here and elsewhere. Some people have learned to some degree, at least in the more superficial realms of life, to decide properly. However, I don't see anyone who has made and is making his emotional decisions this way. Again, here I am giving you strong material with which to work on your path. Think again about all your conflicts and problems. Wherever they exist, in one way or another, you have not made your decisions properly. Do not remain on the surface level; you will have to dig deeper into your emotions in order to find the answer.

Within your emotions sooner or later you must find — *provided you search honestly* — that you have somehow not made a whole decision; you had somehow hoped to gain the advantage without paying the disadvantage. And often you even hope — again without thinking it out in clear-cut words — to gain the advantage of each alternative and to be spared the disadvantage of each side! This amounts to a cheating of life and the result must inevitably be that life will teach you a lesson and you will reap the disadvantages, standing on both or all sides you wished to avoid. If you test this emotional and for the most part unconscious current, what does this amount to? It amounts to greed.

On this sphere most people are greedy, not necessarily materially speaking, but emotionally. And when I say greedy, I mean you want to amass advantages without shouldering the responsibility of paying the price for them. That of course, needless to say, is a violation of one spiritual law. Think about these words I have spoken here, my friends. What I have said will add to the material you need for your progress, if you assimilate it properly, and if you work with it in a very personal way.

The Problem of Individual Empowerment versus Collective Responsibility

Alex Walker

Historical Summary

From the outline presented above we can see that in general terms there has been a slow but steady movement away from the rigidly theocratic system which existed in the early days of the Community. This involved a series of steps in the direction of greater participation and inclusiveness such as publication of Core Group minutes, and certain focalisers being appointed in consultation with the body rather than directly by management. However, only rarely was there a clearly enunciated framework for decision-making procedures to replace the ones preceding it.

This was all very well when the transfer of power was from say Peter to Core Group, as there were very few individuals involved, and all had a relatively clear understanding of the process. However the situation became very confusing when this continued through a series of events that took place over twenty years or more, with no official documentation, and subject to varying interpretations.

Even this was workable when the main thrust of developments was clearly from autocracy towards greater community involvement. However at some point during the 1980s the Foundation reached the point when the understandable desire of the body to have greater say in events began to conflict with efficient day-to-day management. Paradoxically a perception began to grow amongst Foundation 'managers' that too many decisions were being taken in a way that involved the lowest common denominator rather than the highest common factor, but at the same time, a feeling began to emerge in the body as a whole that the managers were becoming an unaccountable oligarchy.

This is part and parcel of the inevitable conflict between efficiency and participation, but what made the problem really

intractable was that there was no suitable 'constitution' to fall
back on. As the Foundation and Community diversified, the
only means of deciding, for example, which groups should
be allowed to come to certain decision-making meetings was
to have the Management Committee reach some kind of arbi-
trary conclusion. Needless to say this state of affairs pleased
virtually no one.

Specific Issues

In order to resolve this deadlock we agreed to take a more
detailed look at some of the specific issues involved. These
seemed to be:

- Confusion about legal, spiritual and administrative 'realms'
- General decision-making procedures
- Line management
- Appointments and reviews
- The role of Foundation-wide meetings

We will look in some detail at each of these in turn, but
first it will be useful to examine some of the general principles that the very process of exploring these issues turned up.

Some Important Principles

Simplicity

As Scott Peck has wisely pointed out, there is a very definite
trade-off between organisation and genuine community. On
the one hand we must organise ourselves to survive, but if
we are to maintain the community spirit which provides one
of our main sources of inspiration here, we must avoid any
semblance of over-government. Thus even those members of
the Community with a fairly analytical bent would view with
absolute horror the thought of someone making a sensible
and agreeable proposal at a meeting, only to have someone
stand up waving a piece of paper and quoting an obscure
sub-section of our 'standing orders' which prohibited such an
action, and throwing the entire meeting into turmoil and angst.
As has been said about another such document:

The Trust Deed does not capture the wholeness of what this place is about. The charity was set up to receive donations. The Deed specified what things could be done legally. However, the Spirit of Findhorn could not be encompassed by the Trust Deed (so said the Trustees at the time!). We must not hold on to it as our only measure, but rather must broaden our vision of what really takes place here.

David Spangler to Education Group, 1993

A first principle in all the discussions was therefore that whatever solutions we arrived at should be **in essence simple and easy for everyone to recall**, rather than some sort of comprehensive written constitution.

Consensus

There are a variety of possible definitions of this word, and the one we have chosen may not suit everyone. However, from the start it was very clear that establishing some kind of agreed consensus was of great importance. Indeed the way in which these agreements themselves were arrived at were a powerful example of how consensus building can work.

This is not to say that by and large most Foundation decisions had not previously been made in a consensual way, but the creation of a clearly defined and explicit means of achieving it has, for the time being at least, increased the general level of confidence in our ability to make clear decisions on complex matters by this means.

Balance

We implicitly agreed that the tension between effective participation and efficient management was one which required a balanced solution rather than an extreme one. For example, as we shall see, some Foundation managers are appointed in an essentially democratic way, while others, whose jobs are of a more technical nature, are selected by Management Committee itself.

Goodwill

These procedures are designed for an organisation which expends considerable effort on community building, and most of the members of which have received some significant training. It is hard to imagine them working in situations where the level of goodwill is low, such as in most modern political fora.

Let us now return to the specific problems listed above. For each issue there will be a short description of the problem, followed by the agreed solution, and a short commentary about the way it was arrived at, and its significance.

Confusion About Legal, Spiritual and Administrative 'Realms'

This challenge is the need to bear in mind that there are three distinct but overlapping worlds within which different procedures apply. It is important to have an understanding of the roles of the key bodies which inhabit them, and which exist to carry out our various objectives.

The Legal Realm

This is both the most durable and the most rigid of the three realms. The situation is very clear here. As a charitable Trust the Foundation is in law controlled entirely by the Trustees, who must act within the terms of the Trust Deed. The Trustees are formally responsible for the administration of the Foundation. The Trust Deed specifies the aims of the Foundation, and the Trustees must not allow its activities to go beyond either the bounds set out in that document, or the limits of financial prudence and legal propriety.

The Trustees accept that the Foundation is largely self-governing, but **no internal policy can ever overrule the principle that any decision on any matter involving the Foundation can be made by a majority of the Trustees.** Period.

There are normally about ten Trustees, some living within the Foundation, the rest elsewhere. The 'internal' Trustees meet at Findhorn regularly; the whole group meets twice a year. All of them have a long-standing connection with the Foundation, most having lived here for several years. Whenever one of the Trustees leaves the Board the remaining

Trustees decide through discussion and meditation who, if anybody, should be invited to join the Board.

The Trust Deed also allows for the creation of a Management Committee to take care of the day-to-day administration of the Foundation, and specifies what it may or may not do. Note that legally speaking the workforce at large have no formal say whatever in the running of the Foundation although obviously the realities are more complex and inclusive than this.

In practice the Trustees tend to act as fail-safe on the overall system, rather than a hands-on management group. Nonetheless, in the legal realm, which is the clearest and most fixed of these states, the situation is and was already perfectly clear.

The Spiritual Realm

This is at the opposite end of the scale to the legal. This realm is the most intangible of the three. Core Group is the Community body appointed to oversee our spiritual affairs. It plays an important part in ensuring that the spiritual integrity of the Community (as opposed to the legal integrity of the Foundation) is maintained at a high level. Here, we are all brothers and sisters in the One Light with total freedom. As in:

> *He offered me no solution for any of my problems and He did not tell me what to do. The Masters never do. They never tell a disciple what to do or where to go, or how to handle a situation, in spite of all the bunk talked by nice, well meaning devotees.*
>
> Alice Bailey, *The Unfinished Autobiography*

The spiritual realm is of course the reality which is hidden behind all the other facades in our life, but the set of issues under consideration here are not primarily concerned with the functioning of a 'spiritual community' in this sense. In fact they are about the third main realm:

The Administrative Realm

This is somewhere in between the other two. It has a degree of structure, but this is for internal convenience, and the organs and personalities within it do not have a strict legal definition for the most part. This realm includes elements of compassion, caring and spiritual work, but it also demands clarity and an agreed line of authority to resolve problems.

The co-ordinating body for the administrative realm is the Management Committee referred to above. The purpose of this committee is three-fold:

a) to co-ordinate discussions of business that concern more than one aspect of the Foundation/NFD.

b) to make decisions for the whole in conjunction with the relevant managers/focalisers of the different aspects (although there is certainly wisdom in the adage that decisions should be taken at the lowest, rather than the highest, possible level in any administrative structure).

c) to perform certain duties on behalf of the Trustees, e.g. approval of budgets and extra-budgetary capital expenditures. As a matter of policy two Trustees are required to attend any meeting where such decisions are made.

The members of this group usually include: the Focaliser of the Foundation; the Focalisers of the Park and Cluny Hill College; the Focalisers of the Personnel, Finance and Education departments; the Managing Director of NFD Ltd.

Solution — Hopefully, simply pointing out the potential for confusion that inaccurate perceptions of these realms can cause will be enough to remedy much of the difficulty they engender, and largely eliminate the problems posed by these apocryphal queries:

Neophyte Associate — "I came here to join a spiritual community, why can't I have a caravan and allowance like all the other members?"

Foundation Member — "What right do the Trustees have to discuss such and such? It should be the members who deal with that issue."

Trustee — "I don't understand all this financial stuff. Isn't it up to the Community to decide how to deal with it?"

General Decision-Making Procedures

This problem essentially concerned a failure of internal education. During the course of the 1980s, most members of the Community generally believed that most decisions were to be made by 'consensus', without there being either a clearly agreed definition of the word, or an identifiable set of circumstances when a lack of consensus could still lead to a clear decision.

After some considerable discussion it was finally agreed that decisions at all meetings should ideally be made by unanimity, failing that by consensus. If consensus cannot be reached, the following applies.

Foundation and Community-Wide Meetings

If the chairperson of the meeting so moves, a decision can be made by a 90% majority of those voting, *at a subsequent meeting*.

The chairperson of a meeting who invokes a majority decision shall be required to place an article in the 'Rainbow Bridge'[10] (or its successor) explaining the background, reasons and decision. This must be done both in advance of and subsequent to the second meeting.

All Other Meetings

If the chairperson of the meeting so moves, a decision can be made at that meeting by a two-thirds majority of those voting. The chairperson is similarly required to advertise the background, reasons and decision.

It was further agreed that these procedures could be amended by a meeting of the Selectorate, but by a two-thirds majority, rather than 90%, if required.

'Consensus' was defined as everyone involved agreeing to the course of action, or agreeing to be a 'loyal minority'. A 'loyal minority' was defined as being made up of those who may disagree with the decision as such but who agree to support the enactment of the decision. It was made clear that it

---

[10] The Foundation's internal weekly newsletter.

should *not* be composed of individuals who agree to go along with a decision but then act in a subversive way afterwards.

Commentary

Much of the discussion of these matters centred around how, if consensus could not be reached, a majority decision of some kind could be made. At first it seemed as if a simple two thirds majority would prevail in all circumstances. However, it was also proposed that for Foundation-wide meetings a 90% majority should be required. This created the spectre of 85% of those involved wanting to change these untested rules, but being unable to do so. Thus 'Pierce's Amendment' — the extraordinary solution of allowing constitutional change to be made by a smaller percentage than that required for an ordinary item of business — was proposed and accepted as a compromise to allow those who felt that 90% was too high a figure to accept the entire package.

It is interesting to note that so much time was spent on dealing with circumstances that most of those involved agreed were likely to be extreme. Instances of a formal vote being taken at a meeting of any kind in the Foundation are very rare, and I can recall only two or three of any significance which I have been involved in over the twelve plus years I have been active in the Community.

Those familiar with constitutions will note the absence of a quorum. This was generally felt to be unnecessary, suggesting a high degree of trust in those responsible for calling meetings (see below), and a low tolerance for those who fail to attend but complain afterwards about decisions made.

Finally on this subject, it is well worth noting that a majority vote, usually thought of as the pinnacle of Western political process, and the safeguard of human rights, is commonly regarded as a failure here.

Line Management

One principle needs to be clearly stated before any sensible examination of this topic can be undertaken. **Leadership and Management are entirely different functions.** Leadership in a spiritual community can be assumed by anyone who, by demonstrating certain qualities of being, can provide inspiration and encouragement for others. It is a personal presence entirely independent of one's job.

Management on the other hand can only be entrusted to a few individuals at a time. It is not possible for all of us to have an overview of finances, personnel needs, the quality of the educational programmes, and the state of the electrics in the Universal Hall. We therefore require some integrated system so that each individual knows how their tasks and responsibilities blend with the whole.

Like any organisation, the Foundation and indeed the Community have their share of individuals who are suspicious of such management necessities. It is therefore worth pointing out that one of the most important features of new age consciousness is that it emphasises personal empowerment, co-creation and synthesis. As one experiences this, perceptions of rigid hierarchical structures imposing their will from above tend to diminish.

Essentially the problem to be resolved in this context was not one of lack of clarity, but lack of communication. The enclosed diagram represents the community structure as agreed at a Foundation-wide meeting in the spring of 1993 and later amended by Management Committee. Further proposals to amend this structure are covered in the section on The Role of Foundation-Wide Meetings below.

Appointments and Reviews

Most positions in the Foundation are filled by a process involving the Human Relations Department (a.k.a. HRD, or Personnel), the relevant area focaliser and the individual him or herself. This simple process needs no elucidation here. HRD have also recently introduced the practice of regular reviews for all Foundation staff. Some positions do however generally require a wider agreement. Prior to the following proposals being arrived at there had never been a clear set of guidelines to cover this subject. The notion at the heart of this

FINDHORN FOUNDATION ADMINISTRATIVE STRUCTURE

TRUSTEES

FOUNDATION MANAGEMENT GROUP

Focalisers of Foundation, Education, Administration plus deputy,
Human Relations, NFD, Cluny and the Park, and others as required

HUMAN RELATIONS	ADMINISTRATION	EDUCATION	CAMPUSES: CLUNY	PARK	OTHER
	Finance & Accounts	*Formal Education:* inc. Guest Dept.	Homecare	Homecare	ERRAID
Employment		Workshops & Trainings	Maint'ance	Maint'ance	IONA
Members	*Asset Administration:* inc. Insurance	LCGs and Longer Progs.			
Associates & Open Community	Rates, Rents, Taxes	Conferences & Events	Garden	Garden	NFD
		External Education	Reception	Reception	(NFD offers some
Self-Evaluation	*Asset Maintenance:* inc. Maintenance,		Dining Room	CC	educational opportunities
Living Education	Health & Safety	*Internal Education:* inc. CAP/COP	Kitchen	Kitchen	for members & guests.
	Park Environment Group	Internal Trainings			This is not a description
Admin:		Children & Families	Transport	Culleme	of NFD line management)
Council Tax	Building Department				
Visas		*Others:*	Sanctuary	Sanctuaries	
DHSS	Universal Hall	inc. Visitors' Centre			
Database		Ecology	Drumduan	Station House	
Members' Health	*Communications:* inc. Media Relations				
	Local Relations	*Admin:*			Note: The Universal Hall might also be
	Fundraising	Programme Co-ord.			considered as part of the Park campus.
	Marketing	Accommodations			
	Mailing List & Mailings	Bursaries			
	Resource Persons	Contracts			
	Stewards	Logistics			
	Visuals	Brochure Production			
	Sundry Tasks: inc. General Secretary				
	Strategic Planning				
	Editorial Board				
	Computer				

section is then that there are certain prominent positions which need some kind of more public review if the management is to continue to receive the blessing of the membership at large. The following is an overview of the currently agreed system.

Foundation Focaliser Appointment and Review

The Selectorate shall appoint the Foundation Focaliser, who shall also seek the approval of the Trustees.

The Foundation Focaliser shall be reviewed by the Selectorate every two years. Any individual receiving less than a two-thirds majority supporting them in the post shall be asked to step down.

Core Group Appointments

A Core Group shall be appointed by the Selectorate every two years by a method to be announced in advance by the Foundation Focaliser.

Managerial Appointments

The **Park** and **Cluny** Focalisers shall be appointed by their respective Families[11] with the approval of the Foundation Focaliser.

The **Education** Focaliser shall be appointed by the Foundation Focaliser with the approval of the Education Group.

The **Administration** and **HRD** focalisers shall be appointed by the Foundation Focaliser with the agreement of the Management Committee.

Managerial Reviews

The Management Committee as a group shall organise an annual meeting of the Selectorate for the purposes of feedback, assessment and dialogue. Should any individual receive less than a two-thirds majority support in their post, the group which appointed them will be asked to review their appointment.

---

[11] The Cluny family comprises those members of the Foundation who live at Cluny Hill. The Park family has a similar composition, although the more complex social conditions there have led to various precise interpretations.

Commentary

The general principle at work here is that the Foundation focaliser is appointed by a widely defined group (the Selectorate) which incorporates not just the workforce of the Foundation, but also others acting in the role of 'elders'. Part of the Foundation focaliser's mandate involves being able to create a suitable management team who shall be selected in cooperation with the group of people they are both responsible for and responsible to. Such appointments will hopefully also give the incumbents of the various positions a clear mandate to get on with their jobs.

The procedures are then a mixture of collective involvement (Foundation, Park and Cluny focalisers) and appointment by a group of colleagues or peers (Education, Administration, HRD). The importance of the former kind is obvious. However it was generally agreed that a process that resulted in all such individuals being appointed by the kind of 'democratic' collective selection process notorious for encouraging short-term popularity at the expense of long- or medium-term needs was undesirable. These two procedures are thus aimed at providing a suitable balance between participation and organisation.

A final footnote is that it was also agreed at some distant point in the past that the **Erraid** focaliser should be appointed by the Erraid family, but he/she should also seek the approval of Management Committee.

The Roles of Foundation-Wide Meetings

This is a complex subject, and was clearly at the heart of much of the confusion which existed. The main remit of the exercise was to address these collective gatherings and determine:

a) Some suggestions for their administration.

b) A clear description of which individuals and groups are empowered to take which decisions.

c) An agreed list of subjects to be brought to this collective forum for a decision.

Organising Foundation-Wide Meetings

There are essentially four purposes for any meeting, or more accurately for any individual item on the agenda of a given meeting.

1) To provide social and spiritual interaction.
2) To disseminate information.
3) To receive feedback on a proposal or idea.
4) To make a decision.

The first item is fairly straightforward and easy to recognise. Meetings usually begin with a meditation, and end with ad hoc socialising, and sometimes these are more useful than the contents of the discussion itself. During the meeting warming up exercises are also frequently used, and the value of these should not be underestimated. Sometimes, in all frankness, we organise meetings just so we can be together — and why not, as that is surely the essence of community?

The second purpose of information sharing is self-evident.

The third purpose of 'testing the waters' is similarly obvious, although sometimes the results come perilously close to a de facto decision.

The fourth purpose is the main subject of this section, but before examining it, it is important to note that these purposes are frequently confused. **It is therefore an important part of any focaliser of a meeting's task to identify clearly for all concerned which category any given event is in,** both at the meeting and in the pre-meeting publicity. It is frustrating for both the managers and supporters of any given event if there is misunderstanding.

It is also vital that as much information as possible about the topic be circulated in advance. Similarly, we sometimes have terrible failures of memory and communication because community meetings are not minuted or properly reported afterwards.

Attendance

As the Community as a whole has become more pluralised than once it was, selecting the appropriate invitees has become something of a learning process in itself. For example inviting 'members' is a guarantee of confusion — members of the Foundation, Associates' group, Community, public, etc.?

In all circumstances it is clearly important that those who call the meeting also make it clear in advance who is eligible to come, and who is eligible to speak, and who is eligible to participate in any decision-making procedures.

After considerable discussion it was finally agreed that: Attendance at Foundation meetings for the purposes of making a decision shall be open to:

To Speak and Decide — Foundation Members[12]; staff builders and Foundation employees who have completed an orientation programme.

Silent Observers — Others as invited from time to time by the chairperson of the meeting.

It was also agreed that:

a) the chairperson of the meeting would ordinarily be appointed by Management Committee

b) the chairperson could invite individuals to assist in the facilitation of the meetings, and

c) that the position of Associates in regard to these meetings would be reviewed at a later date.

Appropriate Decision-Making Subjects

The function of this section is to identify subjects which should come before such a Foundation-wide meeting for a decision. Given that almost all such decisions would probably otherwise be taken by Management Committee, what this boils down to, is 'How shall management be accountable to the body as a whole?'

---

[12] Again, this terminology has been overtaken by events and should presumably be amended to read 'Foundation staff and students' or some variant thereof.

There was clearly a desire for community meetings to be used for more decisions in a structured way. Too few would frustrate and alienate the congregation, too many would place strains on the organisation's efficiency. Above all, lack of clarity about this subject confused everyone.

It was eventually agreed that: Management Committee would be responsible for organising Foundation Meetings to decide upon a variety of subjects, including an annual budget, any asset sales of over £25,000, an annual agreement about priorities for the year ahead, and major land-use planning decisions (the full text is presented below).

Some of these subjects will probably be covered at the annual 'internal conference', when the Foundation personnel take a few days to be together, to review the past year and to set goals for the future. Some sessions are for Foundation staff and students only, and some are open to Associates and longer-term guests of the Foundation, depending on the issues or themes on the agenda.

Final Thoughts

There are a number of related issues which need to be addressed if sound decision-making is to be achieved in any organisation. Here are few pitfalls to watch out for:

1) Firstly, **leadership**, as opposed to management, was mentioned briefly above. If individuals in the organisation do not empower themselves, collective weakness is the only possible result. It is vital to stress once again the importance of taking individual responsibility for decisions and their consequences. It is a key to understanding Community life. If, to paraphrase Section 5, we believe in a Universe created by a God of Love who has offered us free will and the ability to determine our lives within certain self-imposed karmic restraints, then taking full responsibility for our lives must be a prime aim.

Conversely, when the going gets tough, it is all too easy for managers who are under pressure to get things done to imagine that community opposition is created for reasons of personal malice. Sometimes individuals who cause a fuss over a particular issue are playing a role akin to that of a fuse — when they pop, it is to prevent worse damage happening elsewhere. When asked about internal dissent within the PLO, Yasser Arafat once said, "I am not a leader of sheep, I am a leader of freedom fighters. I am proud of opposition![13]"

2) Secondly, the above ideas put a certain onus on **chairmanship**. I believe that is as it should be. Those who seek responsibility should be given the appropriate authority to carry out their tasks. On the other hand, good chairmanship is not an innate gift. It can be learned, but if exercised ineffectively no constitution, however simple or elaborate, will save the day.

3) Thirdly, good decision-making procedures are not designed to avoid **conflict**. On the contrary, they are designed to tease hidden conflicts out into the open where people of goodwill can listen to one another's problems and then find appropriate solutions[14]. In other words they channel conflict in appropriate ways, rather than ignore it or cover it up.

4) We need continually to bear in mind that our work is part of a social and spiritual experiment; we are not cogs in some Divine Master Plan, deviations from which cannot be tolerated. A little **humour** goes a long way.

5) Rather than saying 'No' to a proposal, which might cause offence, we sometimes '**turn it into a process**' with no clear definition or decision attached to it. If an individual or group does not want something to happen it is usually better for everyone to be clear about that from the outset.

6) Similarly, difficult decisions sometimes hide behind '**attunement**'. On the one hand we habitually use 'attunements'

---

[13] Television interview in 1993 shortly after the White House accord.

[14] Community practice has recently found an effective theoretical background to lend it credence in the work of Process Oriented Psychology, which encourages the expression of every voice, even those usually suppressed or dormant, so that an organisation or group can discover the true nature of the 'field of consciousness' they are operating in.

to reach decisions. This is right and proper practice for achieving individual and collective centring, from which space good decisions can be reached. On the other hand it is profoundly disempowering to be told a group did not agree to your proposal because "we attuned". It is better to avoid giving this as the sole reason for a decision.

7) The **tyranny of the minority**. If we are engaged in an important community-building exercise then everyone's contribution is obviously welcome. We need to take into account the ideas of the hurt, the wounded and the shy. On the other hand if 100 people are discussing the new bus timetable and you, and only you, don't like the suggestion you might try going along with everyone else just to see what it feels like.

8) Finally, an organisation without a clear sense of **purpose** may survive, but it cannot thrive. All good job descriptions and the responsibilities they imply should relate to a central vision statement of some kind.

SUMMARY OF AGREED DECISION-MAKING PROCEDURES

This is a complete list of procedures for reference purposes. They were all agreed either by consensus or unanimity at: Selectorate meetings on 24th and 31st May 1994 for Section 1-3, and at Foundation-wide meetings on 31st May, 7th June, 14th June and 20th July 1994 for Sections 4-7.

1. General Decision-Making Procedures

Decision-Making Procedures for All Meetings

1) Meditation and attunement are an integral part of the process by which important subjects are addressed and important decisions are made.

2) Decisions at all meetings shall ideally be made by unanimity, failing that by consensus.

3) If consensus cannot be reached, the following applies.

Foundation and Community-Wide Meetings

4) If the chairperson of the meeting so moves, a decision can be made by a 90% majority of those voting, *at a subsequent meeting.*

5) The chairperson of a meeting who invokes a majority decision shall be required to place an article in the 'Rainbow Bridge' (or its successor) explaining the background, reasons and decision. This must be done both in advance of, and subsequent to the second meeting.

All Other Meetings

6) If the chairperson of the meeting so moves, a decision can be made at that meeting by a two-thirds majority of those voting.

7) The chairperson of a meeting who invokes a majority decision shall be required to place an article in the 'Rainbow Bridge' (or its successor) explaining the background, reasons and decision.

Review

8) These procedures can be amended by a meeting of the Selectorate, using the procedures for Foundation and Community-wide meetings, but by a two-thirds majority, rather than 90%, if required.

Definitions

a) 'Consensus' means everyone involved agreeing to the course of action, or agreeing to be a 'loyal minority'.

b) A 'loyal minority' is made up of those who may disagree with the decision as such but who agree to support the enactment of the decision. It is *not* composed of individuals who agree to go along with a decision but then act in a subversive way afterwards.

c) A 'majority' shall be calculated on the basis that anyone who abstains, doesn't know, is ineligible to vote, or otherwise does not make a clear choice shall not count towards the total votes cast.

2. Foundation Focaliser Appointment and Review

The Selectorate shall appoint the Foundation Focaliser, who shall also seek the approval of the Trustees.

The Foundation Focaliser shall be reviewed by the Selectorate every two years. Any individual receiving less than a two-thirds majority supporting them in the post shall be asked to step down.

3. Core Group Appointments

A Core Group shall be appointed by the Selectorate every two years by a method to be announced in advance by the Foundation Focaliser.

4. Managerial Appointments & Reviews

Preamble

The onus rests with those making the appointments to gather appropriate input and feedback.

Appointments

1) The **Park** Focaliser shall be appointed by the Park Family with the approval of the Foundation Focaliser.

2) The **Cluny** Focaliser shall be appointed by the Cluny Family with the approval of the Foundation Focaliser.

3) The **Education** Focaliser shall be appointed by the Foundation Focaliser with the approval of the Education Group (or its successor).

4) The **Administration** focaliser shall be appointed by the Foundation Focaliser with the agreement of the Management Committee.

5) The **HRD** Focaliser shall be appointed by the Foundation Focaliser with the agreement of the Management Committee. Note: It is current practice for new members of the HRD to come to a Park or Cluny Family meeting for appropriate input and feedback.

Definitions

a) The Park Family shall be as defined from time to time by the Park Focaliser. For the purposes of selecting a Park Focaliser it is currently 'all those working for the Foundation at the Park and not living at Cluny'.

b) 'With the agreement of' and 'with the approval of' mean that both parties have a veto.

Reviews

The Management Committee as a group shall organise an annual meeting of the Selectorate for the purposes of feedback, assessment and dialogue. Should any individual receive less than a two-thirds majority support in their post, the group which appointed them will be asked to review their appointment.

5) Foundation-Wide Meetings

5.1 Preamble

It is an important part of the focaliser of a meeting's task to clearly identify any agenda items requiring a decision. It is also vital that as much information as is possible about the topic be circulated in advance, and that it is made clear in advance who is eligible to come, who is eligible to speak, and who is eligible to participate in any decision-making procedures.

5.2 Attendance at Decision-Making Meetings
Attendance at Foundation meetings for the purposes of making a decision shall be open to:

To Speak and Decide — Members; staff builders and Foundation employees who have completed an orientation programme.

Silent Observers — Others as invited from time to time by the chairperson of the meeting.

Notes:

1) The chairperson of the meeting may also invite individuals to assist in the facilitation of the meetings.

2) The position of Associates in regard to these meetings will be reviewed after the forthcoming Foundation meeting(s) about membership.

5.3 Chairperson
The chairperson of a Foundation-wide meeting for the purposes of making a decision shall be appointed by Management Committee, or Core Group, dependent on which of these two groups called the meeting.

5.4 Decision-Making Subjects
Management Committee shall be responsible for organising Foundation Meetings to decide upon the following items.

Financial
An annual budget
Any item of unbudgeted expenditure of over £10,000
Any asset sales of over £25,000

Annual Reviews
Of any statement of purpose
An annual agreement about priorities for the year ahead
Of administrative/line management structures (preferably after the above item)

Feedback and assessment (but not re-appointment) for Management Committee

Other Items
Changes to the rules of membership[15]
Major land-use planning decisions

Note: 'Major land-use planning' issues would cover, for example, a proposal to apply for outline planning permission for an entire cluster, but would not usually refer to a proposal for an individual house.

5.5 Additional Meetings
In addition to those concerning the above topics, Foundation-wide meetings for the purposes of making a decision may be called by Management Committee or Core Group.

6. Family Meetings
1) Decision-making procedures shall be as outlined for all other meetings, i.e. aim for unanimity, accept consensus, if absolutely necessary have a vote by two-thirds majority.

2) In addition to the appointments outlined above topics to be decided upon shall be introduced at the discretion of the focaliser of the group or his/her appointed deputy.

3) If there is no duly appointed focaliser, responsibility for these meetings shall be taken by the Foundation focaliser.

7. Community-Wide Meetings
Community-wide meetings for the purposes of making a community-wide decision shall be called by Core Group. Core Group shall also appoint a chairperson for such meetings.

---

[15] There are but two — see Section 5.

READING LIST

Roger Benson (editor); *From Organisation . . . To Organism: A New View of Business and Management*; Findhorn Foundation; 1988. Proceedings of the 1987 conference of the same name. See particularly Gerard Endenburg's paper on 'A Model of Sociocracy'.

Roger Benson; *Leadership and Community*; Foundation audio tape of talk given on 6.2.94

Stephen R. Covey and A. Roger Merrill; *First Things First*; Simon and Schuster; 1994

Jim Maynard; *New Age Governance at Findhorn*; Foundation Early Study Paper; circa 1975.

Corinne McLaughlin & Gordon Davidson; *Spiritual Politics*; Findhorn Press; 1994

M. Scott Peck; *The Different Drum: Community Making and Peace*; Arrow; 1990. The quotation is from page 71.

Anne Wilson Schaeff and Diane Fassel; *The Addictive Organisation*; Harper and Row; 1990

Peter Senge; *The Fifth Discipline*; Century Business; 1992

David Spangler; *The Politics of Synergy*; Original Series Study Paper — "Within a group, synthesis of consciousness does not mean the same thing as democracy . . . we have group of people coming together to blend themselves. They have a will to become one, not to find out what the majority thinks." *Evolution of Government*; Original Series Study Paper — "The concept of a spiritual elite ruling the world is one of humanity's dreams but is not a reality. The concept of spiritual educators uplifting the world is the reality." *Growth, Authority and Power — The GAP*; Original Series Study Paper.

David Spangler and William Irwin Thompson; *Re-Imagination of the World*; Bear and Co; 1991. Also appearing in the Section 1 reading list, this volume has some pithy comments to make about the psycho-social dynamics of spiritual communities. See particularly 'Sixteen Years of the New Age' by William Irwin Thompson.

Chogyam Trungpa; *Cutting Through Spiritual Materialism*; Shambhala; 1973

Dick Anthony, Bruce Ecker & Ken Wilber (editors); *Spiritual Choices: The Problem of Recognizing Authentic Paths to Inner Transformation*; Paragon House; 1987. This work contains a wide variety of articles which address the difficulties confronting a spiritual seeker attempting to recognise unhealthy cults from authentic spiritual traditions. Particularly useful (although somewhat weighty and academic in tone) is Ken Wilber's chapter on 'The Spectrum Model' which provides some insight into evaluating decision-making procedures. He identifies three main pitfalls to be avoided, namely the suppression of free and rational enquiry into the teachings offered, the existence of permanent authority figures, and the perpetuation of isolated legitimacy without reference to either external or historical criteria.

Eleven

Thoughts on the Future

Never be afraid of changes ,
Never be afraid of expansion
Simply let go
And allow it all to happen quite naturally.

Open your eyes and see the changes
That take place in nature
How naturally a flower unfolds without any resistance
How a tree changes from bare branches to green leaves
Grows and stretches its branches up and out to its full glory.

Eileen Caddy; *Foundations of a Spiritual Community,* p 128

This section is not about proposed construction projects, ecological initiatives, new businesses, organisations, or prophe-
cies about international events. It is about the development
of spiritual growth, for the most important aspect of change
in life is internal, not external.

Truth about such matters cannot be reduced to a set of
simplistic aphorisms. If it could, then all that could be said
about spiritual guidance would have been written down long
ago. Fortunately life is a more complex and interesting
process, which involves endless growth and evolution, and
the opportunity to express simple truths in a galaxy of new
ways.

Before going on to explore cooperation with spirit further
with some final thoughts by David Spangler, it might be helpful to reiterate one of the most basic precepts. After all, you
may be approaching the conclusion of these introductory
papers, and wondering if they have done you any good, or
brought you any closer to an understanding of the worlds,
seen and unseen, in which you live.

Peter Caddy was fond of saying that much of his early
training was concerned with instilling into him the need to
'love where you are; love what you're doing; love who you're

doing it with'. Much of Eileen's guidance is a re-working of that notion: believe that 'all is very, very, well', — even when you seriously doubt it! Her long training in meditation notwithstanding, Dorothy's love for nature was perhaps the single most important quality she possessed in developing her connection with the devas.

You will always find something of value if you can recall this counsel. The Community is at its best when expressing its love and caring — and at its worst when the challenges of the day become excuses for apathy and factionalism. Be honest with yourself, for authenticity is valued highly in any spiritual tradition worthy of the name, but remember that whatever the question, love is always the answer.

The Future of the Findhorn Foundation

David Spangler

The future of the Findhorn Foundation is reflected in its past. It was born as a centre of demonstration. What it originally set out to demonstrate was three-fold:

- The power of discovering the God within oneself and living in touch with one's own sacred centre which, in turn, is one with the sacred centre of all creation;
- The co-creative cooperation between human and non-human lives, between the invisible and the visible worlds, and between humanity and nature; and
- A new vision — a new imagination — of reality and humanity's role that can be a transformative contribution to the emergence of a new world.

This demonstration took practical form as God's presence and guidance, the cooperation with angels, the nature spirits and other non-physical, spiritual allies, and the idea of the New Age.

The form of this demonstration has changed over the years as the Foundation itself has grown and attracted more and more people, and as the times themselves have changed. At first it was a group, then a community, then a school, and now, perhaps, a village.

In the future, the Foundation may take on other ways of demonstrating its purpose. For example, I think personally the development of the wind park, the eco-village, and so forth, is an important way of demonstrating a social and ecological vision for the future. The Foundation may even wish to re-evaluate and redefine its purpose, though it should do so carefully. To cease to be a place of demonstration — which implies an openness to the public and a willingness to be scrutinised and observed— might well mean ceasing to be the Findhorn Foundation.

This centre is also a place of presence. Essentially, this is the presence of the sacred — of love and wisdom — as mediated through all the people who participate in the life and activity of the centre. However, one might also speak of the presence of spiritual energies or qualities representative of the New Age or the presence of the angelic, faery and elemental worlds. These, as well as others, also add to the quality of the experience a person may have at the Findhorn Community.

This presence, in all its facets, represents one of the factors that attracts people to the Foundation and makes the experience here different from simply being at a workshop centre, a retreat place, or a community. If this presence changes, then the experience of the Findhorn centre will change.

Maintaining its policy of being open to the public as a place of demonstration and nourishing the spiritual presence that weaves through it will probably continue to define the Community's work in the future. However, the Foundation also needs to adapt to changes in the world and in the needs of those whom it wishes to serve. As well, the members of the Community are also creative individuals, capable of new visions and new insights. While the past of the centre should not be disregarded — and major changes in direction and identity taken with care — the history of the Community should not be a limit upon what the future might hold. Everything that is alive grows and changes, adapts and matures, and the Findhorn Foundation should be no different.

For this reason, I cannot predict what the future of the Community will be like. I can only trust that it will be informed by the same spirit that birthed it in the first place. This is the responsibility of every member, not to slavishly hold to the past or the way things used to be done if there is a need to change and equally not to slavishly seek change just for the sake of novelty or fads, but to discern and hold to the informing, incarnating, co-creative spirit of the place.

If this transmission of the essence of the Community is accomplished, then I believe the future will unfold organically and gracefully from all that has been created here and all that you are creating in this moment.

COOPERATION WITH SPIRIT

David Spangler

(Extracts of a transmission entitled 'Cooperation with Spirit — Further Conversations with John'.)

Strategies of Cooperation

You ask what the areas are in which we most seek coopera-tion with you. What are the strategies to be followed? Again, I stress that you ask this question from a human perspective, with a human notion of priorities and differences in scale. This is not our perspective, though in saying that I do not wish to imply that yours is wrong. It is just to explain that my answer may not be what you expect.

For us, you see, all human actions that embody qualities of love and spirit open gateways to us and our power, not to mention the more important attribute of invoking the pres-ence of the Beloved. The scale of the action is less important to us. An act of synthesis between two people and the cre-ation of a healthy family relationship is not less meaningful nor impactful to us than an act of peace between nations. I realise this may be difficult for you to comprehend, but we do not work in a realm of quantity. The love of one person for another is as equal to us as the love of one person for a thousand, if the quality of that love is identical. That, how-ever, is where the difference lies, for usually it is easier for you to love one other person in a specific way than to love a thousand people abstractly. In this case, then, that personal love has more quality and power than the impersonal, abstract feeling that lacks the same precision for you.

In asking us for those areas of endeavour where you may best serve or cooperate with us, recognise that we do not see one area, no matter how vast or vital, as being of greater intrinsic importance than another, no matter how small or triv-ial. We would not have you take up causes to the detriment of the quality of care you give to the immediate affairs of your individual lives, your work, your relationships with friends and family, as well as with seeming strangers, your creative accomplishments, and so forth.

What is important to us, because it affects the quality of the energy you unfold, is the skill of your actions. When you do what is within your range of talents and capacities in the moment, you are more likely to act with skill and create quality. When you attempt too much or you become too abstract, the skill and the quality are lost.

At this time in human history, you have reasonable skill in relating as individuals; where skill is lacking, and hence quality, is in relating as groups. Therefore, developing skill in expressing synthesis on the level of groups and collectives is one area to which we attach importance and would encourage you to give effort to that skill as a practical means of cooperating with us. In terms of honouring this collective energy on a planetary level, we place importance upon your United Nations. Though it has faults, it is still a major centre through which the energy of humanity as a whole can be focused and within which the encounter with yourselves as a whole species can take place. For all its internal conflicts, it is a source of important service in your world. It is at the moment your only true focal point for planetary synthesis. You cannot safely ignore it nor dispense with it. You can only replace it with something better. Until that happens, it is a lens for much energy and attention from my world in particular; to empower it to do its job more qualitatively and effectively is definitely to cooperate with us.

However, we are also concerned with the development of a group life in a less centralised fashion. All groups are under stress at this time, particularly those that identify themselves as being spiritual or oriented towards the emergence of a new age. The stress is to enhance their capacity to embody synthesis. This affects leaders and leadership styles, for the energy of the spiritual worlds cannot manifest where people are used as tools for the objectives of one or a few, and it affects relationships between group members, demanding greater honesty, clarity and mutual empowerment. Not all groups will survive the quickening. Also, understand that by groups I also mean such collective enterprises as communities, neighbour-hoods, villages, and cities. If you would cooperate with us, then explore ways of restoring the sense of communion and community to your organisations. In the days ahead, your graceful passage into a new world depends on your ability to share and cooperate with each other. Your lives are too fragmented, too isolated. Rebuild the human connections that can strengthen and enhance you by allowing you to strengthen and enhance others.

We are concerned in our world not only with humanity but with the integration and wholeness of all life upon earth. Thus, the kingdoms of nature and their well-being are impor-tant to us. We especially see that until you discover how to honour those kingdoms and work with them in a more co-creative fashion, you will not fully experience your own humanness. Also, in this time of quickening for the planet, it only obstructs the deeper incarnation of divinity within the world for humanity and nature to be in disharmony.

Therefore, you cooperate with us by empowering all efforts to establish a more cherishing and interdependent relation-ship with nature. We do not recommend a simple return to the land. It is a matter of discovering how to express your humanness, and its civilisational extensions, in ways that hon-our the land. Towards this objective, we also recommend that you learn from those more ancient cultures, such as the native American culture that lived in that relationship. You are not asked to re-create those cultures, but together you can give birth to a new culture that will learn to extend the spirit of harmony and balance further than any civilisation has yet been able to take it.

It is our interest that each man and woman be uplifted as an important participant in the drama of evolution. Each of you is unique and irreplaceable. In each of you the spirit of synthe-sis grows, and each of you adds to the expression of that spirit in the world. For this reason, you cooperate with us when-ever you discern and support any activity, be it educational, political, economic or artistic, that empowers and honours the development of a creative individuality. To repress this gift of self in oneself or in others is to deny the spirit that seeks incarnation on the earth. Thus, learn how to give to each the freedom to discover his or her unique contribution to the whole.

This means working to bring to your world freedom from all that would repress, be it fear, hunger, neglect, or a failure of love and connectedness. In so doing, keep in mind, though, that not all selves grow and flourish in the same environment. The greatest forms of repression are not always economic or political systems as such, but rather an attitude of disconnectedness and a failure to share, to break bread together in the most basic meaning of that ritual as an act of empowerment.

We find a powerful connection to your world through acts of healing. Do not narrow those acts to a single definition of medicine, but come to understand the many forms that healing can take. It is an attitude of respect and empowerment, as much as an action of removing disease.

Know the healing power that each person has in this context, and practise it quietly. You can each be a comfort and a source of peace to one another through your simple willingness to be compassionate and to love. Understand as well that the gift of peace itself is often the greatest form of healing. At a time when so many of you fear the outbreak of a nuclear war, to heal the causes of conflict, whether in a person, between people, or between nations, is to perform needed service. To heal is to remove all that would threaten life and its potential for growth. To be a healer is to be a peacemaker in all your affairs, and vice versa. To help us and yourselves, practise the spirit of giving peace and of healing the roots of conflict on all levels of human activity.

You cooperate with us when, through the grace and skill of your actions, you fill your world with beauty and harmony and encourage the spirit of creativity. Is this too general? Too abstract? It is the human attitude of overlooking the simple and seeking the glamorous and powerful that too often leaches that skill and quality from your actions and closes the door to our world.

I said once, you do not need me to point out to you the things that need doing in your world. There is suffering in your world; act to diminish it. There is hunger in your world; be a source of nourishment. There is poverty amongst men and women; be a source of abundance and sharing. I have spoken of a new spirit of divinity entering your world and of the quickening that is taking place. Work to understand this vision. Open your eyes and your mind to understand the possibilities for transformative action that are around you. Your culture is changing. Do not fear this. Above all else, do not fear nor be a source of fear for others, for fear is the greatest obstacle we face in sharing our energy with the world. Many people in your society are exploring the shape this new culture might take and strategies for giving it birth. The information and vision is growing about you; seek it out. Do your homework to be a knowledgeable agent for evolution upon your planet. We cannot do this for you. No spiritual power can. This is your role, the reason you are upon earth. It is your challenge that in the depths of your selfhood you discover the spirit and skills of synthesis and love. Acknowledge that spirit and explore those skills. Then we can help. Then your world will be transformed.

Challenges of Cooperation

You ask about the challenges of cooperation and what can be done about them. I would mention five challenges.

The first is to confuse the invisible worlds with the spiritual worlds. There are many dimensions of life which are normally not open to your physical senses. I have spoken, for instance, of the formative worlds and the psychological realms of the so-called astral and lower mental planes. Not all of these have the wisdom or knowledge to interact skilfully with human evolution. Because a person is in touch with some non-physical entity or region through psychic means does not mean a true contact with spiritual realms has been established.

The second challenge is glamour. This might be seen as

the substitution of the unreal for the real, of the image for the substance. It accepts the form but neglects the spirit. Glamour is a loss of perspective and of balance. It bedazzles the individual with visions of power, of superiority, of being different and special. It inflates the self but does not nourish the development of synthesis. To seek contact with spirit because the idea seems glamorous, offering insights into hidden mysteries and secret powers, is to completely misunderstand the nature of the spiritual worlds and the responsibility they offer. One can also, however, have a glamour about being a humble servant of the most high. In either case, the person is really in touch with an image of his or her own emotional and mental needs and is acting on his or her own behalf, not truly on behalf of the greater wholeness.

The third challenge is simple confusion of interpretation. The spiritual worlds are different from yours. Time and space are experienced differently, and communication often uses a language of imagery and emanation which is difficult to translate directly into words. The message or contact may be misinterpreted. This often happens in the case of prophecy. Your tendency is to interpret in terms of physical events and happenings, when the message may deal with psychological and mythic changes.

The fourth challenge is more serious. It represents the loss of personal integration. An individual may tune in to a source of psychological or even spiritual energy beyond his or her capacity to integrate within the personality structure. The result is a loss of inner balance and perspective, even a disintegration of the psychological structure, allowing even more unconscious material to pour into the consciousness. The consequence is what you call a mental or emotional breakdown. When drugs are used to bring about contact with inner worlds, this is even more likely to take place.

The fifth challenge is, from our point of view, the most serious. This is the loss of will and integrity by the individual. The simplest form of this is when a person becomes dependent on guidance from non-physical sources. The person may still have a will with which to act out his guidance, but loses the capacity to think things through for him/herself and make skilful choices. Indeed, the person may become fully passive in the hands or under the influence of an invisible force, as in the case of most forms of mediumship. There was a time when such an approach had value, and even now it may be appropriate for the rare individual; it is not, however, the emerging way of working with spirit, which demands full consciousness, integrity and will on the part of the individual with which to co-create. By will here, of course, I do not mean that wilfulness that can arise from the unintegrated ego but the capacity to direct the energies of one's own identity through moral choice and inner understanding.

To deal with these challenges, I recommend the following. First, discernment is important. Do not attach importance to any message simply because it comes from a non-physical source. Examine the life of the human personality through whom the contact is made. Is it a balanced life? Is that person's behaviour in harmony with the spirit purportedly behind the contact? We encourage creative doubt: not the doubt that shuts out the possibility of spirit altogether, but the doubt that asks you to look twice and to consider a communication in the light of your own values and integrity, not to mention your intelligence.

In this regard, remember all I have said about the spiritual worlds. They are both a level of consciousness and also, most importantly, a function of relationship, one that empowers, elucidates, liberates, and blesses. This relationship is not the sole property of the invisible realms. You may express it as fully as I.

There are spiritual projects within the psychological realms, as well as the spiritual worlds, that can be benefited by human cooperation, and there are beings who seek that cooperation. A person who becomes part of such a project may well receive specific guidance. However, remember that the most precious gift you have is your intelligence and free will, your capacity to think for yourself, to be true to yourself and to grow as a unique expression of divinity. No true worker for spirit, on any level, will seek to abridge this gift. Our responsibility is to nourish the right use of will on all levels. For this reason, you may well be suspicious of any person or force, on any level, that asks you to surrender your inner will. You may give it freely to another as an act of communion, but it cannot be coerced from you without violating the very intent of God for the growth of your being. Unfortunately, there are those who live in the invisible worlds, particularly in what I call the psychological realms, who are the equivalent of your busybodies, still afire with a passion to form schemes and tell others what to do. Be forewarned. Any guidance should strengthen your ability to act with wisdom, without the need for continual guidance, not make you more dependent in the name of a sacred plan.

Honour your human self and its talents. You are not less spiritual or worthy because you happen to have a physical body, nor are we automatically better because we don't. Develop your creative talents and skills; develop your joyous and growing spirit. Rejoice in your ability to accomplish. Never make contact with spiritual realms a reason for your life, nor the only skill you can claim. You are a human being, an incarnation of the divinity, made in the creative image of God, capable of loving and giving birth to the power of the synthesising spirit. Act accordingly and honour the spirituality of your earthly nature, as well as of your unique incarnation. Then you will develop an inner poise and strength that cannot be deceived. Then you will have a wholeness as a person that will call forth to our wholeness and make our communion and cooperation inevitable and graceful.

Cooperation is a community act. It requires more than one person. If you seek cooperation with us, seek it even more so with other human beings. Also, in working with the invisible realms, having others with whom to share, whose perspective and insights you treasure, can help you avoid glamour and confusion and keep you honestly human.

Finally, in seeking the spiritual worlds, remember that what you truly seek is your oneness with God. We are not a sub-stitute for divinity. We are colleagues, if you wish, in tl e endeavours of earthly evolution; we wish to be friends. How-ever contact with us is less than it could be if it takes the place of a spiritual path to the Beloved. Put God first, then we can meet in the mutual embrace of her spirit.

READING LIST

Eileen Caddy and David Earl Platts; *Bringing More Love into Your Life: The Choice is Yours*; Findhorn Press; 1992. *Choosing to Love*; Findhorn Press; 1993

There is also a wide range of New Age written material, usually 'channelled', which attempts to predict possible changes in human culture. A useful guide to their authenticity is the extent to which they stress the inner transformative process, rather than depending on phenomena and cataclysmic prediction. In addition to works by David Spangler and Eileen Caddy some of the more popular ones are:

Ken Carey; *The Starseed Transmissions*; Harper Collins; 1991

Chris Griscom; *Time is an Illusion*; Simon & Schuster; 1988

Barbara Marciniak; *Bringers of the Dawn*; Bear and Co; 1992

James Redfield; *The Celestine Prophecy*; Warner; 1993. This manuscript is a brilliant metaphor masquerading as a real-life drama in true Castaneda style.

Julie Soskin; *Winds of Change*; Ashgrove; 1994. Whilst rightly concentrating on inner dynamics, some of the suggestions about changes in the quality of light in our skies are well worth contemplating.

Twelve

Appendix

NOTES TO THE TEXT

There are a total of eleven *sections* in this volume, plus this Appendix.

Each section is composed of individual *papers*.

The *reading lists* are in three parts, which are, for ease of reference, not exclusive of one another.

i) At the end of each section extra reading material germane to the text has been presented. Wherever possible titles currently available in the Park or Cluny Libraries have been identified.

ii) The second part is a complete index of the *Original Series of Study Papers* as described in Section 2 above.

iii) The third part is a list of *Early Study Papers,* which although used from time to time as internal educational material were never formally collated into a set or single volume. These mostly, although not entirely, pre-date the Original Series.

Copies of both the first series and the early papers are held at both the Park and Cluny, although neither collection was complete at the time of writing.

This usage of 'Original Series' and 'Early Study Papers' as collective terms is a convenient shorthand but not entirely satisfactory. The collections merge somewhat as many articles appear in more than one publication or study paper. Some were first printed for internal use and later edited, compiled and published in book form.

I am indebted to Chris Power whose March 1990 index of the Study Papers forms the basis for this new classification.

Many of the original and early study papers persist in using the word *'Findhorn'* when referring to the Foundation and its associated Community. This was current practice until the early 1980s when, in deference to the views of local people, the Foundation agreed to avoid this usage. Where this occurs the reference has been changed to reflect this policy. There are occasional remaining references to 'Findhorn' meaning the geographical area, or where it is included in the title of a document.

Text in *square brackets* is an insertion of material into the original text.

The *author* of the material is myself unless otherwise stated. The material was also created especially for this volume unless otherwise stated.

STUDY PAPERS

Original Series of Study Papers

Many of the articles in these series have been reprinted singly and some appear in other publications. All are lectures by David Spangler unless otherwise stated. The abbreviation 'tr:' denotes a transmission from a non-physical being through David Spangler. For instance, 'tr: John;' indicates that during a meditation David Spangler made contact with and spoke for a being known as John, and that the article is a transcription of that communication. 'tr: LLT' indicates a transmission from 'Limitless Love and Truth'. Elixir and Divina are the noms de plume Eileen Caddy and Dorothy Maclean used for a time to indicate the source of material was guidance they had received.

THE BROTHERHOOD SERIES

I.   Aspects of the Universal Vision
II. The Melchizedek Priesthood (1)
     (tr: John; 5 May 1971)
III. The Melchizedek Priesthood (2)
     (tr: John; 5 June1971)
IV. Rokoczi and the Brotherhood
     (tr: St. Germain; 8 Nov 1971)
V.   The Meaning of the Brotherhood
     (tr: Higher Self; 9 Nov 1971)

VI.   The College and the Brotherhood
      (tr: John; 22 Nov 1971)
VII. Spiritual Concepts for Those Travelling from Findhorn
      to Other Nations
      (tr: John; 4 June 1972)

THE CHRIST SERIES

I.   From Krishna to Christ
      (Lecture, July 1972)
II.   The Christ
      (Lecture, July 1972)
III. The Christ Pattern
      (Lecture, Sept 1970)
IV.   The Role of Lucifer in Human Evolution
      (tr: Higher Self, 18.5.1971)
V.   Christo-Genesis
      (tr: John; 17 Aug 1969)
VI.   The Christ: Transmutations in Community
      (tr: The Christ; 21.5.1971)
VII. Karma as a Thought Form
      (tr: John; 10 July 1970)
VIII. Sessions with the Christ
      (tr: The Christ; 26 June 1971)
IX.   Letter to Graham, Aug 1972
      (Letter, 22 Sept 1972)

THE NEW AGE VISION

I.   Oedipus and Aquarius
II.   The Four Horsemen of Aquarius
III. The Bearer of the Vision
IV.   The New Man (Man, The Creature of Definition)
V.   The New Age Movement
VI.   Architect of Aquarius
VII. Beyond the Dawn
VIII. Loins of Aquarius
IX.   From Eden to I Am
X.   The Royal Hunt of the Soul
XI.   The New Age and Man
XII. A Personal Vision

THE NEW CULTURE AND CIVILISATION

I.   Art, Civilization and New Age Energies
       (tr: Higher Self, 29 Aug 1970)
II.   New Culture
       (tr: St Germain; 26 Aug 1970)
III.   Cybernetics and Society in the New Age
       (Discussion, 27 Sept 1970)
IV.   Economy
       (Discussion, Apr 1971)
V.   Organization
       (tr: Higher Self, 23 Aug 1970)
VI.   Drugs
       (Lecture, Sept 1970)
VII.   New Age Energies and Seed Atom Concept
VIII. Evolution of Government
       (Lecture, Dec 1971)
IX.   Business in the New Age
       (tr: Higher Self, 28 July 1971)
X.   The City
       (tr: John; 15 Aug 1969)

MAN, NATURE & THE NEW AGE

I.   Man, Nature and the New Age
II.   Man's Relationship with Nature
       (tr: LLT; 7 Aug 1970)
III.   Cooperation with Pan and the Nature Spirits
       (tr: John; 4 Aug 1970)
IV.   Man's Relationship with the Nature Kingdoms: I
       (R. Ogilvie Crombie)
V.   Man's Relationship with the Nature Kingdoms: II
       (R. Ogilvie Crombie)
VI.   The Deva Consciousness
       (Divina; Dorothy Maclean)
VII.   The Devas
       (Divina; Dorothy Maclean)
VIII. Communication from an Angelic Source
       (tr: Elouai; 21 Jun 1970)

The Plan of Light

I.   A Lecture on Power Points
     R. Ogilvie Crombie
II. The Iona Report — The Reconsecration of the Sanctuary at Traigh Bhan
III. Tour Around English Power Points
     (by David, Peter, Eileen & Myrtle)
IV. Britain and the Common Market
     (tr: John; 28 Jun 1971)
V.   Angel of America
     (tr: 14 May 1971)
VI. Sir Francis Bacon to Americans
     (tr: Francis Bacon; 16 May 1972)
VII. The Christ in China
     (tr: John; 26 June 1971)
VIII. Development of Future Light Centres

Series 1: Exploring the New Age

1. The New Age Now
2. The Individual in the New Age
3. The Family of the New Age
4. Man and the Beloved
5. The Spectrum of Man
6. The New Age
7. Wholeness
8. Concepts of Evolution
9. Man, Nature and the New Age
10. Out with the New Age

Series 2, Part 1: Living in the New Age

1. The New Age — Birth Three
2. Revelation: Part I
3. Revelation: Part II
4. Meditation: Parts I and II
5. Meditation: Parts III and IV
6. Meditation: Part V
7. Attunement: The Homecoming

Early Study Papers

This collection is in two parts:

a) Study papers by David Spangler other than those contained in the Original Series.

b) Assorted papers by other authors.

Some of these papers are of course included in part or in whole in this volume.

OTHER STUDY PAPERS BY DAVID SPANGLER

Manifestation
A Report on Manifestation
The New Laws of Manifestation (tr: St Germain; 9 June 1971)
The Laws of Manifestation: Study Guide
Working the Law

Space Contact
Contact with Our Space Brothers — UFOs
Space Contact in the New Age (tr: John; 21 Aug 1970)
Links with Space (tr: Lord Maitreya; 19 June 1970)

Assorted Papers
The Animal Kingdom and Findhorn (tr: John; 2 October 1976)
Creativity and Excellence (Discussion on Education, 19 June 1978)
(with introduction by Michael Lindfield, 23 September 1978)
Group Consciousness (not the same paper as Sex and Identity Series part 6)
Healing: Good and Evil
Identity in Action: The Power of Knowing Who You Are
Karma Paper (tr: John; 11 Jan 1975)
The 1975 Limitless Love and Truth Transmissions (tr: John; 1 Jan 1975)
Also: Limitless Love and Truth: Introduction by Peter Caddy
Midsummer Festival (tr: John, Angel of Findhorn, St Germain; 13 June 1971)
The New Age is Now (tr: Higher Self)
The Pressures Within
An Open Letter from David Spangler (Letter to the Community, 21 August 1974). In this latter David attempts to dissociate himself from the notion that he was in some way the source of, as opposed to

the channel for, Christ energies in the Community, and goes on to discuss glamour ('the greatest challenge facing us today') and to further elucidate his thoughts on the nature of the Christ and the value of family life.

Session with Peter, Lois, Myrtle, Lark and David (tr: John; 10 May 1971)

Transition within the Community: The Mary Principle (tr: Nov 1974)

Universal Aspects of the New Age Vision (condensed transmission)

The Vision of Findhorn in World Transformation (1971)

The Significance of Findhorn (1971)

Cooperation with Spirit

Manifestation (small booklet)

Attunement (small booklet)

New Age (small booklet)

Synergy (small booklet)

Holistic Discipleship (uncovered booklet)

Findhorn: A Place of Vision (pamphlet)

Limitless Love and Truth: Continued Revelation. (Published in four parts and as a whole. Includes an introduction by Peter Caddy, writings by David Spangler, and transmissions from Limitless Love and Truth through David Spangler.)

Assorted Papers by Other Authors

EILEEN CADDY

God Spoke to Me (Elixir — published in four parts)

Why Meditate? (Selections from Elixir compiled by David Earl Platts)

PETER CADDY

The Laws of Manifestation: The Old Laws at Work (15 April 1971)

If It's Right for One It's Right All Round (28 April 1975)

R. OGILVIE CROMBIE

Attunement (Roc at Focalisers' Meeting, Sept 1974)

Conversations with Pan (pp 49-71, *Findhorn Garden*)

ROGER DOUDNA

Living On the Spearhead: A Personal Reflection on Findhorn

FRANÇOIS DUQUESNE

Community, College, University: Toward a University of Light

MYRTLE GLINES
Findhorn: Garden or Jungle?

MICHAEL LINDFIELD
Findhorn: A Learning Experience (1984/5)

DOROTHY MACLEAN
God's Word through Divina
The Soul of Canada: An Overview of National Identity (1977)

JIM MAYNARD
New Age Governance at Findhorn

NICHOLAS ROSE
Findhorn and the Western Mystery Tradition

THE UNIVERSAL FOUNDATION
Light on the Cosmic Plan (November 1968)
For Meditation (June 1969)
Attunement (Autumn 1970)
The Problem and the Answer (1970)

Various Authors

Findhorn: An Agreement to Serve (Core Group; October 1977)
The Findhorn Garden: An Experiment in the Cooperation between Three Kingdoms (with contributions from Sir George Trevelyan, Peter Caddy, Dorothy Maclean et al.)
Moving into the New Age: Blending the Generations (also published as Moving into the New Age: Blending Youth and the Older Generation) (with contributions from Peter Caddy, Eileen Caddy, John Michel, Anthony Brooke, Sir George Trevelyan; September 1969)
The Transformation of Findhorn (1972)
Sanctuary Pamphlet

Findhorn Press Publications in Print

BY EILEEN CADDY

Dawn of Change	£5.95
Flight Into Freedom	£7.95
Footprints on the Path	£5.95
Foundations of a Spiritual Community	£5.95
God Spoke to Me	£5.95
Living Word	£3.95
Opening Doors Within (hardback)	£10.95
Opening Doors Within (paperback)	£6.95
Spirit of Findhorn	£5.95

Video

Opening Doors Within	£17.95

BY EILEEN CADDY & DAVID EARL PLATTS

Choosing to Love	£5.95
Bringing More Love into Your Life: The Choice is Yours	£11.95

ABOUT THE FINDHORN COMMUNITY

Findhorn Community — Carol Riddell	£8.95
Findhorn Garden — Findhorn Community	£9.95

OTHER TITLES

Canoeing Through Life — Nick Inman	£1.95
Chronicles of the White Horse — Peter Please	£3.95
Earth at Omega — Donald Keys	£2.95
Maze and the Arc of Light — Hope Tod	£6.95
My Life My Trees — Richard St Barbe Baker	£5.95
New Economic Agenda — ed. Mary Inglis & Sandra Kramer	£4.95
Sacred Times — William Bloom	£5.95
Spirit of Dance — Anna Barton	£3.50
Spirit of Dance: The Next Steps — Anna Barton	£3.95
This New Age Business — Peter Lemesurier	£4.95
Tower at the Edge of the World — William Heinesen	£2.50
To Honour the Earth — Kathleen Thormod & Dorothy Maclean	£9.95
Australian Bush Flower Essences — Ian White	£11.95
First Steps — William Bloom	£4.95

NEW TITLES

Healing the Cause — Michael Dawson	£6.95
Hands-On Spiritual Healing — Michael Bradford	£7.95
Astral Sex to Zen Teabags — Gerry Thompson	£5.95
Art of Living in Peace — Pierre Weil	£5.95
Spiritual Politics — Corinne McLaughlin & Gordon Davidson	£8.95

Note of Thanks

In addition to the authors and publishers of the quoted material I am indebted to: Patricia Andersson, Katherine Bischoff, William Bloom, Karin & Thierry Bogliolo, Eileen Caddy, Richard Coates, Gordon Cutler, Aziz Dikeulias, Roger Doudna, Dianne Falasca, Eric and Angela Franciscus, Ben Fuchs, Craig Gibsone, Linda Hall, Alan Harfield, Mari Hollander, Mary Inglis, Ike Isaksen, Tony Judge, Sandra Kramer, Robbie Laing, Vidura Le Feuvre, Muriel MacVicar, Bill Metcalf, Judith Meynell, Patrick Nash, Chris Power, Christina Rindt, Nick Rose, Mike Scott, Andrew Shorrock, Susan Tulloch, Kathy Tyler, David Spangler, Vita de Waal, Frank Whaling, Stephan Wik, Carol Williamson and the staff of Forres Library for their help and kindnesses along the way.

Thanks to Alan Watson for the use of one of his photographs for the cover of this book.

I am particularly grateful for the support of my wife Pauline, and to John Brierley for his able assistance with matters both small and large.

The many deficiencies which remain are of course my own.

Alex Walker, September 1994

And when he was demanded of the Pharisees when the kingdom of God should come, he answered them and said, "The Kingdom of God cometh not with observation: Neither shall they say, Lo here! or Lo there! for, behold, the Kingdom of God is within you."

The Gospel According to St Luke 17:20